Impact!

Civic, Social and Political Education for Junior Certificate

Fifth edition

Jeanne Barrett
and
Fiona Richardson

Gill & Macmillan

CSPE

Gill & Macmillan Ltd
Hume Avenue
Park West
Dublin 12
with associated companies throughout the world
www.gillmacmillan.ie

978 0 7171 4529 4

Artwork by Peter Bull Art Studio, East Sussex, UK
Colour reproduction by Typeform, Dublin
Design and print origination by Mike Connor Design and Illustration, UK

The paper used in this book is made from the wood pulp of managed forests. For every tree felled, at least one tree is planted, thereby renewing natural resources.

CONTENTS

ACKNOWLEDGMENTS

The authors would like to acknowledge the help and advice given by the following:

80:20, ActionAid, Afri, ALONE, Amnesty International, ARASI (Association of Refugees and Asylum Seekers Ireland), Senator Ivana Bacik, Ballymun Partnership, Barnardos, John Byrne, Camara, Ann Carroll, Childnet International, Christian Aid, Citizen Traveller, *Clare Companion*, Tom Clonan, Coalition to Stop Child Soldiers, Combat Poverty, Concern Worldwide, Council for People with Disabilities, Courts Service of Ireland, Brian Crowley MEP, Dáil na nÓg, Councillor Clare Daly, DEFY, Detective Garda Cathal Delaney, Department of the Environment, Department of Justice, Equality and Law Reform, Department of An Taoiseach, Proinsias De Rossa MEP, Shane Doyle and Gorey Skate Club, Dublin Simon Community, Clare Dunne, ECO UNESCO, ENFO, Equality Authority, Fairtrade Mark Ireland, Fianna Fáil, Fine Gael, Focus Ireland, Foróige, Free the Children, Peter Gaynor, GOAL, GoodWeave, Green Party, Ciaran Halford, Holocaust Educational Trust of Ireland, Irene Hughes and Ashbourne Community School students and Green School Committee members, International Labour Office, Councillor Kealin Ireland, Irish Aid, *Irish Examiner*, Irish Fair Trade Network, *Irish Independent*, Irish Red Cross, *Irish Times*, Irish Traveller Movement, ISPCA, Nellie Joyce, Kick it Out, Craig Kielburger, Labour Party, *LifeTimes*, Local Planet, Longford County Council, Grant Masterson, Mairead McGuinness MEP, MiCandidate, Catherine Murnane, Margaret Murphy, National Children's Office, National Youth Council of Ireland, NewsFour, Senator David Norris, Caoimhghín Ó Caoláin TD, Anne O'Donnell, Office of the Minister of Children and Youth Affairs, Offices of the European Parliament, Ombudsman for Children, Outreach International, Oxfam, Pavee Point, Pride of Place: Co-operation Ireland, Councillor John Ryan, Trevor Sargent TD, Save Tara/Skryne Valley Group, Sinn Féin, Socialist Party, SpunOut, Sustainable Energy Ireland, An Taisce, Trócaire, Trust, UNICEF, United Nations High Commission for Refugees (Ireland), URBAN Ballyfermot, Vincentian Partnership for Social Justice, Mark Waddock, Jake Walsh (Tipperary South Comhairle na nÓg), *Western People*, *Wexford Echo*, Wicklow County Council, World Development Movement.

For permission to reproduce extracts, the authors are grateful to the following:
Adrian Mitchell for his poem 'Back in the Playground Blues' and Jacqueline Wilson for her novel *Secrets*.

The authors extend their thanks to the teachers and students of Killinarden Community School, Tallaght and Loreto College, St Stephen's Green.

Jeanne Barrett would like to dedicate this edition of *Impact!* to the memory of her mother Nance Barrett.

eTest.ie – what is it?

A revolutionary new website-based testing platform that facilitates a social learning environment for Irish schools. Both students and teachers can use it, either independently or together, to make the whole area of testing easier, more engaging and more productive for all.

Students – do you want to know how well you are doing? Then take an eTest!

At eTest.ie, you can access tests put together by the author of this textbook. You get instant results, so they're a brilliant way to quickly check just how your study or revision is going.

Since each eTest is based on your textbook, if you don't know an answer, you'll find it in your book.

Register now and you can save all of your eTest results to use as a handy revision aid or to simply compare with your friends' results!

Teachers – eTest.ie will engage your students and help them with their revision, while making the jobs of reviewing their progress and homework easier and more convenient for all of you.

Register now to avail of these exciting features:

- Create tests easily using our pre-set questions OR you can create your own questions
- Develop your own online learning centre for each class that you teach
- Keep track of your students' performances

eTest.ie has a wide choice of question types for you to choose from, most of which can be graded automatically, like multiple-choice, jumbled-sentence, matching, ordering and gap-fill exercises. This free resource allows you to create class groups, delivering all the functionality of a VLE (Virtual Learning Environment) with the ease of communication that is brought by social networking.

Chapter 1

Citizen You

Civic, Social and Political Education looks at what it means to be a **citizen** and how each of us can **take part** in the **different groups or communities** of which we are members. We are all members of a family community, a school community, a local community, as well as a national community and a world community. Being a member of a community means that we have certain **rights** but it also means that we have duties and **responsibilities** to the other people in that community.

STUDY 1 WHAT IS CSPE?

Civic, Social and Political Education (CSPE) is about finding out what it means to be an active citizen.

Learning about citizenship is about getting involved in my school, my community, my country and the wider world.

The 7 Concepts of CSPE

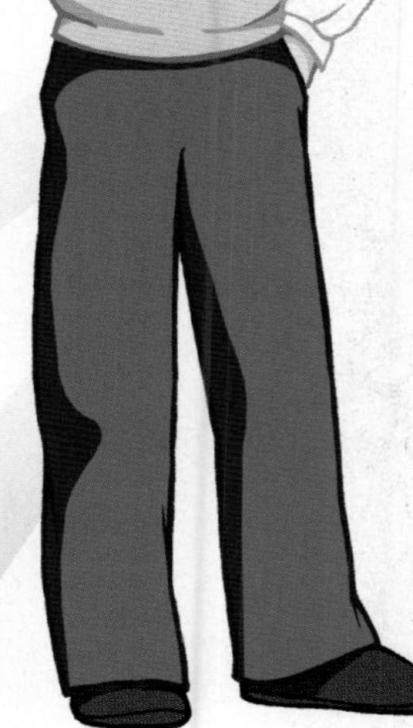

Concept 1

Rights and Responsibilities

You need to know that while you have rights you have a **responsibility** to protect the **rights** of others.

Issues like ...

- Respect
- Bullying
- Racism
- Organisations that look out for human rights

Concept 2

Stewardship

We are all stewards or carers of the planet. We all have to be responsible for looking after the local **environment** and the world.

Issues like ...

- Litter
- Pollution
- Recycling
- Global warming

Concept 3

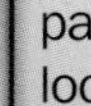

Development

How you can take part in improving your local **community**, what happens when people want different things, and what can block change in the developing world.

Issues like ...

- My local community
- Local government
- Planning
- What development means in other areas around the world

It means that I find out about things going on and learn how to take action and bring about change.

Concept 7

Interdependence

You will learn that we all **depend on one another** and how our actions as people – even what we buy – can have an impact in places that we have never been to.

Issues like ...

- Child labour
- Fair trade
- World debt
- Being part of big groups like the EU, UN

Concept 6

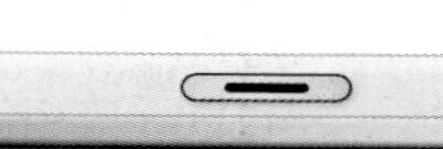

Human Dignity

This means learning that every person should have their **basic needs** met, like the need for water, food, shelter, education, health.

Issues like ...

- Respect
- Bullying
- Racism
- Organisations that look out for human rights

Concept 5

Law

We need to understand why rules and laws are needed, and that they are a way of making sure people's **rights are protected**.

Issues like ...

- The Constitution
- The courts system
- Different laws
- The Gardaí

Concept 4

Democracy

You will learn about how you can **play your part** in the world at a local level, at a national level, at an EU level and at a UN level.

Issues like ...

- Student councils
- Elections
- Voting
- Political parties

ACTIVITIES

1. What does Joe say citizenship is about?
2. What does Jane say citizenship is about?
3. Fill in the correct CSPE concept in each of the following sentences:
   a) Making sure that people's basic needs are met means respecting everyone's human ________.
   b) __________ is another way of describing how we look after our planet.
   c) If I learn about voting and elections I will understand better how __________ works.
   d) While you have many __________, you also have a __________ to protect others.
   e) Learning that the actions I take, such as the way I shop, could have an impact in another part of the world, shows how __________ we all are.
   f) Using __________ is one way to make sure people's rights are protected.
   g) When change happens in communities we call this __________.

Communities often come together to take action on the environment

Protesting about an issue that concerns you is one way of taking action

Nelson Mandela addresses a crowd in South Africa to highlight issues of national concern

What are these students taking action about?

Why Action?

CSPE is about being an active citizen. An **action project** shows how you can take action over an issue that concerns and interests you. Read what some famous people have said about **taking action** and making an **impact** in the world.

Never doubt that a small group of thoughtful, committed citizens can change the world; indeed, it's the only thing that ever has.

Margaret Mead (1901–78), American anthropologist

Have a bias toward action – let's see something happen now. You can break that big plan into small steps and take the first step right away.

Indira Gandhi (1917–84), Indian politician and prime minister

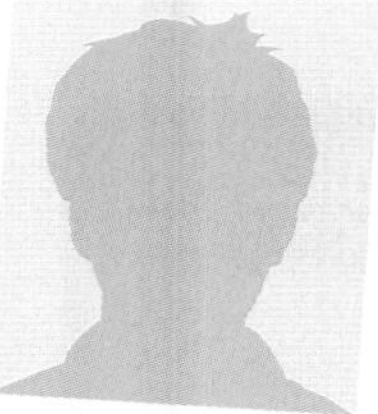

Remember, people will judge you by your actions, not your intentions. You may have a heart of gold – but so does a hard-boiled egg.

Anonymous

It is easy to sit up and take notice. What is difficult is getting up and taking action.

Honoré de Balzac (1799–1850), French novelist

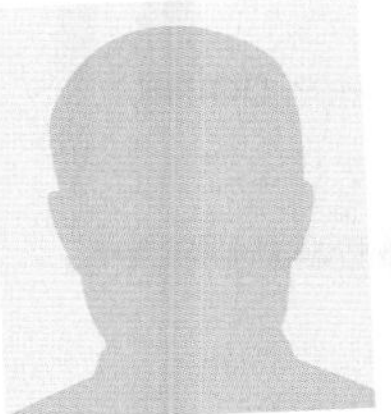

Be the change you want to see in the world.

Mahatma Gandhi (1869–1948), Indian philosopher

Knowing is not enough; we must apply. Willing is not enough; we must do.

Johann Wolfgang von Goethe (1749–1832), German writer

Don't wait. The time will never be just right.

Napoleon Hill (1883–1970), American author

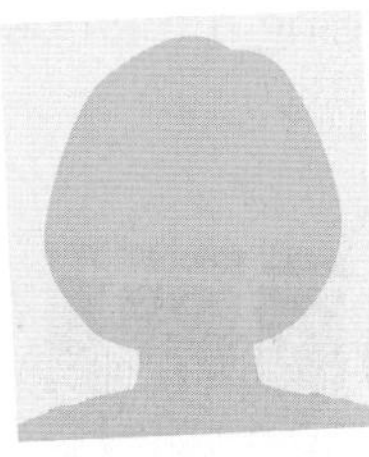

Many fine things can be done in a day if you don't always make that day tomorrow.

Anonymous

The activist is not the man who says the river is dirty. The activist is the man who cleans up the river.

Ross Perot (1930–), former American presidential candidate

In Chapter 6 you will find details of how to go about doing an action project. Make sure you read Chapter 6 before doing an action project.

What's an action project?

Doing an action project means taking action on an issue that concerns and interests you, like doing something so that more people will know about the issue. Maybe you could take action over the environment – there are hundreds of different things you could do!

ACTIVITIES

1. How did Margaret Mead suggest that the world could be changed?
2. How did Indira Gandhi think you could get change happening?
3. What did Balzac say it was more difficult to do?
4. What do you think Mahatma Gandhi meant by his words?
5. How did Ross Perot describe an activist?
6. Do you think it would be useful to keep these statements in mind when you are doing your action project?

STUDY 2 A NEW BEGINNING

You are now a member of a new school, a new **community**. There are different rules and responsibilities that come with being a member of this community.

Students Entrance

Moving from primary school to secondary school can be both an exciting and an anxious time. How do you think this move could be made easier for students?

Playing sports is one way of getting involved and meeting people in your new school community. What other ways are there?

Read what Sam thinks of his first week in school.

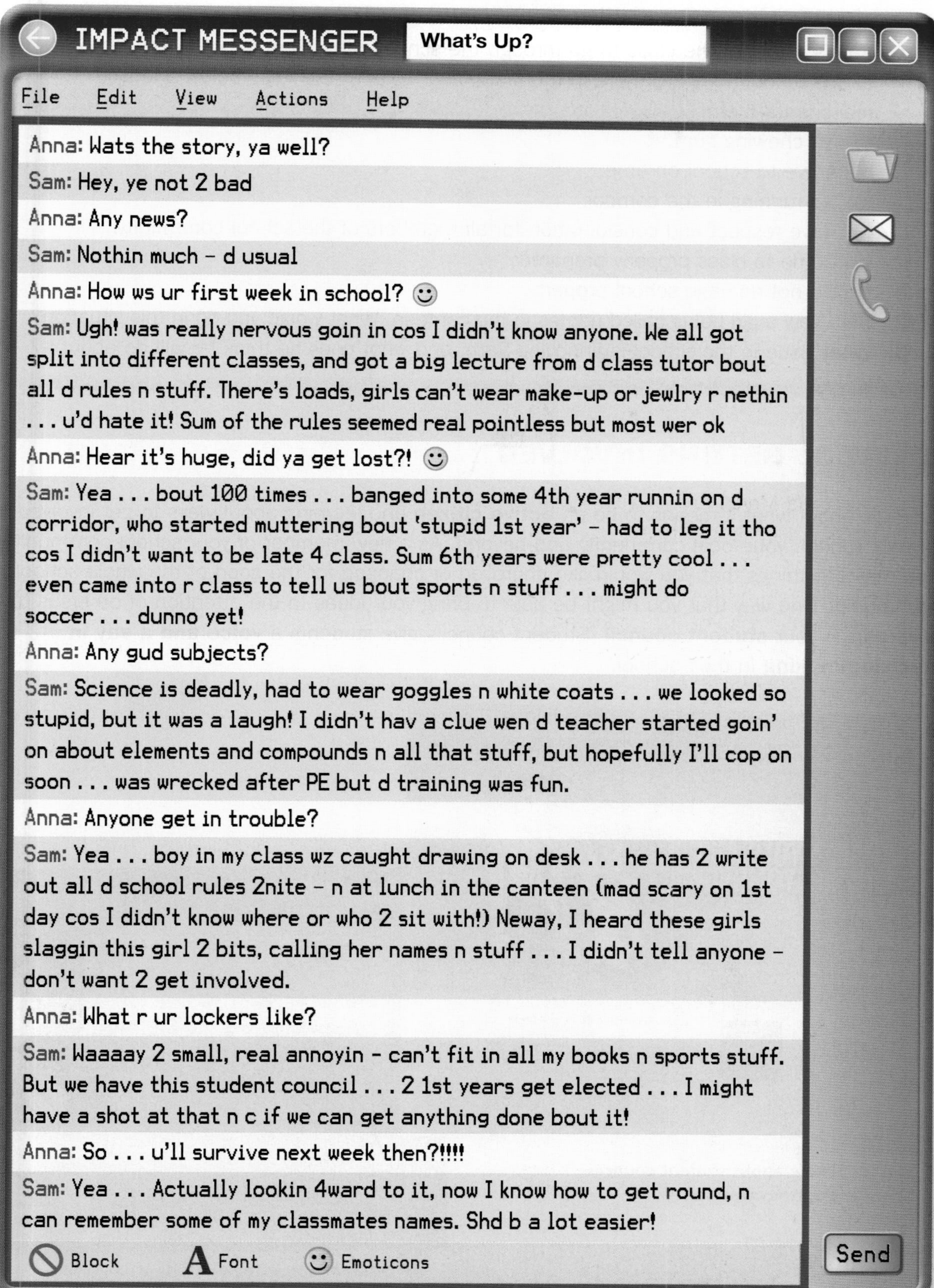

IMPACT MESSENGER
What's Up?
File Edit View Actions Help
Anna: Wats the story, ya well?
Sam: Hey, ye not 2 bad
Anna: Any news?
Sam: Nothin much – d usual
Anna: How ws ur first week in school? ☺
Sam: Ugh! was really nervous goin in cos I didn't know anyone. We all got split into different classes, and got a big lecture from d class tutor bout all d rules n stuff. There's loads, girls can't wear make-up or jewlry r nethin . . . u'd hate it! Sum of the rules seemed real pointless but most wer ok
Anna: Hear it's huge, did ya get lost?! ☺
Sam: Yea . . . bout 100 times . . . banged into some 4th year runnin on d corridor, who started muttering bout 'stupid 1st year' – had to leg it tho cos I didn't want to be late 4 class. Sum 6th years were pretty cool . . . even came into r class to tell us bout sports n stuff . . . might do soccer . . . dunno yet!
Anna: Any gud subjects?
Sam: Science is deadly, had to wear goggles n white coats . . . we looked so stupid, but it was a laugh! I didn't hav a clue wen d teacher started goin' on about elements and compounds n all that stuff, but hopefully I'll cop on soon . . . was wrecked after PE but d training was fun.
Anna: Anyone get in trouble?
Sam: Yea . . . boy in my class wz caught drawing on desk . . . he has 2 write out all d school rules 2nite – n at lunch in the canteen (mad scary on 1st day cos I didn't know where or who 2 sit with!) Neway, I heard these girls slaggin this girl 2 bits, calling her names n stuff . . . I didn't tell anyone – don't want 2 get involved.
Anna: What r ur lockers like?
Sam: Waaaay 2 small, real annoyin – can't fit in all my books n sports stuff. But we have this student council . . . 2 1st years get elected . . . I might have a shot at that n c if we can get anything done bout it!
Anna: So . . . u'll survive next week then?!!!!
Sam: Yea . . . Actually lookin 4ward to it, now I know how to get round, n can remember some of my classmates names. Shd b a lot easier!
Block
Font
Emoticons
Send

ACTIVITIES

1. Sam's tutor got the class to go through the school rules. Sam is not sure why some of the school rules are there in the first place. Look at the rules below and give reasons for them.
   a) No chewing gum.
   b) Arrive to school on time.
   c) No running in the corridor.
   d) Have respect and consideration for all members of the school community.
   e) Come to class properly prepared.
   f) Do not damage school property.
2. Sam saw a girl being called names in the canteen. What would you do in this situation?
3. What issue in the school is annoying Sam, and what does he think he will do about it?

STUDY 3 GETTING INVOLVED

CSPE is about what it means to be an **active citizen** and learning about ways to get involved in your school, your local community and beyond. As a new member of your school community you may see things that you would like improved or changed for the good of the whole school community. One way that you might be able to bring your ideas to the attention of others is to take part in your **student council**. Student councils give students a **voice and a say in decision-making** in their school.

Find out more about student councils at www.studentcouncil.ie

Student councils give students a voice and a say in decision-making

Usually the student council works with a teacher, who is the link person between students, staff and management in the school. Taking part in your student council means you first have to convince your classmates that you have good ideas, and that you would act in a responsible way and take your job seriously. The student council is one group in the school that works to make sure that school life is a good experience for everyone. Other groups, such as the staff, the board of management and the parents' association, also hold meetings to discuss issues and ideas that are important to the whole school community.

Look at this student's election leaflet for the student council and see how she tried to convince her classmates that they should vote for her. Then answer the questions that follow.

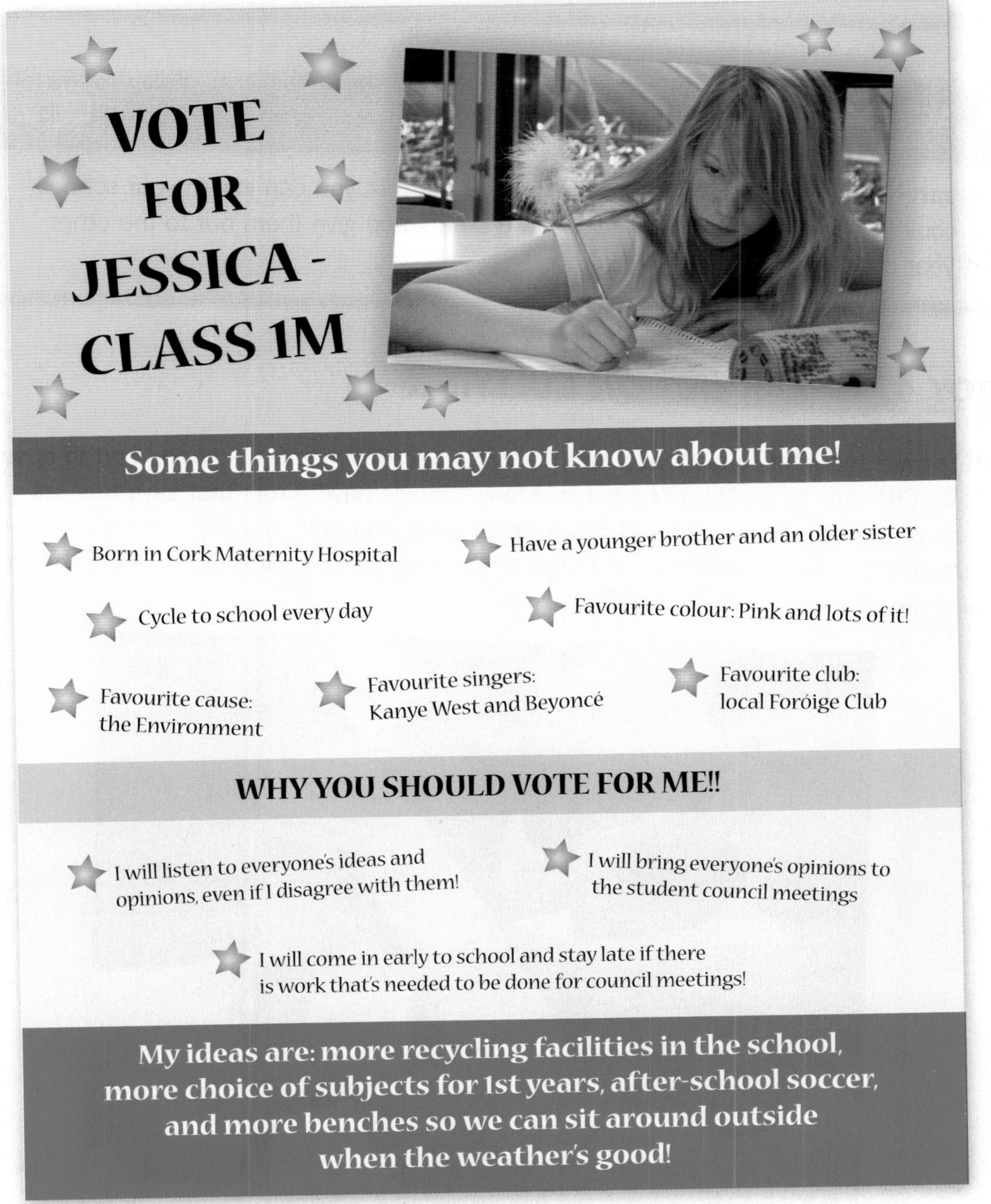

VOTE FOR JESSICA - CLASS 1M
Some things you may not know about me!
Born in Cork Maternity Hospital
Have a younger brother and an older sister
Cycle to school every day
Favourite colour: Pink and lots of it!
Favourite cause: the Environment
Favourite singers: Kanye West and Beyoncé
Favourite club: local Foróige Club
WHY YOU SHOULD VOTE FOR ME!!
I will listen to everyone's ideas and opinions, even if I disagree with them!
I will bring everyone's opinions to the student council meetings
I will come in early to school and stay late if there is work that's needed to be done for council meetings!
My ideas are: more recycling facilities in the school, more choice of subjects for 1st years, after-school soccer, and more benches so we can sit around outside when the weather's good!

(Adapted from leaflet produced by Catherine Murnane, Loreto College, St Stephen's Green)

 ACTIVITIES 

1. Give **two reasons** why you would vote for Jessica.
2. Name **two concerns** you have as a first year.
3. Design your own election leaflet telling other students:
   a) something about yourself
   b) reasons why they should vote for you.
4. If you were the class rep on the school council, what issues would you raise that are of concern to first years?

 ACTION IDEA 

Research: Find out about all the clubs and teams that you can join in your school. You could make a list of all these clubs and teams and give them out to the other first-year classes.

STUDY 4 SPEAK OUT ON BULLYING

Students have the right to feel **safe and secure** when they come to school, and to have friends and be able to learn and have fun. Many schools have a rule that says that 'all members of the school should **treat each other with respect**'. Bullying means a person is not treated with respect, school is no longer enjoyable and it is not a place where they feel safe and secure.

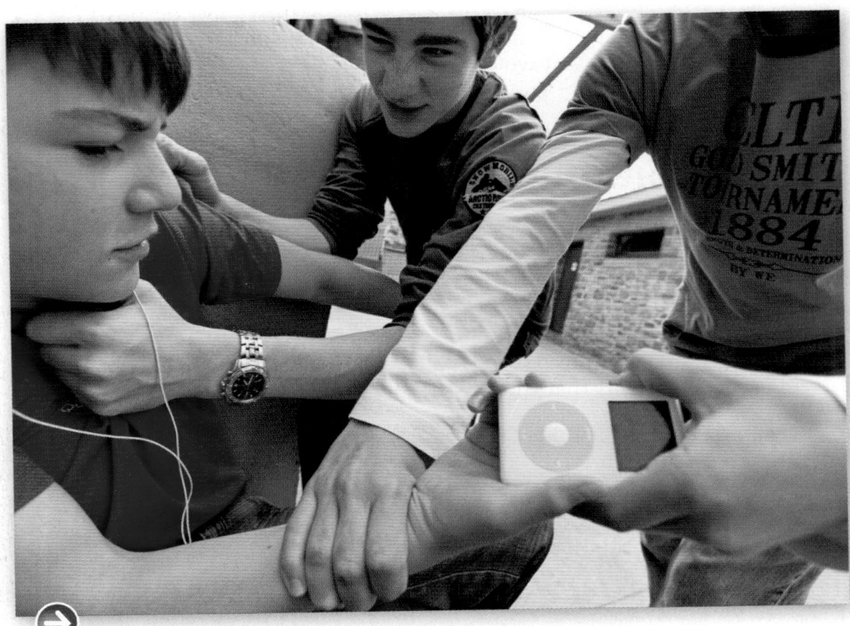

How can everyone in the school community make sure that school is a safe and happy place for all?

Playground Blues

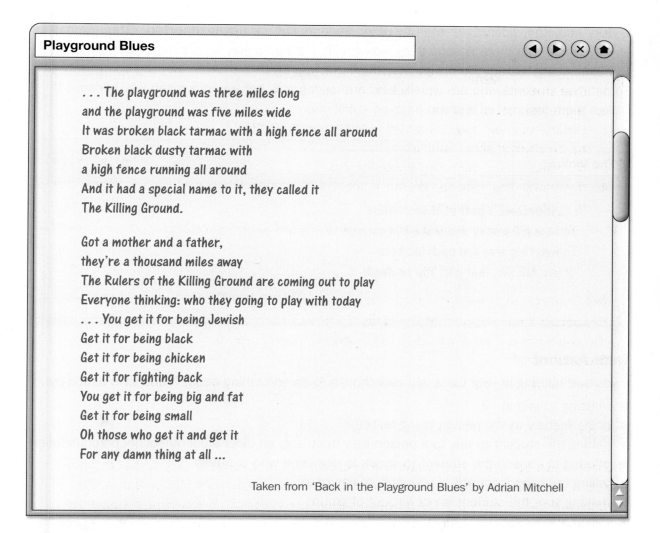

. . . The playground was three miles long
and the playground was five miles wide
It was broken black tarmac with a high fence all around
Broken black dusty tarmac with
a high fence running all around
And it had a special name to it, they called it
The Killing Ground.

Got a mother and a father,
they're a thousand miles away
The Rulers of the Killing Ground are coming out to play
Everyone thinking: who they going to play with today
. . . You get it for being Jewish
Get it for being black
Get it for being chicken
Get it for fighting back
You get it for being big and fat
Get it for being small
Oh those who get it and get it
For any damn thing at all ...

Taken from 'Back in the Playground Blues' by Adrian Mitchell

People do not have a right to hurt others. Bullying is a behaviour that is hurtful, done on purpose and lasts for weeks, months or even years. It is often very difficult for those being bullied to defend themselves.

What is Bullying Behaviour?

- Spreading rumours about people, including online gossiping.
- Name-calling and teasing.
- Threatening people or making them do things they don't want to.
- Kicking, hitting or punching them.
- Saying or writing nasty things about them.
- Sending mean text messages.
- Taking and hiding their things.
- Saying racist or sexist things.
- Ignoring them or leaving them out on purpose.

What kind of bullying does this poster highlight?

A lot of bullying incidents are seen by other students but are **never reported**. Often there is an unwritten rule that there is something wrong with 'ratting'. If you do nothing when you see someone being bullied, the bullies may think that you agree with what they are doing. Sometimes students who are usually kind and caring may behave in a mean way because it makes them feel part of a group.

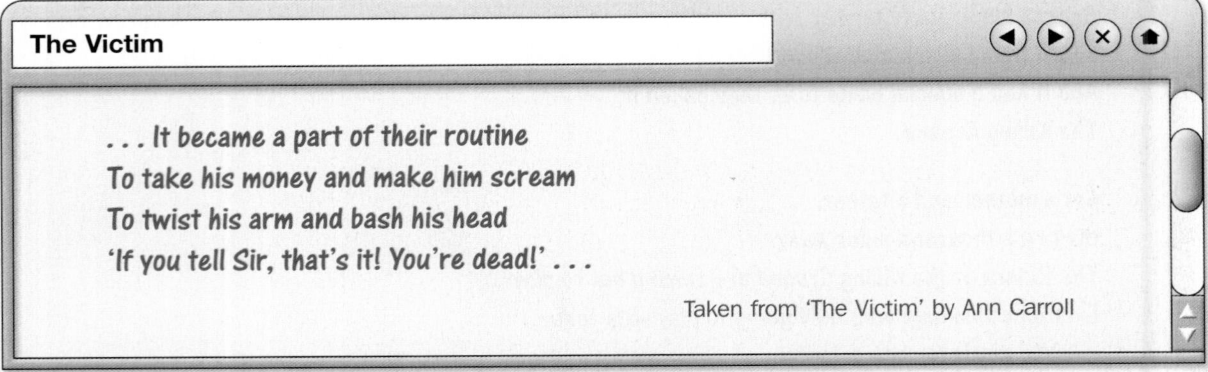

The Victim
... It became a part of their routine
To take his money and make him scream
To twist his arm and bash his head
'If you tell Sir, that's it! You're dead!' ...
Taken from 'The Victim' by Ann Carroll

Take Action!

If you see bullying in your class you can choose to do something about it and take action by:

- refusing to join in
- being friendly to the person being bullied
- getting the student to talk to a person they trust, e.g. an older student/teacher/parent/relation
- offering to go with the student to speak to someone who can help
- telling the school council (if your school has one)
- making sure the student is not left out of groups
- telling a teacher.

Cyber Bullying

Mobile phones and the internet can be great for keeping in touch with friends via texts and using sites like Bebo, Facebook, MySpace and Twitter to chat, but they can also be abused and used as a way of bullying – this is **cyber bullying**.

Cyber bullying can be very painful for victims because the audience may be very large, with messages or images being forwarded from one group to another.

In Ireland, if you take away someone's good name by saying or writing nasty stuff about them, you could be guilty of breaking the law.

Cyber Bullying and How to Protect Yourself

1. Always respect others – be careful what you say online and what images you send.
2. Think before you send – whatever you send can be made public very quickly and can stay online forever.
3. Treat your password like your toothbrush – keep it to yourself. Only give your mobile number or web address to trusted friends.
4. Don't intentionally exclude someone from an online group, like a buddy list or game, or share someone's secrets or embarrassing information online.
5. Block the bully – learn how to block or report someone who is behaving badly, and don't reply.

6. Save the evidence – learn how to keep records of offending messages, pictures or online conversations.
7. Check the service provider's website to see where to report incidents and have content removed.
8. Make sure you tell a trusted adult, a teacher, or someone responsible for anti-bullying in your school.
9. If you see or know that cyber bullying is happening in your school or to your friends, support the victim and report the bullying.

Text adapted from document written by Childnet International for the Department of Children, Schools and Families in the United Kingdom

Be a good cybercitizen – don't take part; don't let cyberbullies use you to embarrass and torment others. As Martin Luther King Jr once said, 'In the end we will remember not the words of our enemies but the silence of our friends.'

Take Action!

In 2009, 17 social networking sites, including Bebo, Facebook and MySpace, signed a European Union (EU) pact on **child safety**, in order to stop online bullying and to let young people know how to protect themselves. Measures they decided on included the introduction of an easy-to-use **'report abuse' button** on their sites.

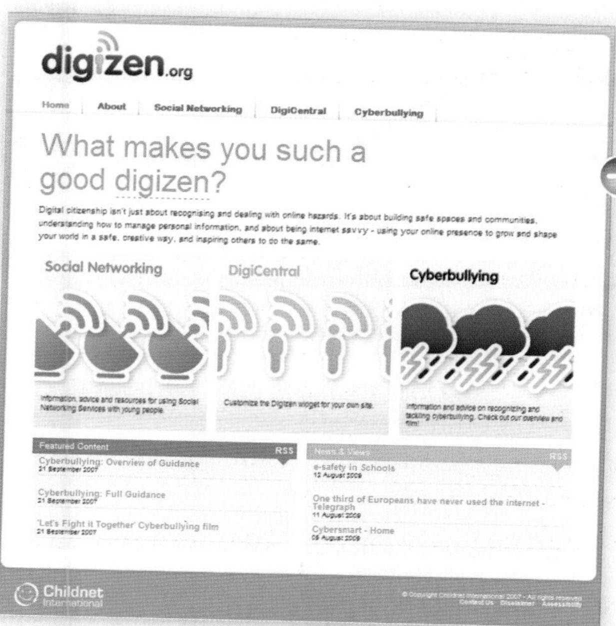

For more information and advice on recognising and tackling cyber bullying, check out www.digizen.org, which is all about digital citizenship and how you can be a good citizen in cyberspace and use your online presence in a safe and creative way

Whether in cyberspace or not, there is never a reason for bullying. We all have a right to come to school and feel safe there. Bullying is a behaviour that denies people the right to be treated with **dignity and respect**. Everybody in the school community should . . . **Speak Out and Take Action on Bullying!**

ACTIVITIES

1. Design an anti-cyber bullying poster. Make up a slogan to go with it.
2. In the poem 'Back in the Playground Blues', how does the young person show that they are afraid of the playground?
3. Why does the person in the poem feel that their mother and father are 'a thousand miles away'?
4. Write another verse for 'Playground Blues' or a poem of your own that describes the effects of cyber bullying on a person.
5. In the poem 'The Victim', why do you think the bullies' behaviour is allowed to continue?
6. Who could you report a bullying incident to in your school?
7. Students who are being bullied are sometimes afraid to tell anyone about what is happening. What signs can parents and teachers look out for in pupils who might be being bullied?
8. If you became aware of someone being bullied, what could you do to help? (*Hints:* hang out with them at break time, walk home with them, report the incident to the website service provider, etc.)
9. Give two ways your school council could help make your school a bully-free zone.

ACTION IDEA

Design a cyberbullying information leaflet. Using the websites listed below, put together a leaflet on how to prevent cyberbullying for your school community.

Check out:
www.thinkb4uclick.ie – a CSPE resource all about cyberbullying and what to do about it
www.webwise.ie – find out how to be a wise web user
www.watchyourspace.ie – for more tips on cyber safety.

ACTIVITIES

1. Look at the list below. Put each item under either 'Need' or 'Want'.

Healthy food	CD player	Water
A home	Skateboard	Clean air
Mars bar	Medical care	Pocket money
Sports gear	Have opinion listened to	Protection from abuse
Own bedroom	Somewhere to play	

2. Choose **five rights** from the UN Declaration of Human Rights and rank them from 1 to 5 in descending order of importance.
3. Make a Charter of Rights for:
   a) students
   b) teachers
   c) parents/guardians.
4. Looking at the four categories of rights in the UNCRC, which category do you think is the most important? Give reasons for your answer.
5. Look again at all the rights included in the UNCRC, and decide on **three further steps** that you think need to be taken by the Irish Government to improve the lives of children in Ireland. Give reasons for your answer.

STUDY 6 STANDING UP FOR CHILDREN'S RIGHTS

Dr Janusz Korczak

Henryk Goldsmit was born in Warsaw, Poland in 1878. He took the pen name of Dr Janusz Korczak when he became a writer of popular children's books, and he was known by this name for the rest of his life. As well as an author, he was also a children's doctor, and a passionate **defender and promoter of the rights of children**.

Dr Janusz Korczak

Henryk Goldsmit gave up his successful medical practice to open two orphanages in Warsaw, one for Jewish children and the other for Catholic children. He tried to make sure that children were really listened to by setting up the children's own **parliament and court** in the orphanages. He did this because he believed that '*children are not people of tomorrow, but people today*', and that showing respect to them as young citizens would in turn help them develop a sense of responsibility towards others.

Dr Janusz Korczak

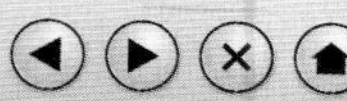

He also started the first ever section of a newspaper especially for young people. This was called the *Little Review* and it was published every Friday with the main Polish newspaper. The *Little Review* published stories by children on every topic from hobbies to pets to politics. The paper also had a section for letters, where children wrote in about problems that were bothering them. Some of these letters were from Jewish children, who wrote about **anti-Semitism** (policies and actions that harmed or discriminated against Jewish people) in their schools.

In Dr Korczak's orphanages, children had their own parliament and court

Children in the Warsaw ghetto during World War II

In 1939, Germany invaded Poland and World War II began. The following year, the Nazis decided to create a 'special quarter', or **ghetto**, in the city of Warsaw. All Jewish people, including Korczak's orphans, had to move to the ghetto. Inside the ghetto, Korczak continued to hold lessons and concerts for the children, and he had to beg other Jewish residents in the ghetto and Christians beyond the walls for food for the 192 children in his care.

On 6 August 1942 Nazi SS officers arrived at the door of the orphanage to tell Korczak that the children were being transported by train to the East . . . exactly where wasn't explained. Korczak was again offered the chance, as he had been many other times since the beginning of the war, to leave the children and save himself, but he refused to do so.

Dr Korczak's orphans were taken to the concentration camp at Treblinka

Dr Janusz Korczak

Dressed in their best clothes and holding little toys, the children marched and sang on the way to the transport area, with Korczak doing everything he could to protect them and keep them calm. The train took Korczak and the children to the concentration camp at Treblinka. None of them survived to tell their story.

Many hospitals, streets and schools in different European countries are named in Korczak's memory, and he remains a powerful example of a life dedicated, to the very end, to the **rights and dignity of children**.

The belongings of those who were taken to Treblinka and did not survive

To this day Dr Korczak is still remembered in many European countries as a defender of children's rights

The story of Korczak and the children being sent to Treblinka concentration camp is written about in Wladyslaw Szpilman's book *The Pianist*, which was later made into a film

ACTIVITIES

1. Why did Dr Korczak give up his medical practice?
2. How did he make sure that children in his orphanage were listened to?
3. What problem did some Jewish children write to the *Little Review* about?
4. Where did the Nazis move Korczak's orphans after World War II began?
5. Where were Korczak and the orphans finally taken?

ACTION IDEA

Guest speaker: There are still a small number of Holocaust survivors in Ireland today, who lived as children in concentration camps in World War II. You could contact the **Holocaust Educational Trust Ireland** for information on Holocaust survivors and programmes specifically tailored for secondary schools: 01 669 0593 or info@hetireland.org.

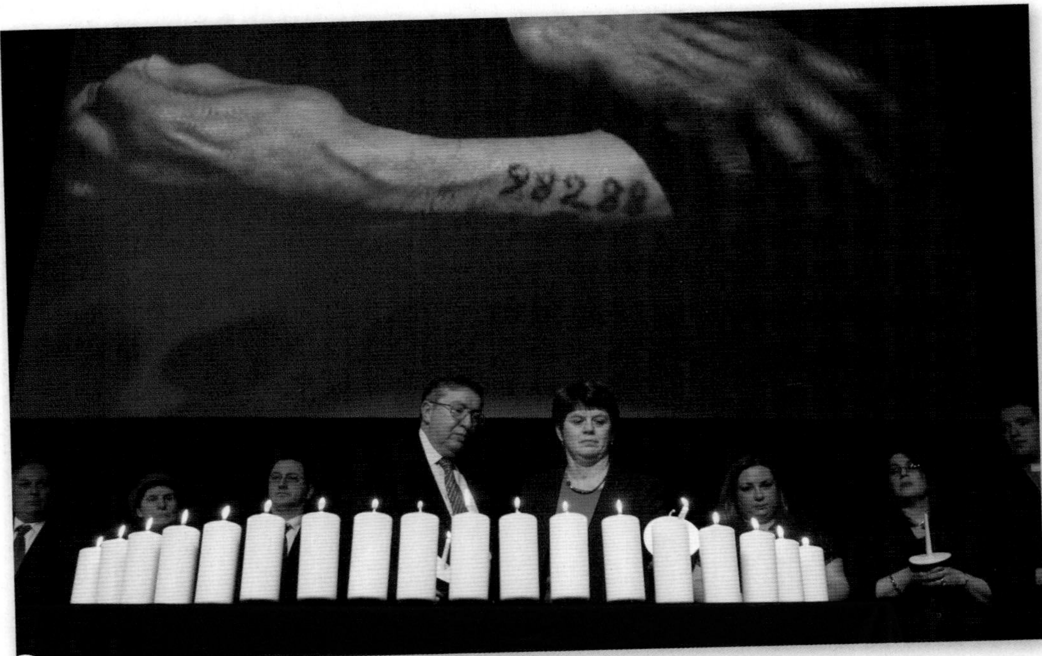

Lighting candles during the Holocaust Memorial Day commemoration at the Mansion House, Dublin, where President McAleese said, 'Never forgetting is our duty and our responsibility'

The Holocaust Educational Trust Ireland educates and informs people about the Holocaust in order to address anti-Semitism and all forms of racism and intolerance in Ireland. See www.hetireland.org.

STUDY 7 RIGHTS ON OUR DOORSTEP

The first article of the **UN Declaration of Human Rights** says, *'Everyone is born free and equal'*, yet many people are not treated equally. They are unable to join or fully take part in society. In our society, **some groups of people do not have equal rights**. These groups include people who are homeless, people with disabilities and people living in poverty.

Here is an example of some of the rights that these groups can be denied.

People who do not have equal rights	Rights included in the UNDHR
Homeless people	Right to housing
People with disabilities	Right to work
People living in poverty	Right to food and clothing
Members of the Traveller community	Right to be treated equally and with respect

Looking Out for Others

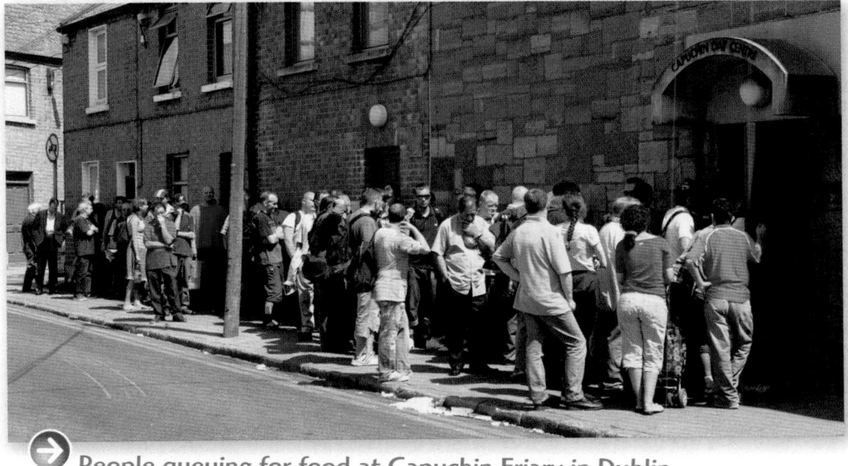

People queuing for food at Capuchin Friary in Dublin

There are many organisations that concern themselves with the rights of certain groups, **raising awareness** of their situation and helping them. For example, **Focus Ireland** and the **Simon Community** are concerned with the needs and rights of people who are homeless. **Pavee Point** and the **Irish Traveller Movement** are concerned with the needs and rights of the Traveller community; **ALONE** with the needs and rights of elderly people; the **Irish Society for the Prevention of Cruelty to Children** with the rights and needs of children; and the **Irish Wheelchair Association** with the rights of people with disabilities.

These organisations **rely on people to support them** in their work and provide opportunities for individuals to volunteer and give their time to help support others.

Read the following story of one person who volunteered his time and took action to support the rights of others.

Taking Action

View from a Volunteer

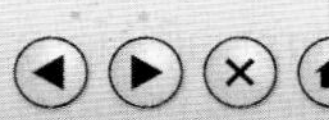

Simon Community volunteers on a soup run

I joined the Simon Community as a volunteer just over a year ago. I suppose I probably signed up for the same reasons that a lot of other people do: I'd seen people begging around town and wanted to do something other than throwing coins into a cup, but had no idea how to go about it. I heard about Simon, went for the interview, the ladies who interviewed me listened to what I had in mind and suggested that I attend the Social Club in Capel Street on Monday nights.

Before I attended the Social Club, I'll be honest, I had a idea of a 'typical homeless person'. I think it's fair to say that notion has been shattered over the last year! At the club, I've met some of the funniest, most intelligent people I've ever been lucky enough to meet. Every week I'll learn something new, the broad knowledge some of the guys have on so many subjects is genuinely breath-taking and I've also had the misfortune of being humiliated at Scrabble on far too many occasions.

Not that I'm trying to paint a completely idyllic, rose-tinted picture. Obviously there are people who attend the club that you wouldn't leave unattended with your wallet, but in my experience the good far outnumber the bad. Initially I would have preferred to have been assigned to the soup run, but now I'm delighted with the way things have worked out. By meeting the same 'users' week in, week out in Capel Street, I think I've been able to get to know them much better, and hopefully build up a bond of trust and friendship with some of them. The same goes for the other volunteers, of course. Everybody from day one was very friendly and very helpful, for which I'm very grateful.

Warren

(Taken from *Dublin Simon Newsletter*, December 2007)

ACTIVITIES

1. Can you name other groups in Ireland who do not have equal rights? What rights do they not have?
2. Who do you think is responsible for making sure that everyone has equal rights in Ireland?
3. How well does your school meet the needs of people with disabilities? Make a list of the changes that would have to be made in your school so that a wheelchair user and a person who is blind could take part fully in school life.
4. How was Warren's image of a 'typical homeless person' changed by his experience as a volunteer?
5. Name **three other ways** in which people support the work of organisations such as Simon.

STUDY 8 DISCRIMINATION ON OUR DOORSTEP

If people **label** a certain group or community as being bad, blame them when things go wrong and give them no help to improve their situation, this is called **discrimination**. Often, people are discriminated against because of **stereotyping** and **prejudice**.

Ok – let's organise the experiment. Seán, you sort out the computer. Kevin, you get the chemicals. And Ann…well, maybe you might be best at cleaning up afterwards.
That's always my job!

An example of a stereotype is to say that all Irish people drink too much, or all women are better than men at minding children. Stereotyping can give rise to **prejudice**. Prejudice means **prejudging** a person or group. It is having a view of a person or group without really knowing them. The Traveller community are often stereotyped and experience discrimination. Pavee Point is an organisation that **promotes Travellers' human rights**. There are approximately 24,000 Travellers in Ireland, and:

- only 3.3 per cent are aged 65 or over
- 48 per cent have no piped water
- 50 per cent have no toilet
- 54 per cent have no access to electricity.

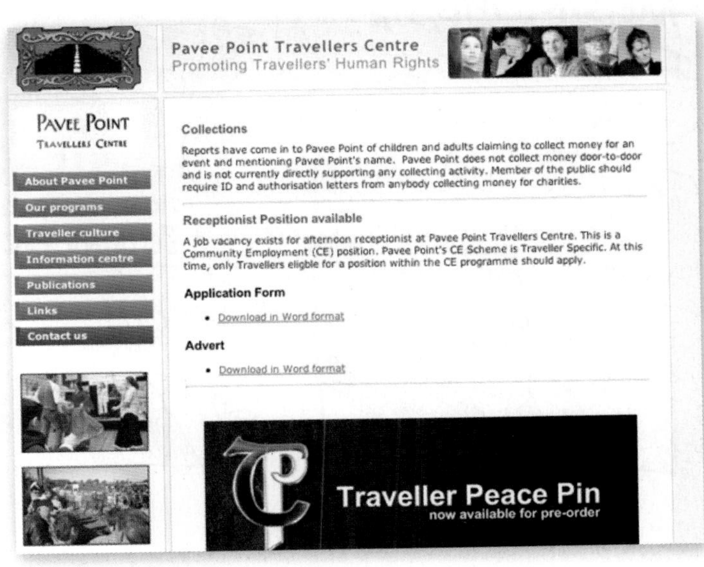

Our programs

Contact us
Collections
Reports have come in to Pavee Point of children and adults claiming to collect money for an event and mentioning Pavee Point's name. Pavee Point does not collect money door-to-door and is not currently directly supporting any collecting activity. Member of the public should require ID and authorisation letters from anybody collecting money for charities.
Receptionist Position available
A job vacancy exists for afternoon receptionist at Pavee Point Travellers Centre. This is a Community Employment (CE) position. Pavee Point's CE Scheme is Traveller Specific. At this time, only Travellers eligble for a position within the CE programme should apply.
Application Form
Download in Word format

Download in Word format
Traveller Peace Pin
now available for pre-order

Noel Know-All

Read about Noel Know-All and see the ways he prejudges his classmate.

Thanks to Pavee Point for permission to reproduce this cartoon

What are these people taking action about?

ACTIVITIES

1. Explain in your own words what discrimination means.
2. Name some other groups in society that are often stereotyped, and describe the stereotyping. (Hints: teenagers/football fans/teachers.)
3. What is Noel Know-All's information about the Traveller community based on?
4. What stereotype does Noel show when he says, 'But you look like a normal person ... You're not supposed to know more than me'?
5. What does Mary say all Travellers 'are really asking for'?
6. List **four facts** Mary tells us about the Traveller community.
7. Look at the poster and answer the questions that follow:

a) What message is this poster trying to get across?
b) How do the words on the poster help get the message out?

STUDY 9 RIGHTS ACROSS THE GLOBE

Amnesty International is an organisation that campaigns for **human rights**. It was set up by British lawyer Peter Benenson in 1961 after he read about two Portuguese students who had been sentenced to seven years in prison for raising their glasses in a toast to freedom. At the time, Portugal was run by a military dictatorship.

Today Amnesty has over 1.8 million members in over 150 countries. There are also over 3,500 youth and student groups worldwide, including 150 groups in schools across the Republic of Ireland. You can find out about Amnesty using:

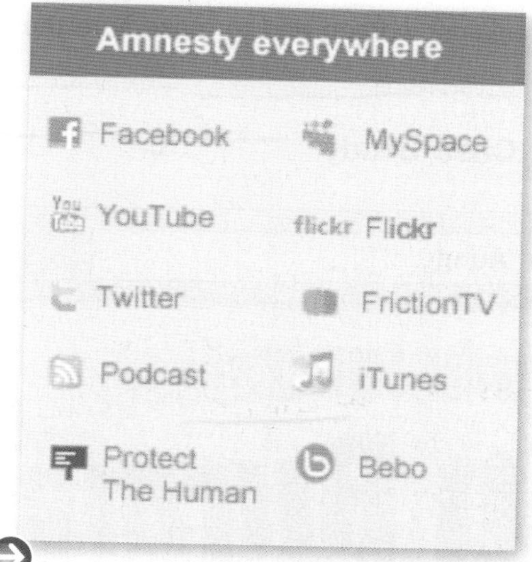

In what way can social networking sites support the work of organisations like Amnesty?

Amnesty's famous symbol of a candle and barbed wire was inspired by the Chinese proverb, 'It is better to light one candle than to curse the darkness.'

As Peter Benenson himself put it: 'The candle burns not for us, but for all those whom we failed to rescue from prison, who were shot on the way to prison, who were tortured, who were kidnapped, who "disappeared". That's what the candle is for.'

These words can be seen around the 'Eternal Flame' near the Customs House in Dublin city centre. They are also to be found on posters, T-shirts and postcards in lots of languages all over the world. The candle is seen everywhere as a **symbol of hope, justice and freedom**. Amnesty's vision is of a world in which every person enjoys all the human rights written in the **Universal Declaration of Human Rights** and other international human rights documents.

There are hundreds of Amnesty school groups in Ireland. Does your school have an Amnesty group?

The Aims of Amnesty

The work of Amnesty includes promoting awareness of human rights and working to stop specific abuses of human rights such as:

- torture and cruel treatment of prisoners
- the death penalty
- the imprisonment of people because of their beliefs, ethnic origins, sex or colour
- executions and disappearances.

Amnesty members have always worked on behalf of people in countries around the world. Now they can also act on issues which affect the countries in which they live. For example, Amnesty members in Ireland have worked to raise awareness of racism and have campaigned for fair treatment for asylum seekers and refugees in Ireland. They have also campaigned to stop violence against women and to make sure the human rights of children in Ireland are protected.

Amnesty Takes Action: Case Study

Student Activist Thet Win Aung

Protesting for human rights in Burma

Ko Thet Win Aung, a student and human rights activist, was arrested in 1998 and sentenced to 52 years' imprisonment in Myanmar (Burma). This was later increased to 59 years. He was arrested with other students for his part in organising peaceful small-scale student demonstrations which called for improvements to the educational system in Myanmar and for the release of political prisoners.

He and other students are believed not to have had access to lawyers, and when they asked prison officials and the presiding judge to see a lawyer, the judge is reported to have made no response. They were denied the right to speak in their own defence.

Ko Thet Win Aung was badly tortured during his imprisonment, and also suffered from a variety of health problems, including malaria. In 2006 Ko Thet Win Aung, student leader and prisoner of conscience, imprisoned for exercising his right to freedom of expression, died in prison.

Amnesty International is concerned that many prisoners of conscience are continuing to be denied their freedom, as Thet Win Aung was, solely on the basis of their peaceful exercise of basic rights.

As a member state of the United Nations, Myanmar must uphold all of the rights outlined in the Universal Declaration of Human Rights. Amnesty International calls on the Burmese authorities to grant the immediate release of all prisoners of conscience in Myanmar (Burma).

Source: Amnesty International, www.amnesty.org

The Power of the Pen or Mouse

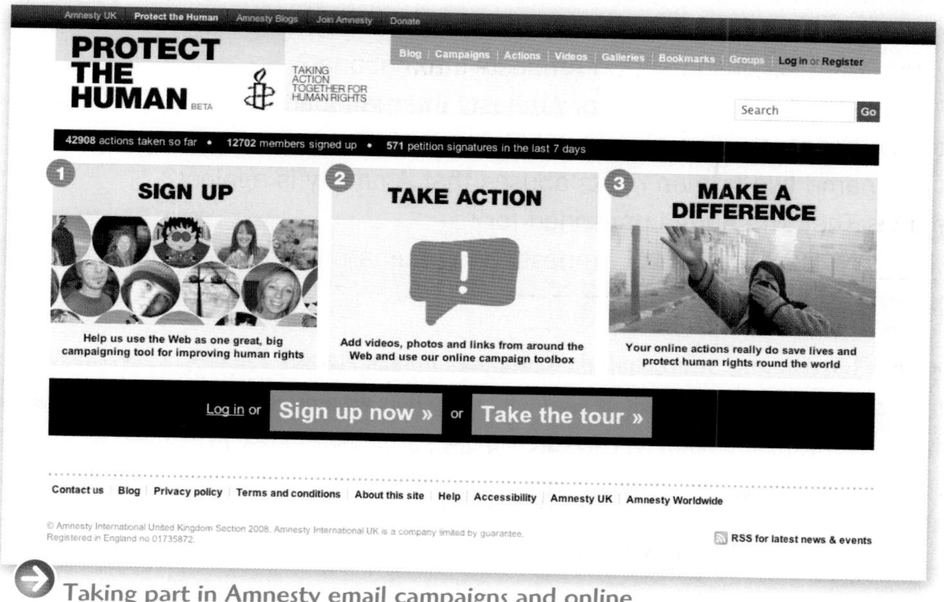

Taking part in Amnesty email campaigns and online petitions is one way you can support human rights

One of the ways Amnesty brings human rights abuses to the attention of governments is through letter writing and email campaigns. Amnesty members and supporters write to governments, prison officials and other people of influence. They sometimes write to the prisoners themselves. This puts pressure on those holding prisoners and gives hope and comfort to those being held. It has helped to get prisoners released and to improve their conditions.

Amnesty often receives letters from those who have been released.

Constantino Coronel, released prisoner of conscience, Paraguay:

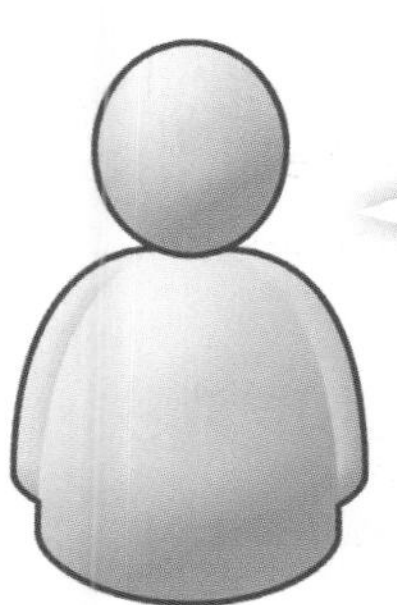

For years I was held in a tiny cell. My only human contact was with my torturers. For two and a half of those years I did not experience the glance of a human face, see a green leaf. My only company was the cockroaches and mice . . . On Christmas Eve the door of my cell opened and the guard tossed in a crumpled piece of paper . . . It said simply 'Constantino, do not be discouraged; we know you are alive.' It was signed 'Monica' and had the Amnesty International candle on it. Eight months later I was set free.

Former torturer, El Salvador:

If there's a lot of pressure, like from Amnesty International, we might pass the political prisoners on to a judge. But if there's no pressure, then they're dead.

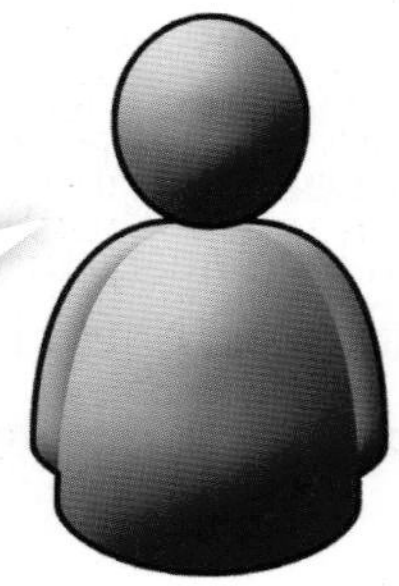

ACTIVITIES

1. Why did Peter Benenson set up Amnesty International?
2. What does the famous symbol of Amnesty International stand for?
3. What is Amnesty's vision of the world?
4. Can you name two human rights abuses that Amnesty is against?
5. What was Thet Win Aung imprisoned for?
6. In what ways do members of Amnesty bring human rights abuses to the attention of governments?
7. *People often ask me, 'what can I do to support human rights? I'm only an ordinary worker – but I do care!' To the woman or man who asks that vital question I have a simple answer. 'Great! Why not join Amnesty?' Amnesty helps caring individuals to connect with political prisoners, with issues of violence against women, with the campaign against small arms that kill so many – all the key human rights issues. You can make a difference – sign on!*

   Quoted in *Amnesty Newsletter*

Barack Obama awarded former Irish president Mary Robinson the US Presidential Medal of Freedom, America's highest civilian honour, for her contribution to world peace and human rights.

   a) What 'human rights issues' does Mary Robinson refer to?
   b) What is Amnesty's main weapon in their work to stop human rights abuses?

ACTION IDEAS

Guest speaker: If there is an Amnesty group in your school, invite one of the members to give a talk to your class on Amnesty's work.
Research: Find out about Amnesty's latest campaign by visiting their website – www.amnesty.ie. You could make an information leaflet about the campaign and give it to other students in your school.

STUDY 10 TAKING ACTION

Pastor Niemöller

Pastor Niemöller talks about what can happen when people do not look out for the rights of others. Rights and responsibilities go hand in hand, and we all have the responsibility to look out for the rights of others. In doing so we are also protecting our own rights. If you don't speak out for the rights of others, who will speak out for you?

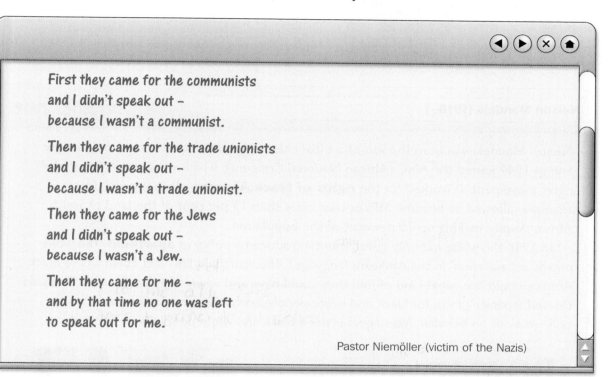

First they came for the communists
and I didn't speak out –
because I wasn't a communist.

Then they came for the trade unionists
and I didn't speak out –
because I wasn't a trade unionist.

Then they came for the Jews
and I didn't speak out –
because I wasn't a Jew.

Then they came for me –
and by that time no one was left
to speak out for me.

Pastor Niemöller (victim of the Nazis)

Amnesty International
Will you stand up for human rights ?

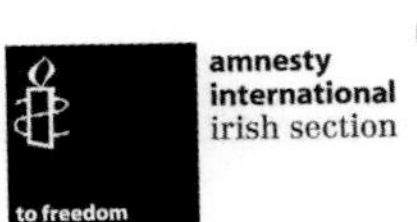

Why do you think it can be difficult to speak up for the rights of others?

Nelson Mandela

One person who spoke out against the denial of human rights in his country was Nelson Mandela.

Nelson Mandela said, 'A nation should not be judged by how it treats its highest citizens, but its lowest ones – and South Africa treated its imprisoned African citizens like animals'

Nelson Mandela (1918–)

Nelson Mandela was born the son of a tribal chief in South Africa. He became a lawyer and in 1944 joined the ANC (African National Congress), which was a non-violent civil rights movement. It worked for the **rights of black Africans** who were not, for example, allowed to become MPs or own more than 13 per cent of the land of South Africa, despite making up 75 per cent of the population.

In 1948 the white minority government introduced a policy of **apartheid** (the word means 'separateness' in the Afrikaans language). The apartheid laws laid down where black Africans could live, what kind of jobs they could have and where they could study. The laws created separate places for black and white people, such as separate toilets, and 'whites only' sections on beaches. Marriages between black and white people were banned.

In Ireland, workers in Dunnes Stores refused to handle fruit and vegetables from South Africa. The strike lasted nearly three years and was only ended when the government banned the importation of South African goods. In Johannesburg, a street is named after Mary Manning, one of the strikers. Outside the Dunnes Stores branch on Henry Street there is a plaque, given by the South African government, dedicated to the workers who stood up against apartheid.

In 1960 the government banned the ANC, and in 1962 Mandela was **sentenced to life imprisonment** for being involved in ANC activities.

Nelson Mandela spent the next 27 years in prison. During this time he became a hero to many millions of people. People in different countries showed their support by refusing to buy South African goods. In Ireland, for example, Dunnes Stores workers refused to handle any goods from South Africa.

Nelson Mandela (1918–)

In 1990 Nelson Mandela was finally released from prison and the new South African government, led by F. W. de Klerk, lifted the ban on the ANC. In the same year de Klerk ended the apartheid system.

In 1993 Nelson Mandela and de Klerk were **awarded the Nobel Peace Prize** for their efforts to bring about equality among all South Africans. In 1994 the first elections in which blacks were allowed to vote took place. Nelson Mandela became the **president of South Africa**.

On the day he became president, Mandela talked about his struggle and what he called 'the long road to freedom'. He said:

> *I have walked that long walk to freedom. But I discovered that after climbing a great hill, one only finds that there are many more hills to climb. I have taken a moment here to rest, to steal a view of the glorious vista that surrounds me, to look back on the distance I have come. But I can rest only for a moment, for with freedom comes responsibilities, and I dare not linger, for my long walk is not yet ended.*

Nelson Mandela being sworn in as president of South Africa

ACTIVITIES

1. How did the apartheid system affect the lives of the citizens of South Africa who were not white?
2. Why was the apartheid system a denial of human rights as set down in the UNDHR? (See United Nations Declaration of Human Rights, page 15.)
3. Why did Nelson Mandela and F. W. de Klerk win the Nobel Peace Prize?
4. What do you think Mandela meant when he said, 'with freedom comes responsibilities'?

Martin Luther King

In the USA in the 1950s Martin Luther King campaigned for equal rights for black people. He believed in peaceful protest.

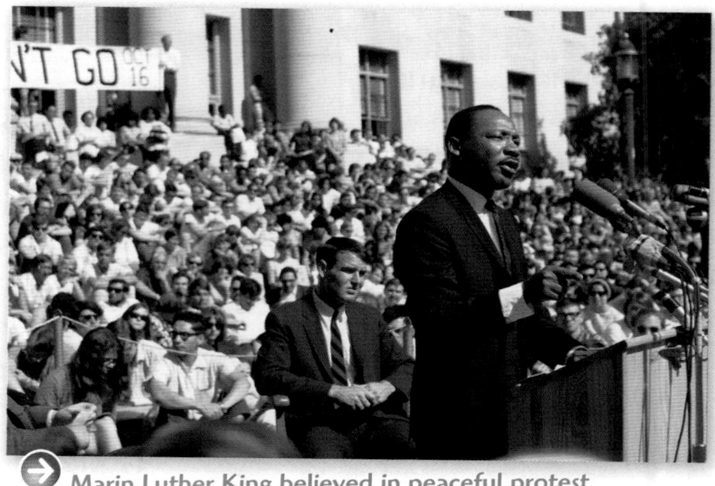

Marin Luther King believed in peaceful protest

Martin Luther King (1929–68)

Martin Luther King was born in Atlanta, Georgia, in the USA, in 1929. He became a Baptist minister like his father. When he was studying in college he read about Mahatma Gandhi and was impressed with his ideas of **non-violent protest**.

In America during the 1950s there were many laws that were unfair to black people. They had to sit in separate parts of restaurants and at the back of buses, and they even had to give up their seats on buses if a white person wanted to sit down.

One day a black woman named Rosa Parks refused to give up her seat on a bus for a white person. Martin Luther King organised a campaign in Montgomery, Alabama in which all black people refused to get on any public buses. They walked to work instead.

Rosa Parks refused to give up her seat on the bus to a white person

A crowd being water-hosed by police in Birmingham, Alabama during the 1960s civil rights protests

After 381 days, during which time Martin Luther King was put in prison, a new law was declared allowing black people to sit in any part of a bus they wanted; and they didn't have to get up to let a white person sit down any more.

Martin Luther King (1929–68)

  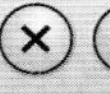 

Martin Luther King went on to lead many peaceful campaigns to get better education and housing for black people. In 1963 he led a demonstration of nearly 500,000 people for better rights for black people in front of the White House in Washington. He made a famous speech in which he said:

> *I have a dream that one day the State of Mississippi will be transformed into an oasis of freedom and justice. I have a dream that my four little children one day will live in a nation where they will not be judged by the colour of their skin . . . when all of God's children, black and white, Jews and gentiles, Protestants and Catholics, will be able to join hands . . .*

Martin Luther King continued to campaign peacefully for black people's rights until he was **assassinated in 1968**.

In memory of Martin Luther King Jr, the third Monday of January every year was made a national holiday in the USA. Many Americans now call this day the **King National Day of Service** and honour Dr King by volunteering at projects helping out those in need in their communities – delivering meals, painting and repairing schools and community centres, or collecting food and clothes for those in need.

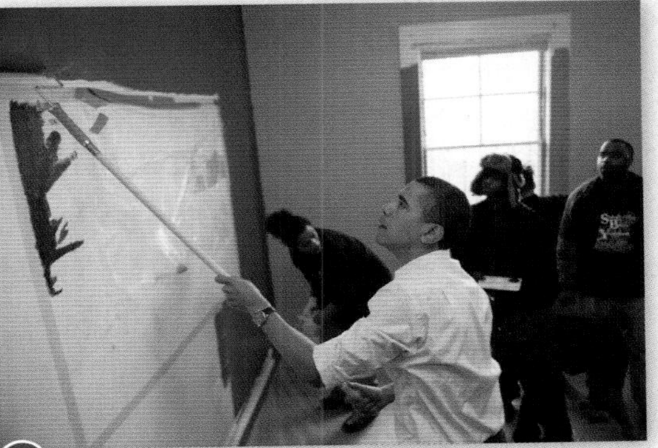

On the day before Barack Obama became the 44th president of the United States, he spent the afternoon repainting the walls of a community centre to mark King National Day.

ACTIVITIES

1. What rights did Martin Luther King campaign for?
2. What was the main message of the speech Martin Luther King gave outside the White House?
3. Name some other people who have campaigned for human rights.
4. Do you think it would be a good idea to have a National Day of Service in Ireland? It so, what national figure would the day honour? Can you come up with a list of candidates?

The Global Elders – Campaigning for Good

In 2007, in Johannesburg in South Africa, a group of people who had been involved in campaigns for human rights most of their lives came together as a group known as the Elders. The group includes Nelson Mandela, Desmond Tutu, Kofi Annan, **Mary Robinson**, Muhammad Yunus and Aung San Suu Kyi among others. (You can read the biographies of the elders at www.theelders.org.)

The Global Elders was formed to help solve world problems such as poverty, HIV/Aids and climate change

The idea behind this group came from the former President of South Africa, Nelson Mandela, the businessman Richard Branson and the musician Peter Gabriel. They had discussed the fact that the world is becoming more like a village, and had the idea that a group of global elders could help solve global problems in the way that traditional village elders were trusted to try and settle conflicts in their communities.

They hope to be able to use their long experience to help solve problems like poverty, HIV/Aids and climate change. Another aim is to be able to use their experience to try and help solve conflicts in the Middle East, Africa and wherever they may occur around the world. Nelson Mandela said:

This group can speak freely and boldly, working both publicly and behind the scenes on whatever actions need to be taken. Together we will work to support courage where there is fear, foster agreement where there is conflict, and inspire hope where there is despair.

Kofi Annan, former General Secretary of the United Nations, said of this campaign:

I'm sure if we all work together and we all take the attitude of 'what can we do', 'how can we organise ourselves to do it?', we can make a difference to this world of ours. These thoughts are similar to what a former campaigner for human rights, Mahatma Gandhi said, 'Be the change you want to see in the world.'

Check out www.everyhumanhasrights.org

The Elders have also started a major campaign called 'Every Human Has Rights' to try to ensure that the rights laid out in the United Nations Declaration of Human Rights becomes not just a vision for what all people should have, but a reality and what everyone is entitled to, regardless of their religion, colour, gender or where they were born in the world. **They believe that the biggest enemy of human rights in the world today is silence.**

ACTIVITIES

1. In what ways has the world become more like a global village?
2. In what ways can the Global Elders fight for the rights of others?
3. Why would 'silence' be the biggest enemy of human rights?

ACTION IDEA

Find out more about how other people have stood up for human rights by researching their stories on www.everyhumanhasrights.org.

STUDY 11 IDEAS FOR ACTION PROJECTS

See how you might go about doing an action project by reading the interview below. Then look at the other ideas for action projects that follow and see what other issues your class could take action over.

Doing an Action Project – the Brief Guide

So why did you choose this action?
We were talking in CSPE class about how lost we all felt in first year and how we didn't know how to get involved in clubs and school life.

Who did you communicate with?
The whole school community, the student council and school staff.

Why were these people involved in the action project?
We had to talk to lots of different teachers and senior students to find out what was going on in the school. We also had to ask the student council to give us a hand.
Can you list the different activities or tasks you were involved in?
Sure:
- We brainstormed to find the best ideas to help students
- We voted on doing a factsheet
- We divided into groups to research all the different clubs and sports
- We made a factsheet
- We asked the Principal if he wanted to add anything
- We went to the student council and asked the student reps to give it to everyone.

Can you describe one thing that you did?
I was responsible for going to the student council and telling them why we thought a factsheet would be really helpful, especially for first years and new students.

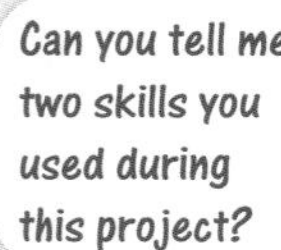

Can you tell me two skills you used during this project?
I improved my communication skills when I had to talk to the council. I improved my presentation skills when I showed them different designs we'd come up with for the factsheet.

Action Project Ideas on . . .

Your School

1. You and your classmates could put together a charter stating the kind of behaviour that shows respect for everyone's human rights.
2. Find out if your school has an anti-cyber bullying policy. Such policies need to be updated because technology is changing so fast. You could bring your suggestions to the student council and school management.

Rights and Responsibilities

1. Contact a voluntary organisation and design an information poster about their work. This could be displayed around the school.
2. Many national organisations like the Irish Red Cross have local branches. Invite a local member of one of these organisations into your school to talk about their work.
3. Run a poster campaign or awareness week in your school highlighting human rights abuses in national and international situations.
4. Organise a fundraising event (e.g. a cake sale) for an organisation whose work you are interested in.
5. Invite a member of a senior class who is involved in an Amnesty International club or St Vincent de Paul group to give a talk to your class on what they do.
6. Carry out a survey to find out how wheelchair-friendly your school is.

- See what other action ideas you and your classmates can come up with!
- Remember to look back over the action ideas that are suggested throughout the chapter for more topics for an action project.
- In Chapter 6 you will find advice and helpful hints on how to make posters and leaflets, and on conducting surveys, interviews, petitions and fundraising events.

STUDY 12 REVISION QUESTIONS

Section 1

Answer ALL questions. (Total: 18 marks.)

1. **(a)** Which of the following organisations are concerned with promoting and supporting human rights? Put a tick in the box opposite the correct options. **(4 marks)**

(i) Irish Refugee Council ☐
(ii) Barnardos ☐
(iii) Simon Community ☐
(iv) Bank of Ireland ☐
(v) Alone ☐

(b) Indicate whether the following statements are true or false by putting a tick in the correct box. **(4 marks)**

(i) Bullying always involves physical violence.
True ☐
False ☐

(ii) Amnesty International does not oppose the death penalty.
True ☐
False ☐

(iii) Children have the right to play.
True ☐
False ☐

(iv) A compromise is when two sides meet each other halfway to solve a conflict.
True ☐
False ☐

2. Fill in the missing words in the following sentences. **(4 marks)**

(a) To say that all football fans are hooligans is called ________________.

(b) ________________ won the Nobel Peace Prize for his efforts to bring about equality between all South Africans.

(c) The organisation known as the ___________ ________________ _____________________ concerns itself with the needs and rights of people with disabilities.

(d) One type of rights covered in the United Nations Convention on the Right of the Child are d____________ rights.

3. In the boxes provided below match the letters in row X with the corresponding numbers in row Y. The first pair is completed for you. **(6 marks)**

X	A	B	C	D	E	F	G
Y	7						

X
A. Pavee Point is
B. The United Nations Declaration is
C. The family is
D. The Global Elders are
E. Rights and responsibilities
F. Dr Janusz Korczak was
G. 'Cyber bullying' describes

Y
1. an early defender of children's rights.
2. the most common unit in society.
3. using new technologies in a harmful way.
4. an organisation that is concerned about poverty, HIV/Aids and climate change.
5. go hand in hand.
6. a charter of rights to which every human is entitled.
7. an organisation concerned with Travellers.

Section 2

Answer ALL the questions numbered 1, 2 and 3 below.
Each question carries 14 marks.

1. Look at the pictures below and answer the questions that follow.

(a) Name a human right you think the people in each of these pictures are being denied. **(2)**
(b) Name one document drafted by the United Nations for the protection of human rights. **(2)**
(c) Name two countries that you know of where human rights are being denied. **(4)**
(d) Name two organisations that concern themselves with the protection of human rights. Describe two actions that one of these organisations has taken to protect human rights.
First organisation **(1)**
Second organisation **(1)**
First action **(2)**
Second action **(2)**

2. Examine the photograph and answer the questions that follow.

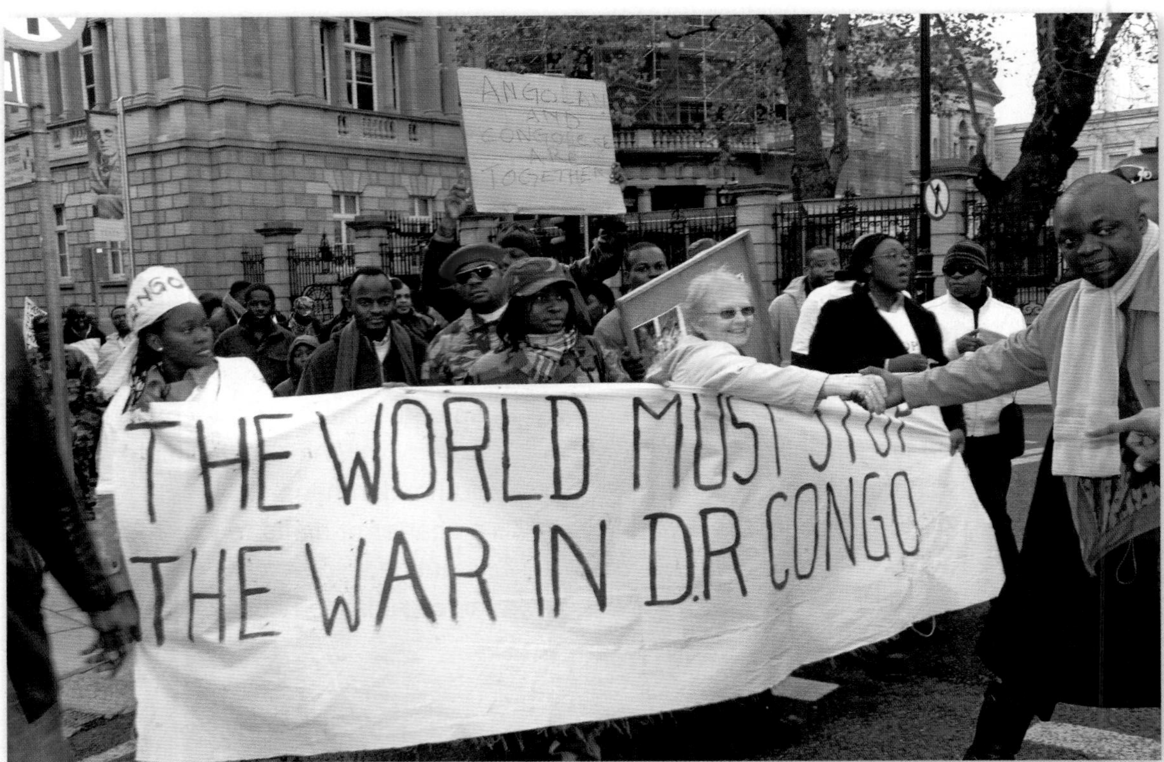

(a) What are these people protesting about? **(2)**

(b) Name two other ways a group like this could highlight their concerns.

Method 1 **(2)**

Method 2 **(2)**

(c) Name two skills you think are necessary to be a good campaigner.

Skill 1 **(2)**

Skill 2 **(2)**

(d) Describe two actions you could take in your school to highlight the issue of the denial of human rights in a particular situation.

Action 1 **(2)**

Action 2 **(2)**

3. Look at the poster below and answer the questions that follow.

(a) What is the name of the organisation mentioned on the poster? **(2)**
(b) What issue is the organisation trying to highlight? **(2)**
(c) Whose help do they believe is needed to solve this problem? **(2)**
(d) What is the slogan of this organisation? **(2)**
(e) Besides this organisation, can you name another that concerns itself with the rights of children? **(2)**
(f) Suggest two actions you could take that would help with this problem.
Action 1 **(2)**
Action 2 **(2)**

Section 3

Answer ONE of the questions numbered 1, 2 and 3 below.
Each question carries 20 marks.

1. Amnesty International's main weapons are letter writing and lobbying.
   (a) Describe how you would organise a campaign in your school to highlight the work of Amnesty International.
   (b) Describe in words or draw an outline of a poster which would highlight a right contained in the UN Convention on the Rights of the Child.

2. 'I object to violence because when it appears to do good, the good is only temporary – the evil it does is permanent.' Mahatma Gandhi
   (a) Write an article for your school magazine on solving conflict situations peacefully. In your article use examples from recent history of well-known people who have successfully done this.
   (b) Make up a slogan that would help students understand the importance of compromise.

3. Imagine you have invited a member of Pavee Point to talk to your CSPE class.
   (a) Describe how you would organise and prepare for the visit.
   (b) Outline the type of issues you would discuss with your visitor.
   (c) Describe how you would organise a campaign to highlight the dangers of stereotyping and prejudice in your school.

Chapter 2

Your Environment, Your Responsibility

As individuals born on the planet we are the temporary owners or **stewards** of the earth. We are responsible for caring for the earth. We can all play our part to make sure that the planet is kept in good order for those who will be stewards after us. Everything we do, from turning on a light switch to eating a burger, has an environmental impact somewhere in the world. So how can each of us make choices that have a positive impact on our planet?

STUDY 13 CLIMATE CHANGE AND HUMAN RIGHTS

A Rising Tide For Climate Justice
www.risingtide.org.uk

What does this poster suggest could happen as a result of climate change?

When the **UN Declaration of Human Rights** was written in 1948, with the aim of bringing about peace and security in the world, no one imagined that one of the threats to that peace and security would be **climate change**. Climate change affects people's rights, such as the right to housing, food and even the right to life. For example, if your house is destroyed because of rising sea levels, you have no shelter; if your crops are destroyed because of drought, your food source is gone. The increased frequency of hurricanes and cyclones is also a risk to life.

Flooding in Papua New Guinea

Water, Water Everywhere . . .

In January 2006, the Waghi River in the western highlands of Papua New Guinea flooded. After months of drought my family had been praying for rain. We needed water for the vegetable gardens where we grow our food and for the coffee plantation we work on. When the rains came they didn't stop. The river burst its banks and washed everything away. Everyone in the village fled into the hills, but our homes, our gardens, our animals, the plantation . . . everything was under water. We thought the worst was over when the water receded, but we were wrong. Everything was covered in a thick layer of mud and sand and debris. The bodies of drowned animals began to decay and we got sick from malaria because the puddles and ponds were ideal breeding places for mosquitoes. It took four months of cleaning and repairing before my family could move back home.

The bitter irony of the flooding was that even though we had prayed for rain and the water came, we were dying of thirst. After the flood there was no access to safe water for drinking or washing because the usual streams that we took water from were destroyed or polluted with dead animals. We had to rely on bottled water! Even a year later things still haven't returned to normal.

From *Water Rights and Wrongs: A young people's summary of the United Nations Development Report 2006, Beyond scarcity: Power, poverty, and the global water crisis.*

Flooding in Papua New Guinea

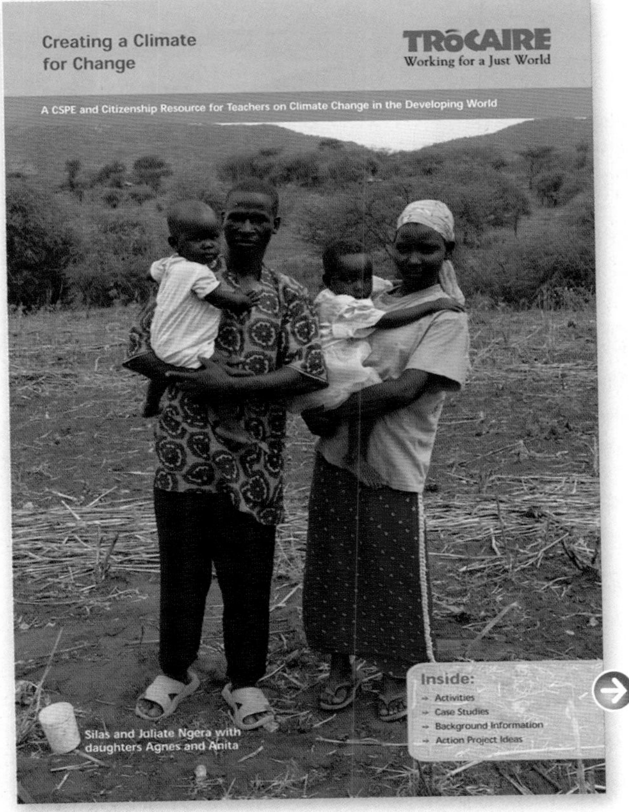

Creating a Climate for Change
TRÓCAIRE
Working for a Just World
A CSPE and Citizenship Resource for Teachers on Climate Change in the Developing World
Silas and Juliate Ngera with daughters Agnes and Anita
Inside:
Activities
Case Studies
Background Information
Action Project Ideas

Find out more about climate change in this resource, available at www.trocaire.org/resources/schoolresources

ACTIVITIES

1. How are human rights and climate change linked?
2. Describe how the people in Papua New Guinea were affected by climate change. Which of their rights were threatened?
3. What other environmental crises have you heard about?
4. Can you think of any ways in which Ireland has been affected by climate change?

It's a Global Problem

Climate change and **human rights** are linked in a very real way. The developed world is the biggest polluter of the earth's atmosphere, but this pollution also affects people in the developing world as they experience droughts, hurricanes and floods. Every action that we take or don't take on the environment impacts not only our own lives into the future, but also the lives of people that we have never met. So our care of the earth, or our **stewardship** of the earth, is important.

Many environmental problems are **global**. These include:

- ozone layer depletion
- global warming
- acid rain
- deforestation
- nuclear pollution
- danger to wildlife.

Global Warming

Burning fossil fuels creates greenhouse gases

Melting ice caps are a result of global warming

Cause: Burning **fossil fuels** like coal, gas and oil produces **carbon dioxide**. Carbon dioxide, methane gas and chlorofluorocarbons (CFCs) are often called **'greenhouse gases'**. Global warming happens when heat from the sun gets trapped by these gases and cannot go into the earth's atmosphere.

Effect: Global warming causes **climate changes**. Higher temperatures on the earth's surface cause the ice caps to melt. This in turn will cause sea levels to rise and flooding will occur. Small changes in temperature can have a huge effect, including crop failure and drought.

Solution: **Green energy** (energy created by renewable resources like solar power, wind and water power) could be used more in industry and in our homes. In Ireland, most of our energy is still made by burning fossil fuels.

Ireland has some of the best conditions in the EU for producing wind power

Ozone Layer Depletion

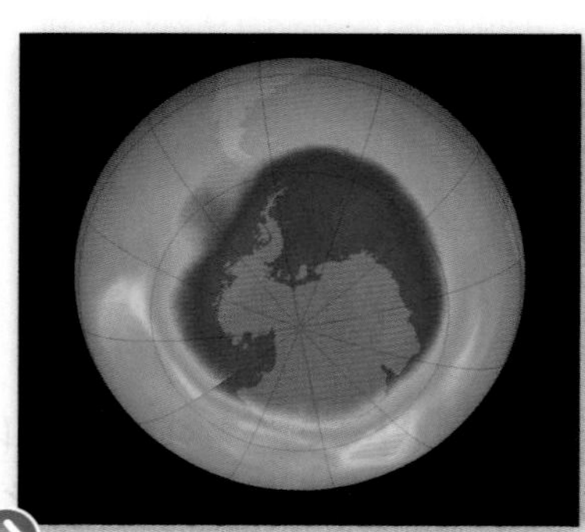

Cause: When we release artificial chemicals like CFCs into the earth's atmosphere they destroy the ozone layer.

Effect: Less ozone means more exposure to harmful **ultraviolet rays** from the sun, which cause skin cancer. This can also lead to eye diseases, damaged crops, smog pollution and climate change.

Solution: Cut down on CFCs, which are used in items like fridges, freezers, aerosols and glues.

This photo is of the Antarctic ozone hole. The blue and purple colours are where there is the least ozone, and the greens, yellows, and oranges are where there is more ozone.

Less ozone leads to more smog pollution in cities

CFCs in aerosol cans destroy the ozone layer

Acid Rain

Changing to eco-friendly cars will reduce acid rain

The effects of acid rain

What type of energy is this car using?

Cause: **Acid rain** is another result of burning fossil fuels (gas, coal, oil). Acids in the gases produced by power stations, factories and car exhausts mix and fall in rain.

Effect: Acid rain damages trees, fish die in rivers and lakes, and buildings are damaged. As the pollution can travel in the air, the problem affects many countries. For example, half the acid rain that falls in Canada comes from the USA.

Solution: Put in place more pollution laws for power stations, factories and cars. Using **renewable sources of energy** like wind, solar and wave power will cut down on the amount of acid rain.

Deforestation

Cause: Trees are often cleared to make way for new roads and housing developments. **Rainforests are disappearing** because of farming, dams, ranching, logging for fuel and mining.

Why are the rainforests disappearing?

Planting trees helps to create 'carbon sinks'

Effect: We need trees to take in harmful carbon dioxide and release oxygen, which we need to breathe. Burning trees adds to the amount of carbon dioxide in the air, which adds to global warming. Since 1960, 50 per cent of the rainforests of South America have disappeared and rainforests now cover less than six per cent of the earth's surface.

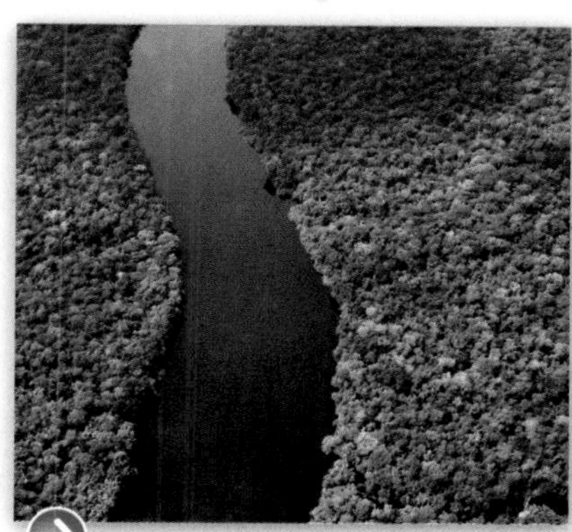

Trees absorb carbon dioxide and produce oxygen, which we breathe

Solution: Take part in **tree-planting schemes** and only buy timber products that have an FSC mark. The FSC mark means that the timber made to use the product you are buying came from a forest that has been looked after properly. Ireland imports €145 million worth of tropical hardwood trees, such as mahogany and rosewood, which come from rainforests.

Nuclear Pollution

Cause: Another way of creating electricity is by nuclear power, which creates radioactive waste.

Effect: Radioactive waste remains a threat to the environment for up to 10,000 years. The effects of accidents at nuclear plants like the one in Chernobyl in Belarus are well known to Irish people through the work of Adi Roche and the Chernobyl Children's Fund.

Solution: Use **renewable energy sources** like wind, solar and wave power to make electricity and introduce more controls on safety in nuclear power plants.

Ireland does not have any nuclear power plants. Sellafield nuclear plant, on the coast of Cumbria in England, is the nearest one to Ireland.

This sign at Chernobyl means the landscape is still radioactive

Wave power can be used to produce electricity

Danger for Wildlife

Cause: Different species of wildlife are disappearing because of deforestation and habitat loss as the human population grows (possibly to more than nine billion by 2050). This means that more forests and habitats will need to be cleared to make way for more arable land and cities. Also, the demand for luxury goods such as fur coats and ivory leads to illegal wildlife trading.

Effect: Many species of animals are becoming extinct. Now, less research is possible into new drugs from plants because of disappearing forests.

Solution: We should have more wildlife parks, as well as more controls on the destruction of forests and farmland.

The illegal trade in elephant tusks endangers the elephant population

Cross River Gorilla. Habitat: Nigeria and Cameroon. Number: Fewer than 300 in the world.

Wildlife parks protect many animals from extinction

 ACTIVITIES 

1. Why is climate change a global problem?
2. What is green energy?
3. What is global warming?
4. Why is the ozone layer important?
5. What damage is caused by acid rain?
6. What is the effect of the rainforests being cut down?
7. Why are certain species of animals in danger of extinction?
8. List **two** ways:
   - you can take positive action on the environment
   - your school community can take positive action on the environment
   - your local neighbourhood can take positive action on the environment
   - the government can take positive action on the environment.
9. According to this poster, what does the doctor prescribe?

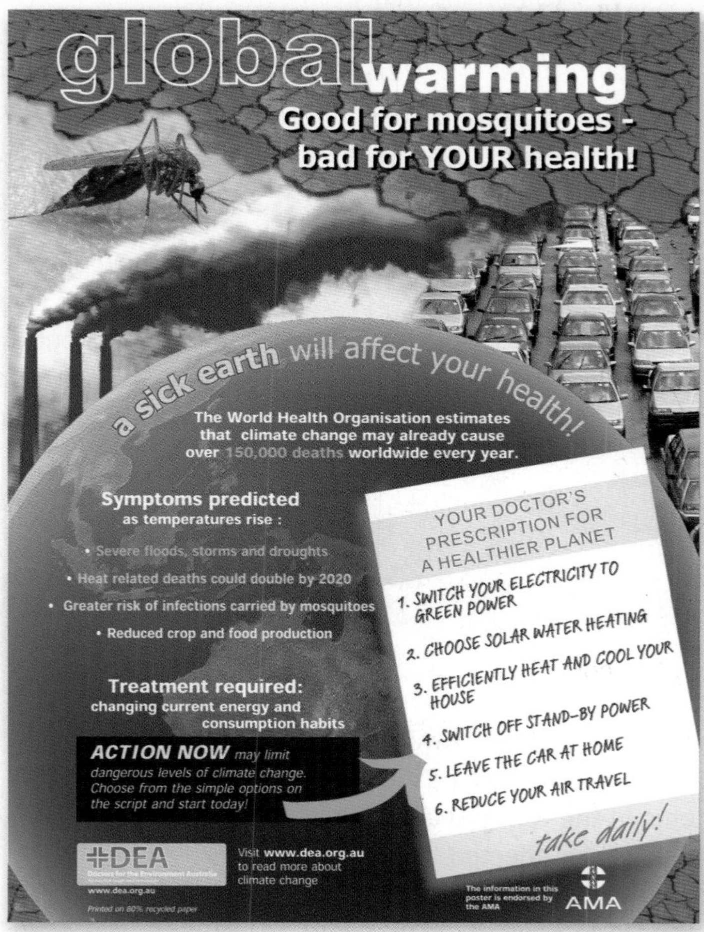

10. Design your own poster about one of the environmental issues mentioned in the study and 'prescribe' some medicine!

STUDY 14 LEAVING YOUR MARK

Your **carbon footprint** measures how much you are adding to climate change. The carbon footprint of the world's poorest billion people is only about three per cent of the world's total carbon footprint. Western countries are the worst offenders. For example, public buildings in England and Wales are pumping out 11 tonnes of carbon dioxide a year, more than Kenya's entire carbon footprint.

What are you doing about your carbon footprint?

What about Ireland?

Everyone in Ireland likes to talk about the weather – especially farmers, whose living depends on it. For example, if there is a very wet summer, it may be very difficult to harvest crops, or if the ground is frozen in spring it can be more difficult to sow seed. The increase in **changing weather patterns** due to global warming may even some day make Ireland unsuitable for growing potatoes, a food that always been associated with this country.

The last ten years in Ireland have been the warmest decade since records began, but these records have also shown changes in rainfall patterns. The West of Ireland and the North now have a higher number of days with heavy rainfall, and more rain throughout the year. This has meant higher river levels and **increased flooding**.

Global warning means there is a greater risk of flooding on our own doorstep

If **global warming** continues at its current pace, it will mean rising water temperatures. This in turn will affect storm patterns in the North Atlantic. This means that costal areas will be affected by stronger storm surges, and extreme weather, which will leave our coastlines very exposed to flooding. Higher sea levels will also mean more erosion of the coastline.

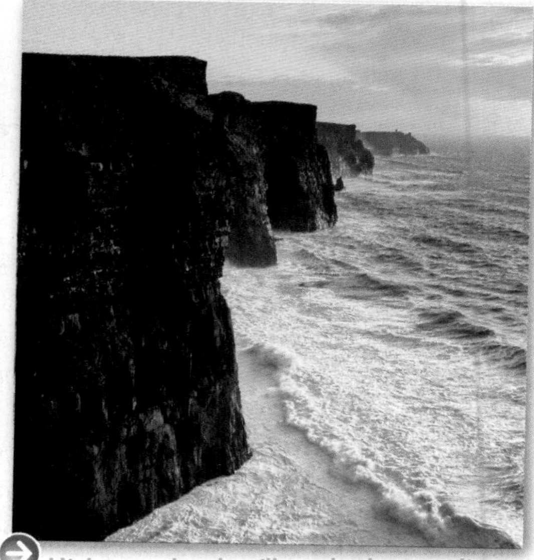
Higher sea levels will erode the coastline. Can you name these famous cliffs?

Where Ireland Stands on Climate Change

Under the ***Kyoto agreement**, Ireland agreed to limit our emissions. However, by 2005 we had already gone over the target agreed and will have to pay fines. Work is being done to introduce more measures to reduce our carbon emissions.

The government has written a **National Climate Change Strategy**, which includes targets in different areas, such as:

- **Energy supply** – 15 per cent of our electricity is to be generated from renewable sources by 2010, and 33 per cent by 2020.
- **Transport** – more money is to be put into public transport to make it easier to make the choice of making a journey by bus, Dart, Luas or train rather than using a car.
- **Homes** – change to low-energy lightbulbs. Homes are to have an energy rating certificate (BER – Building Energy Rating). Grants for renewable energy heating in homes.
- **Public sector** – Biomass heating in schools (biomass means organic materials like wood, plants, etc.). All street lighting and traffic lights to be energy efficient.

The National Climate Change Strategy also includes increased spending on climate change awareness campaigns, such as the **Power of One** campaign.

*Kyoto Protocol: 183 countries around the world agreed to take measures to limit greenhouse gas emissions by 2012.

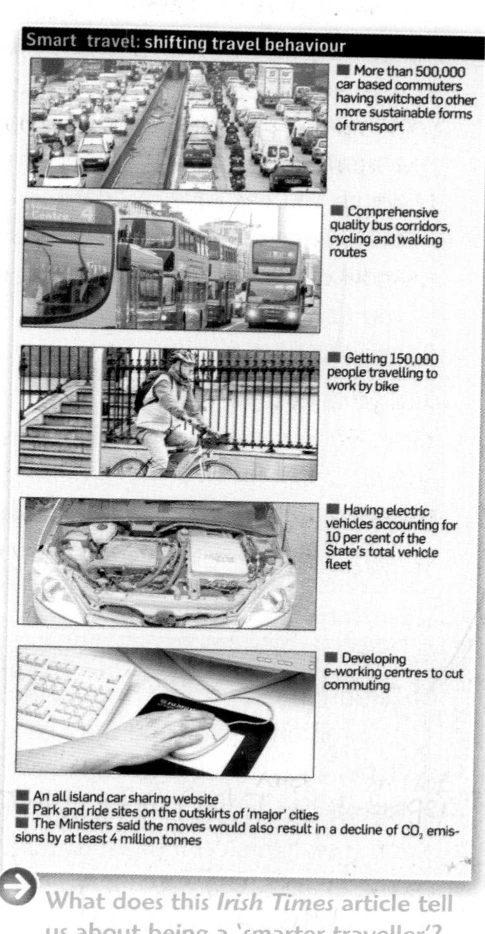
Smart travel: shifting travel behaviour

- More than 500,000 car based commuters having switched to other more sustainable forms of transport
- Comprehensive quality bus corridors, cycling and walking routes
- Getting 150,000 people travelling to work by bike
- Having electric vehicles accounting for 10 per cent of the State's total vehicle fleet
- Developing e-working centres to cut commuting
- An all island car sharing website
- Park and ride sites on the outskirts of 'major' cities
- The Ministers said the moves would also result in a decline of CO_2 emissions by at least 4 million tonnes

What does this *Irish Times* article tell us about being a 'smarter traveller'?

Take Action!

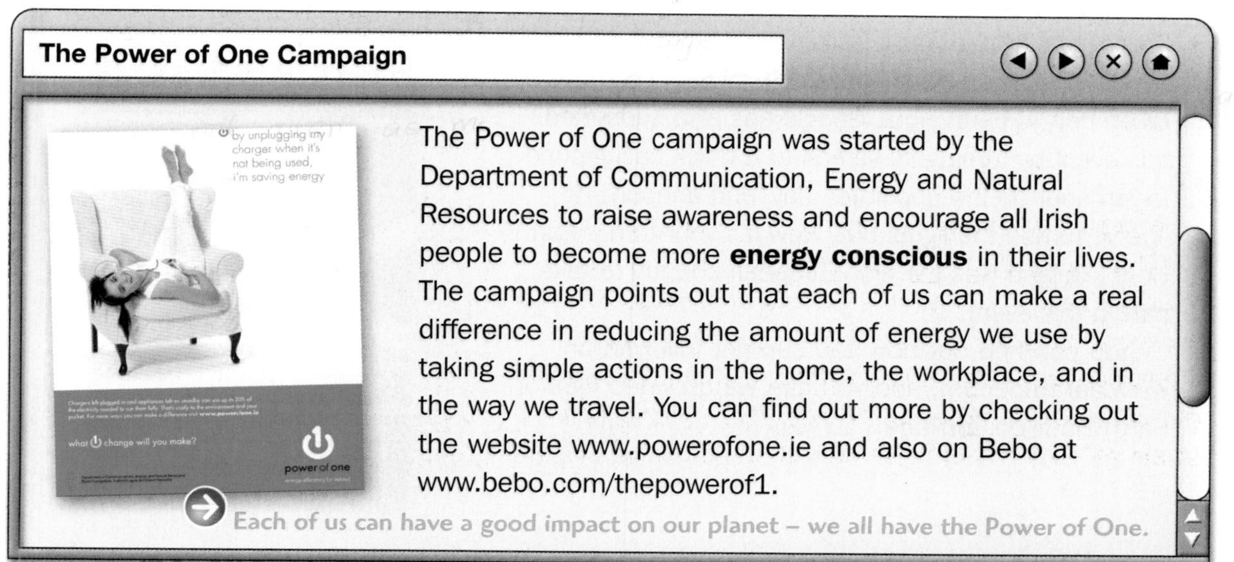

The Power of One Campaign

The Power of One campaign was started by the Department of Communication, Energy and Natural Resources to raise awareness and encourage all Irish people to become more **energy conscious** in their lives. The campaign points out that each of us can make a real difference in reducing the amount of energy we use by taking simple actions in the home, the workplace, and in the way we travel. You can find out more by checking out the website www.powerofone.ie and also on Bebo at www.bebo.com/thepowerof1.

Each of us can have a good impact on our planet – we all have the Power of One.

Calculate for Change

One way to find out how you are contributing to climate change is by measuring your own carbon footprint. You can do this by going on to the website www.change.ie, where you can take the **carbon calculator challenge**. Once you know what your carbon footprint is you can decide what actions you need to take to reduce it.

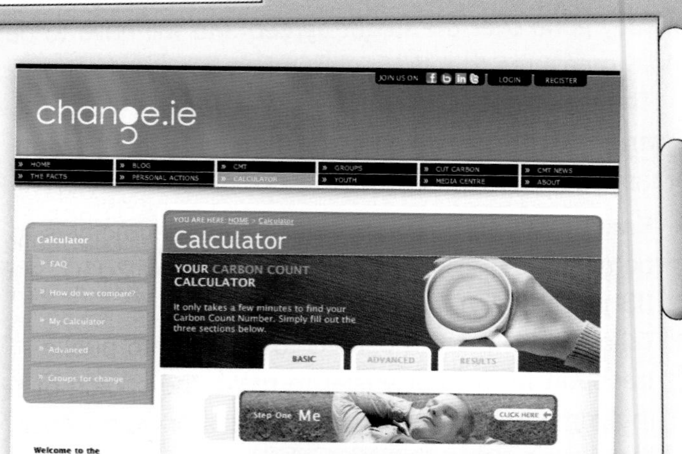

Earth Hour

Earth Hour started in Sydney, Australia in 2007 when 2.2 million homes and businesses turned off their lights for an hour. This has now become a **global campaign** to get citizens from all over the world to turn off their lights on the last Saturday in March every year. The event was created by the World Wide Fund for Nature. Homes, businesses, cafés, schools, etc. all get involved, and the lights of famous buildings are also turned off for one hour.

Buildings like Sydney Opera House, the Coliseum in Rome, the Empire State Building in New York and the famous Wat Arun Buddhist temple in Bangkok have all taken part in Earth Hour. Google has also supported this event by turning its screen to a black background for an hour on the appointed day, and announcing 'We've turned the lights out. Now it's your turn – Earth Hour'. Ireland was the first European country to take part in this event.

You can find out how you can get involved on www.earthhour.org, and you can watch video files of Earth Hour on YouTube.

ACTIVITIES

1. Do you think the gum target is a good idea? Give **three** reasons for your answer.
2. What argument would you give people who said the gum target was 'unsightly'?
3. Can you think of another way to get people to dispose of their gum properly?
4. List **three** ways the students in Galway researched climate change.
5. Why do you think it is important to research a topic?
6. Name **five** ways in which the Galway students raised awareness.
7. Think of **four** ways the internet and other technology could help a group spread their message.

Concern Worldwide

Do you know how useful your old mobile phone can be? Many aid agencies have noticed the importance of mobile phones in the developing world, where telephone companies often do not have enough land lines, and where it can also be very expensive to have a land line installed even where it is possible.

Mobile phones are really important in the case of disasters, as they can make it much easier to reach and communicate with people in need and with aid workers. They can also make it much easier to try and reunite families who have been separated during an emergency.

Put your Old Mobile Phone Back to Work

In 2008, the Irish aid agency Concern were for the first time able to use mobile phone technology to text aid to people in crisis in Kenya. Secure text messages from Concern Worldwide put credit on people's SIM cards which they could then use to collect as cash from mobile phone agents. (You can see how this was done by watching the video 'Mobile phone cash transfers in Kenya' on YouTube.) The cash was then used to buy food produced locally. This can be a much more efficient way of delivering aid quickly, instead of waiting for delivery trucks of aid to arrive to remote areas, which can take too much time.

However, it was not possible to reach everyone in need via text aid, because many people did not have mobiles, and many others could not read: so groups of ten shared a mobile.

So recycling your old phone will not just be good for the environment, but may some day be used to help someone in an emergency in a developing country.

ACTIVITIES

1. Why are mobile phones useful in an emergency?
2. Why might it not be possible to reach everyone via text aid? Suggest one way in which this could be improved.
3. Design a poster to get people to recycle or donate their old mobiles.

ACTION IDEA

Research: For more information on how to do a campaign around this issue, check out Oxfam's Cool Planet website www.oxfam.org.uk/coolplanet/kidsweb/

3. Look at the poster below and answer the questions that follow.
   (a) Why, in your opinion, is the thermostat shown next to the earth? **(2)**
   (b) Who does the poster suggest controls climate change? **(2)**
   (c) What FOUR actions does the poster encourage you to take that would be good for the environment? **(2)**
   (d) What action, in your opinion, would have the most effect? Explain your answer. **(2)**
   (e) If the earth's temperature increases by another two degrees, name ONE possible effect this will have. **(2)**
   (f) Suggest ONE way you could bring the 'Change' message to the attention of your school community. **(2)**
   (g) Suggest TWO more actions that you could take that would help control climate change. **(2)**
   Action 1
   Action 2

Section 3

Answer ONE of the questions numbered 1, 2 and 3 below.
Each question carries 20 marks.

1. Imagine you have invited a member of a local environmental group to talk to your CSPE class.

(a) Describe how you would organise and prepare for the visit.

(b) Outline the type of issues you would discuss with your visitor.

(c) Describe how you would organise a campaign to keep your school a litter-free zone.

2. 'Only when the last tree has died and the last river been poisoned and the last fish been caught will we realise that we can't eat money' – Cree Indian proverb.

(a) Write an article for your school magazine on the importance of looking after our environment. Begin by explaining what is meant by the proverb above.

(b) Draw a sketch of a poster that you would design to appear with the article, highlighting one of the main causes of global warming. You should include an appropriate slogan with your sketch.

(c) Apart from the article and poster, name and describe two other ways in which you could raise awareness of environmental issues in the wider community outside school.

3. Imagine that your family, and other families in your local community, have been affected by an environmental disaster (for example a landslide, a hurricane, or flooding). The families have now decided to set up a local action committee to look for aid. You have been chosen as a youth representative on this committee.

(a) Name ONE organisation that the action committee should approach to ask for aid. Give TWO reasons why you think this organisation should be asked.

(b) Prepare a script for a local radio show to convince the community of the need to see the increase in environmental disasters as the result of global warming.

(c) Describe TWO actions that your local committee could take to try to reduce the impacts of landslides, hurricanes or flooding in the community.

(Adapted from DES exam paper)

Chapter 3

Your Community and Development

In Chapter 1 you saw that you are a member of a community – a school community. We are also members of a **local community**. In a local community people meet and come together for different reasons. We can all take part in our community and bring about change on issues that interest and concern us. Being a member of a local community also means you have certain rights and responsibilities.

STUDY 19 WHAT IS A COMMUNITY?

We belong to many communities at the same time. For example:

The **family community** is the first and most important community of which we are members. Other members of our family could be parents, guardians, brothers, sisters, grandparents, aunts and uncles.

The **school community** is usually the next group that we join and this group is made up of other students as well as school staff such as teachers, secretaries and caretakers.

The **neighbourhood community** is made up of families who live near each other and who often meet each other.

The **local community** is made up of many of these neighbourhoods together, for example in a housing estate, village or town.

Each larger community is made up of many smaller communities and we all **take part in these communities** in different ways.

Your Local Community Quiz

How much do you know about your local community and how much do you take part in it? The following questions can help you to gather information about your community. Either answer them yourself or use the questions to interview a classmate about his or her community and then use the answers to make a tourist brochure about your area.

What places, people, events or activities make you proud to be a member of your local community?

1. What type of community do you live in? (Hints: county, city, town, village, large, small.)
2. What services are in your community? (Hints: doctor, sports, post office.)
3. Are there any famous people from your community?
4. What historic buildings or landmarks are there in your area? (Hints: castle, old church, round tower, Celtic cross, spire.)
5. Which festivals take place in your area and what happens at them? (Hints: music festival, summer festival, writers' festival, poetry festival, St Patrick's Day festival.)
6. Name an area in your locality that you find interesting and say why. (Hints: park, town centre, river, sports centre.)
7. What activities are there for young people?

Pride of Place Awards

The Pride of Place Awards is an all-Ireland competition in which local groups are nominated for the award by their local authorities because they have done something to **make improvements in the life of their communities**.

Special Award for Community Empowerment – Larne, County Antrim

This award was given to a group that undertook to:

1. develop a 'state of the art' play park on what had been a run-down public space
2. improve relations between young people in the area and the local police.

Both projects were very successful. The play park is visited regularly and is a source of great local pride. The success of the second project has seen a 34 per cent drop in crime in the area in one year. The annual bonfire night – previously overseen by police vans and riot police – is now a trouble-free, family-friendly celebration which is overseen by police on foot dressed in ordinary uniforms.

(Adapted from case stories at www.prideofplace.ie.)

Larne, Co Antrim

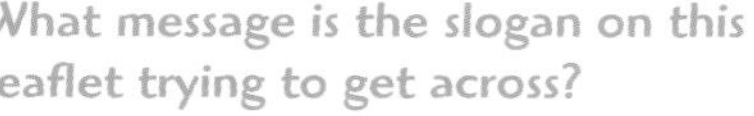

What message is the slogan on this leaflet trying to get across?

ACTIVITIES

1. In groups, make a poster or tourist brochure about your area using the information you gathered from the quiz.
2. What improvements would you like to see in your area?
3. Do you know of any competitions your community has been involved in (e.g. Tidy Towns)?

ACTION IDEA

Research: Communities change over time. Find out how your community has changed in the past 50 years by interviewing an older member of your community.

STUDY 20 FIND YOUR SPACE!

There are many ways of getting involved in your community. Throughout Ireland many young people have got involved in their communities and have won awards for their participation.

Getting Involved

Foróige clubs are youth development groups for young people from the local community. Founded in 1952, Foróige comes from the Irish word meaning 'development of youth'. There are currently over 420 active Foróige clubs all over Ireland. They help young people to experience democracy by electing their own club committees and by being involved in running the clubs in co-operation with adult leaders.

Foróige Youth Citizenship Programme

This programme aims to help young people develop the values and skills of good citizenship. Club members study their local area and take action to improve the community. The citizenship programme aims to empower young people to:

- understand what is happening in their community and society
- take action to bring about improvement
- develop good community values
- make a real difference to the world and the lives of others.

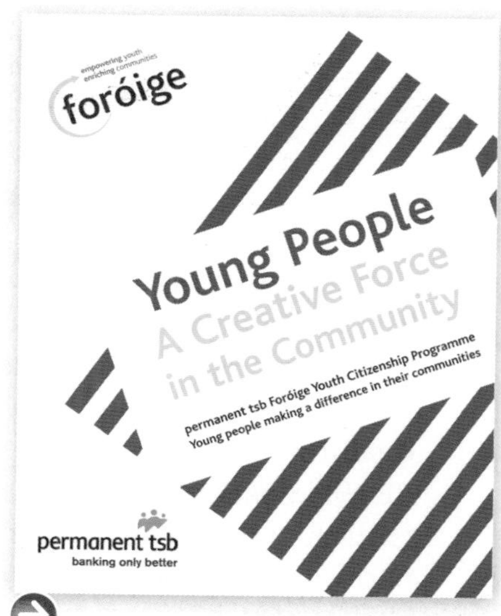

Find out about the Permanent TSB Foróige Youth Citizenship Programme in your area

Read the descriptions below of a number of projects that have been entered in the Permanent TSB Foróige Youth Citizenship programme.

Templeport Foróige Club, County Cavan

Crossing Generations

Templeport Foróige Club organised a number of citizenship activities to benefit both the older and the younger members of their community. They hosted a disco, using the proceeds to buy a park bench, a bird table and lots of flowers, which they planted to make the garden of a local nursing home a more enjoyable place for the residents. They also organised a children's Christmas party for the younger members of the community.

Cheeky Cheetahs Group, Dublin 24

Autism Awareness

The Cheeky Cheetahs Group ran an autism awareness campaign because they felt that their school mates didn't know much about the condition and didn't understand the growing number of young people with autism in their school. They researched the topic thoroughly and presented their findings to the school.

Maree Foróige Club, Co Galway

Accessibility for All

The club decided to run an Accessibility Project to improve facilities for people in the community who have a physical disability. They made designated disabled parking spaces outside the local church and GAA pitch and had a pathway constructed from the gate to the shelter at the pitch.

Bundoran Neighbourhood Youth Project, Co Donegal

Staying Safe in the Water

For their Water Safety Project, the Bundoran Neighbourhood Youth Project worked closely with the local rescue service, the RNLI. They designed posters, made presentations on water safety at the local primary school, organised a first aid course and produced a water safety booklet.

Killinarden Junior Estate Management Committee, Dublin 24

It's Playtime

Killinarden Junior Estate Management Committee cleaned up the basketball court in their local community centre to encourage young people to use the amenity. They got permission from Dublin County Council and project managed the timetable and what jobs everybody would do on the day.

Bonniconlon Foróige Club, Co. Mayo

Alarm Bells

The members of Bonniconlon Foróige Club became aware that a number of elderly people in their community didn't have smoke alarms in their homes. They held a car wash and cake sale and raised over €350 to buy the much-needed smoke alarms. The young people then visited elderly people in the community and installed the alarms.

Thanks to Foróige for permission to feature these projects.

ACTIVITIES

1. Name some of the clubs you can join in your area.
2. What links can you see between the Permanent TSB Foróige Youth Citizenship programme and CSPE?
3. Look at the activities the clubs above were involved in and name the skills they would have used to take action.

Visit the Foróige website, www.foroige.ie/, to find out about clubs in your area.

STUDY 21 LOCAL GOVERNMENT

Every local community includes different **amenities and services** that people in the area use every day. Here are some of the facilities that might be in your area:

- post office
- fire station
- public park
- sports club
- swimming pool
- car park
- Garda station
- library.

How does having a post office benefit a local community?

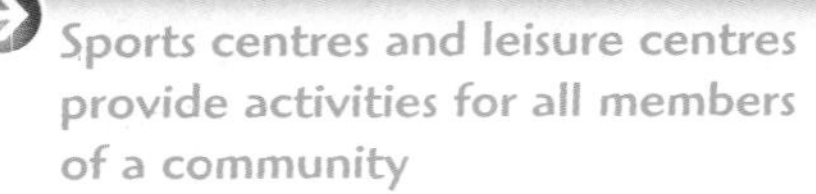

Sports centres and leisure centres provide activities for all members of a community

Green spaces add to the natural beauty of communities

Many of the services and amenities that we use every day, from getting water from the tap to visiting the park, are the responsibility of the **local authority**.

There are four different kinds of local authority in Ireland.

- 29 county councils, e.g. Fingal.
- 5 city councils, e.g. Cork.
- 5 borough councils, e.g. Kilkenny.
- 75 town councils, e.g. Killarney.

There are 114 local authorities in Ireland. Local authorities are part of the local government system. The Department of the Environment, Heritage and Local Government is responsible for the local authorities.

What do Local Authorities do?

Local government gives people a chance to **make their voices heard** and bring about change to improve their area.

Local councillors and city and county managers run local government. They in turn report to the Minister for the Environment, Heritage and Local Government. Local councillors are elected by the people of an area **every five years**. Anyone over 18 years of age can run for office.

Most local authorities hold meetings every month. At these meetings important decisions are made on how much will be spent in an area and on what. Decisions made by the councillors are reached by **voting**.

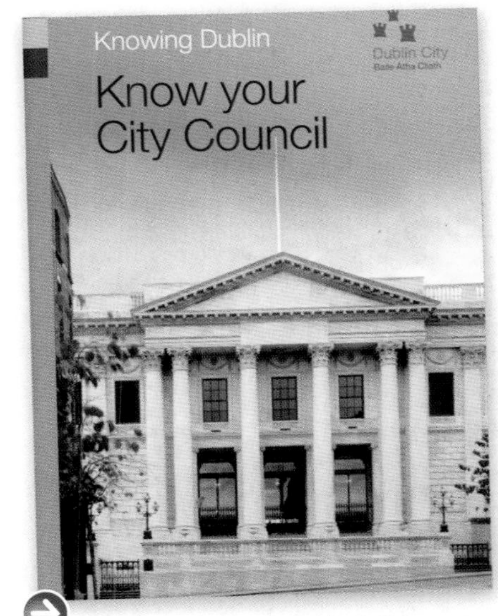

Local councils provide information on the services and amenities available to local people

The offices of the Department of the Environment, Heritage and Local Government are in the Customs House, Dublin

Local councillors meet once a month to discuss issues of importance to the community they represent

Some of the areas that local authorities are responsible for are:

- housing and building
- roads and safety
- water supply and sewerage
- environmental protection, including rivers, lakes, air and noise
- recreation and amenities – parks, playgrounds, libraries
- planning.

Providing playgrounds is the responsibility of the local authority

Planning for Change

Each local authority is responsible for drawing up a **development plan** for its area. This is usually done every five years.

A development plan covers:

- the development of run-down areas
- the development and improvement of parks and public areas
- road improvements
- looking after historical buildings
- what sort of land should be used for housing, schools, factories and shops. This is called **zoning of land**.

When the local councillors agree on the development plan it is put on public display for at least three months, in places such as libraries. Any person in the area can then let the councillors know what they think of the planned changes for their community.

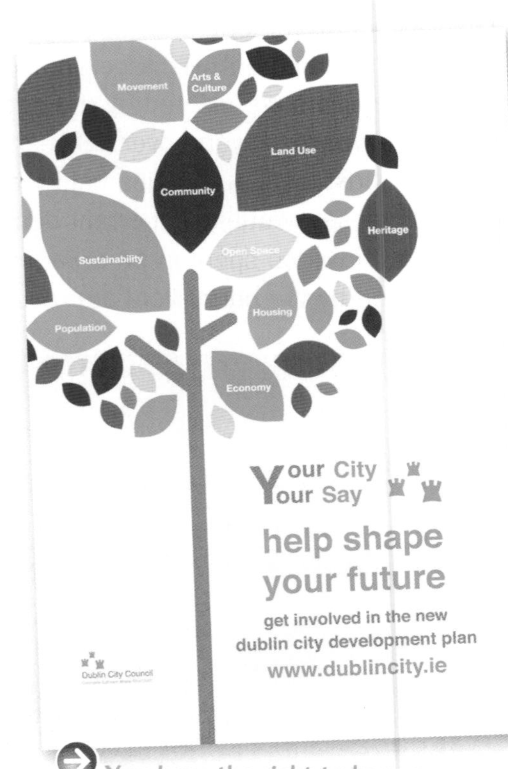

You have the right to have a say in the plans for your area

Permission to Build?

Every building must have **planning permission**. If any person or group disagrees with a decision made by a local authority – either granting or refusing planning permission – they can go to **An Bord Pleanála***. An Bord Pleanála will look at the case again.

Everyone has the **right to a say in the future planning and development of their area**.

Plans for your local area can be seen in local council offices, libraries, etc.

Take Action!

Read the following case study to see how residents in Dunmore East took action over an issue that concerned them.

Residents win battle over mobile phone antennae

Residents of a small Waterford fishing village have won a three-year battle to have mobile phone antennae taken down from the roof of their local shop.

An Bord Pleanála, in two separate decisions, has ruled in favour of residents of Dunmore East, who are now celebrating their victory over three communications companies – Hutchinson 3G, Meteor and 02.

The 12 antennae and dishes on the roof of the village's Londis store were erected initially without planning permission and residents claimed they only became aware of them when their television sets started picking up interference.

But following a ruling by An Bord Pleanála, the locals now plan to demand that the equipment, over which they had expressed health concerns, be taken down.

'This is a significant result for the group of determined residents who came together and battled against something they felt was just not right,' said solicitor John Reedy.

Residents complained that the equipment was located only yards from homes, shops and also a playschool attended by 30 children. Residents had said that while there was no proof of risks, there was no proof to the contrary either.

Meteor and 02 had lodged a joint application for planning retention for their equipment, while Hutchinson 3G had applied alone. At the height of the dispute, Meteor and 02 had claimed that their antennae could help in future sea rescues in the fishing village.

(*Source:* Jennifer Long, *Irish Times*.)

*An Bord Pleanála is a body set up by the government to deal with planning applications that cause difficulty or controversy.

ACTIVITIES

1. What services and amenities would be available in your ideal community? Draw a map of your ideal area. Remember to include essential services, like hospitals and schools, as well as recreational facilities such as parks, etc.

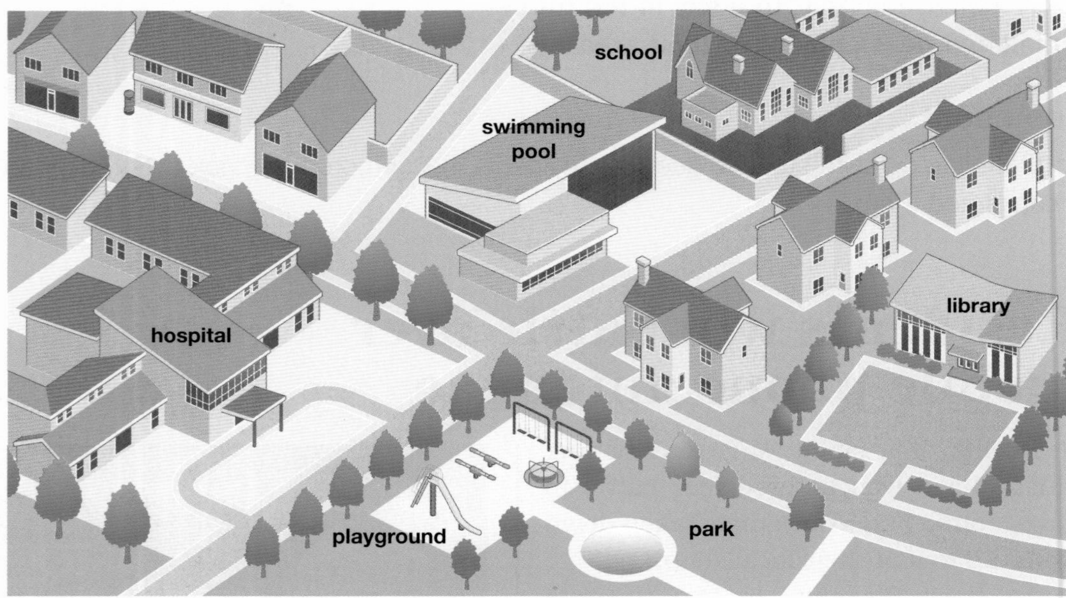

2. Why do we have local government?
3. How often are local councillors elected?
4. How do local authorities make decisions?
5. Name a local councillor from your area.
6. In your opinion, why would a person want to become a local councillor?
7. What does a development plan cover?
8. How can you influence your area's development plan?
9. What were the 12 antennae and dishes on the roof of Dunmore East's Londis store put up without?
10. Why were the residents of Dunmore East concerned about the dishes?

ACTION IDEA

Research: Using your local newspapers, find out what issues have caused problems or conflicts at council meetings. Present your findings to the class.

Check out www.environ.ie (you can get your local council's web address here).

STUDY 22 COUNCILLORS OUT LOUD

Look at what the following people had to say about being a councillor, why young people should be involved in their local communities and the importance of voting.

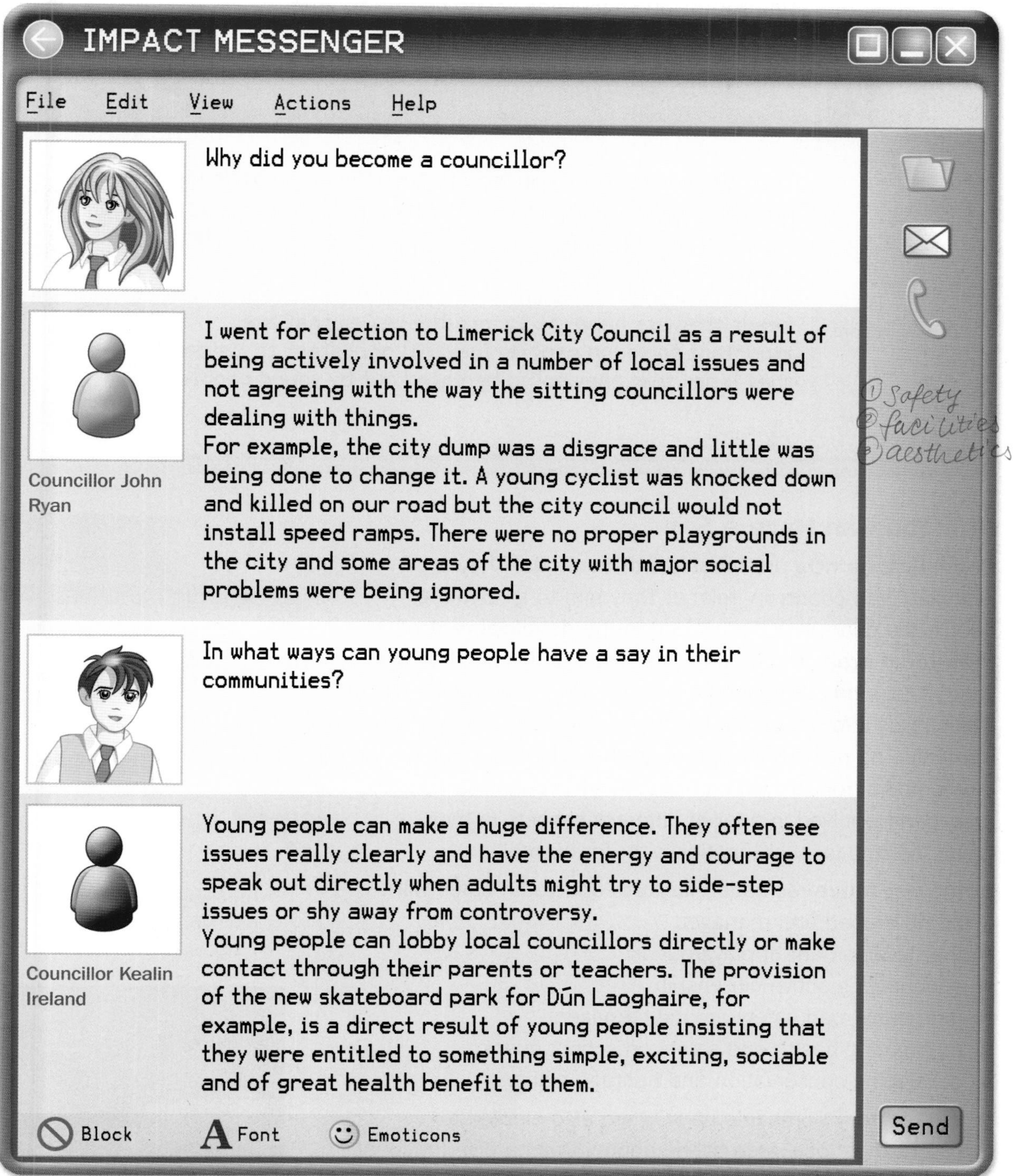

Why did you become a councillor?

Councillor John Ryan

I went for election to Limerick City Council as a result of being actively involved in a number of local issues and not agreeing with the way the sitting councillors were dealing with things.

For example, the city dump was a disgrace and little was being done to change it. A young cyclist was knocked down and killed on our road but the city council would not install speed ramps. There were no proper playgrounds in the city and some areas of the city with major social problems were being ignored.

In what ways can young people have a say in their communities?

Councillor Kealin Ireland

Young people can make a huge difference. They often see issues really clearly and have the energy and courage to speak out directly when adults might try to side-step issues or shy away from controversy.

Young people can lobby local councillors directly or make contact through their parents or teachers. The provision of the new skateboard park for Dún Laoghaire, for example, is a direct result of young people insisting that they were entitled to something simple, exciting, sociable and of great health benefit to them.

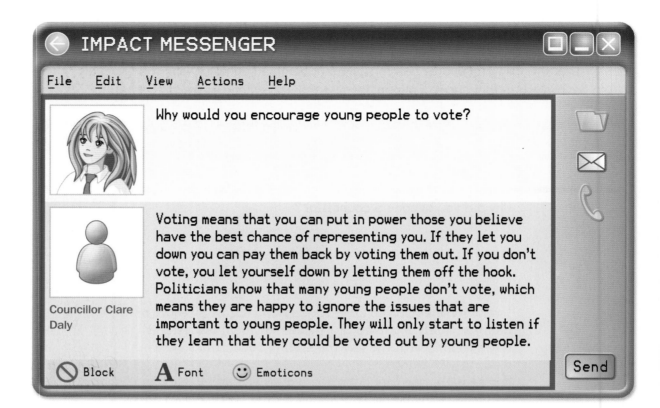

IMPACT MESSENGER

File Edit View Actions Help

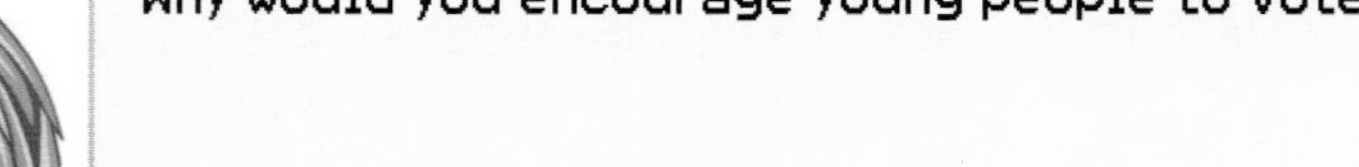

Why would you encourage young people to vote?

Councillor Clare Daly

Voting means that you can put in power those you believe have the best chance of representing you. If they let you down you can pay them back by voting them out. If you don't vote, you let yourself down by letting them off the hook. Politicians know that many young people don't vote, which means they are happy to ignore the issues that are important to young people. They will only start to listen if they learn that they could be voted out by young people.

Block Font Emoticons Send

How You Can Have a Say

Comhairle na nÓg are **local youth councils**. They are in every city and county in Ireland. They aim to give young people the chance to be involved in the **development of their local area**. The Office of the Minister for Children and Youth Affairs has developed a website for Comhairle na nÓg which gives information on Comhairle na nÓg and links to Comhairle na nÓg websites around the country.

Members from the different comhairlí around the country have been involved in a lot of different projects in their areas, helping local authorities with, for example:

- the way future recreation facilities and youth cafés will be developed and managed
- the development of playgrounds
- encouraging active citizenship
- promoting road safety among teenagers
- highlighting health and safety on school buses
- developing conservation and heritage plans.

Delegates from Comhairle na nÓg are also elected to represent their local area at the annual Dáil na nÓg (national youth parliament).

On the next page are some examples of how young Comhairle na nÓg members are finding their space and making a difference in the lives of young people in their communities.

You can click on the map of Ireland to find out what is happening in your local Comhairle, in whatever county you live in

A meeting of Donegal Comhairle na nÓg youth council

www.youthconnect.ie

Teenagers in Roscommon Comhairle na nÓg designed a website to meet the needs of young people in the county. The website is a one-stop shop where young people can connect with other young people on social issues as well as getting practical advice on topics of concern. The website also informs young people about what is happening throughout the county and keeps people informed about the work of the Comhairle na nÓg. A subgroup of the Comhairle na nÓg monitors and updates the site.

Alcohol Brochure

Young people from Westmeath Comhairle na nÓg designed and developed an excellent information leaflet on alcohol, as 'alcohol' was selected as a priority issue by young people. The Comhairle na nÓg invited the members of their Agency Support Structure and in particular HSE staff to view their draft leaflet and received very valuable feedback, which was taken into account. The brochure lists:

- facts about alcohol
- advice for young people
- things that young people can do that don't involve alcohol
- the law and rules about underage drinking
- what can happen when you get drunk
- alcohol services and further information.

ACTIVITIES

1. What **three issues** led Councillor Ryan to stand for election on Limerick city council?
2. According to Councillor Ireland, how do young people often see issues?
3. How did the new skateboard park in Councillor Ireland's area come about?
4. According to Councillor Daly, why do some politicians ignore issues that are important to young people?
5. What does she think will make politicians listen to young people?
6. Where can you find out about Comhairle na nÓg?
7. Why do you think Comhairle na nÓg was set up?
8. If you were at a meeting of Comhairle na nÓg in your area, what issues would you raise and why?

ACTION IDEA

Interview a local councillor to find out why s/he became a councillor and how they want to improve their area.

- Find out more at www.comhairlenanog.ie.
- Want to know what a council meeting is like? You can watch Dublin City Council meetings by logging on to www.dublincity.ie. Click on *Council Meetings* under the *Your Council* section of the site. As well as looking at live webcasts of meetings, you can also view past meetings.

STUDY 23 DEBATING DEVELOPMENT

The process of development in any community can cause problems, because what one person sees as being good for their community may be seen as bad by another person.

How the community develops sometimes causes **conflict** in a local area. **Different groups may have different views** about how a piece of land, for example, might be developed.

Imagine . . . a piece of land is about to be put up for sale in the middle of a town. There are many people who live and work in the area who would like to see the land developed in a particular way.

Read what the various groups in the community want to do with the land and answer the questions that follow.

We, the members of the community association, think that the site should be used as a community centre. It could be used as a drop-in centre for the unemployed, for social evenings for the elderly and as a place for young people to meet. We have been fundraising for a number of years and, with the help of a government grant, we could afford to buy the site and build the community centre. We think it would be a great way to get young people off the streets and reduce crime and vandalism in the area.

Mr Kymlicka – chairperson of the local community association

I want to build a cinema, a small shopping centre and a nightclub on the site. I already have tenants for the shops and the nightclub if I can buy the site. This would bring more jobs to the area, which I believe would help tourism, especially the local hotel and B&Bs.

Mr Brown – local property developer

We think that the area should be turned into a park. We believe that the area needs more trees and open green spaces, not car parks creating more pollution.

Ms Nolan – member of the local environmental group

The idea to put a nightclub on the site is totally unacceptable to the local residents. We would be kept up all night with the noise of people shouting on their way home, revving cars and beeping horns. If the local authority gives permission for Mr Brown's development, the residents' association will appeal the decision to An Bord Pleanála.

Mr Naipaul – local resident

I want to do what is best for the community. I think that Mr Brown's proposal is the best because it would bring business to the area. I feel that the environmentalists don't appreciate the benefits of this.

Ms Akerele – local politician

ACTIVITIES

1. There are **three** ideas for the development of this site. Choose one and give reasons why you think that idea should go ahead.
2. Which idea do you think would most benefit the community? Give reasons for your answer.
3. Imagine that you are a supporter of Mr Kymlicka or Ms Nolan or Mr Brown. In groups, prepare a role play that you would argue at a public meeting. Two students could chair the meeting and decide which group makes the best case.
4. Imagine you are a newspaper reporter. Write an article briefly describing the main arguments of each group and how the meeting ended.
5. Develop a list of arguments for and against the following facilities in your area:
   - youth café
   - Travellers' halting site
   - incinerator
   - homeless shelter.

ACTION IDEA

Debate/Essay: 'Community development should only be carried out by councillors and community leaders.'

STUDY 24 A COMMUNITY TAKES ACTION

Different people come together in communities over issues that concern them and affect their lives. Groups are often formed in local areas to **bring about change**. Read the case study below of how a group of young people decided to do something about the lack of skateboarding facilities in their local town.

Campaign for Gorey Skate Park

A group of young guys in Gorey, County Wexford, including Grant Masterson, Mark Waddock, Ciaran Halford and Shane Doyle, were mad about skateboarding and in-line skating, but back in 1997 there was nowhere in Gorey where they could practise their sport. They decided to put some ramps in the car park near the fire station, but as skateboarding was seen as a dangerous activity, their ramps were taken away by the local council and they couldn't even get them back.

What they dreamed of was having a proper skate park, and were aware of skate parks being built in lots of public parks in the USA and Europe. They also found out that there were already a few skate parks in Ireland. So instead of feeling defeated when their ramps were taken away, they decided to organise themselves and lobby the county council to build a skate park in Gorey.

They first went to their local TD (Ivan Yates, who also happened to be a Government minister at the time) and asked him for advice about what to do and how they might get funding. He advised them to set up a proper skateboarding club, with a bank account and members who would take jobs on a committee, like a chairperson, treasurer and public relations person. (This turned out to be good advice, as local or national government/authorities need to see official records of how any monies given to voluntary groups or clubs in a local community are spent.) They were able to show that any monies they raised were spent in the name of the club.

The big problem they then faced was that the county council was afraid that if they gave money for a skate park, and someone skating hurt themselves, the council would be sued. The cost of insuring against this would be massive. So when they met with council officials they were well prepared.

Pictured at Gorey's car park beside the garda station looking for a proper place to skate - front - Ciaran Halford, Ciaran McCarthy, John Dunne, back: Eve Stack, Mark Waddock, Grant Masterson, Conor Stafford, Dan Smith and Danny Smith.

They had business plans, and showed how this problem was overcome in other countries. They were also able to show the council the surveys they had done of school students, youth clubs and sports clubs in the South East, which showed how many young people really wanted facilities like this in their local areas. They had to convince the council that skateboarding and in-line skating was not just a dangerous fad.

Other actions they took to get as many people as possible aware of their campaign was to set up a website called www.goreyskateclub.com, and to set up meetings in the town asking young people and their parents to come along, and get involved in the campaign.

Finally, after a long, hard eight-year struggle, their dream came true, and the national government decided to give a grant of £110,000, which Wexford County Council said they would match, so there was a fund of £220,000 to build the skate park in the county. The reason Gorey was chosen was because of their campaign, which showed they could operate a skate park.

When asked to explain why their campaign was successful in the end, Grant said, 'We didn't lose track of the main goal, we never took no for an answer, and we looked for funding everywhere. We also looked for support in our community, with meetings of young people and parents, informing everyone of what was happening at each stage of our campaign. The media were very helpful too – when we contacted the local newspapers and local radio, they did stories which helped our campaign to get public attention.'

The advice that Grant would give to other young people trying to bring about change for the good of their communities is, 'if you feel what you are trying to chase is going to benefit all the people in your area, there should be no limit to the time and effort you should put in'.

(Thanks to Grant Masterson for this article.)

ACTIVITIES

1. What did the group of young people in Gorey do when their skateboarding ramps were taken away?
2. What advice did Ivan Yates give the group and why was it important?
3. What problem was the county council afraid of if they got involved in this project?
4. How did this group make as many people as possible aware of their campaign?
5. What **skills** did the group use to make their campaign work?
6. Why does Grant Masterson think that their campaign to get a skate park in Gorey was successful in the end?

STUDY 25 ACTION INTERNATIONALLY

Around the world young people have been getting involved in the development of their own communities. Read the following story of Dariana and a group of young people in Bolivia, who were determined to improve their community with the help of a development agency called Outreach International.

Take Action!

Outreach International – Bolivia

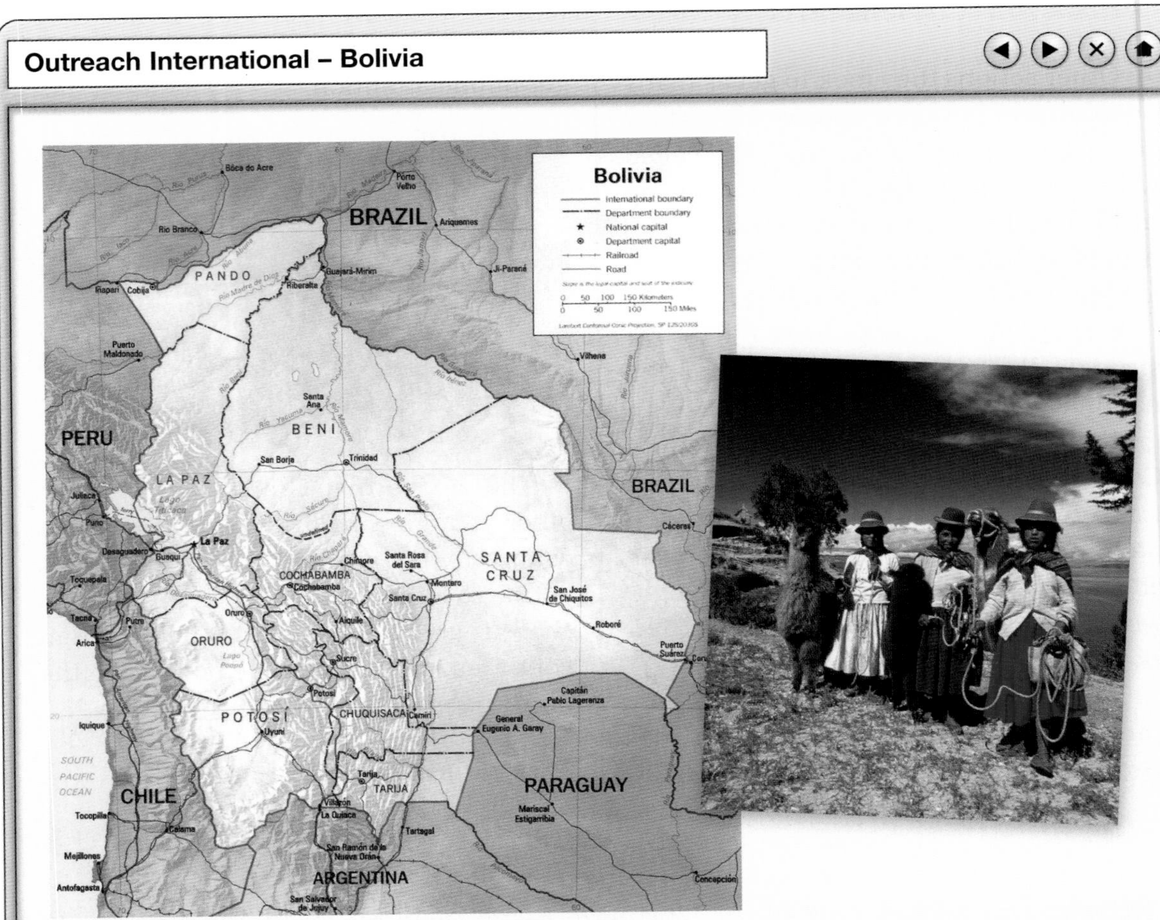

'Why don't we have fruit?' asked 14-year-old Dariana, after returning from a visit to a community a day's distance from her village, Sacaba, Bolivia. 'People in other places have apples and peaches – why can't we?' Her mother and father didn't know how to answer; there hadn't been fruit available in their village for as long as they could remember. They thought she would drop the subject in a few days.

Instead, Dariana got about 25 other young people aged between 14 and 25 to join her campaign. She knew that fruit trees were growing in another community where Outreach International was working. And although it was unheard of to take initiatives without parental consent, this group of youths began to meet together to make it happen. When the young people asked for the issue to be recognised within the community group, parents were amazed at the efforts they had taken to achieve their dreams.

Outreach International – Bolivia

For example, the youth group had talked to their schoolteachers and had researched latitudes, longitudes, wind patterns and rainfall, finding their local conditions were similar to other fruit-growing areas. With facts in hand, there was no stopping their enthusiasm. Parents were quickly drawn into their efforts, proud of the leadership and critical thinking of their children. They invited agricultural experts to visit, and found out which fruit varieties were most drought-resistant and cold-hardy.

The community group then planted 180 apple trees and 60 peach trees. The trees are now thriving, and the community has enjoyed two harvests, and planted more trees. Besides enjoying the fresh fruit, the youth group constructed a dehydrator to dry the fruit, which they could sell at the market to earn continuing education funds.

Dariana's parents are proud. Not only did she achieve her dream of having fruit, but she is now focused on having a brighter future than that of her parents. 'How could we not be happy?' say her parents, smiling.

(Adapted from 'Stories from the Field', available on the Outreach International website, www.outreach-international.org.)

ACTIVITIES

1. Over what issue in their community did Dariana and her friends take action?
2. What kind of research did the group do to find out if what they planned to do would work?
3. What are the group doing with the money they earn at market?
4. How do you think the actions of Dariana and her friends have helped their community?
5. What skills did the group use to make their campaign work?

STUDY 26 IDEAS FOR ACTION PROJECTS

See how you might go about doing an action project in a local community by reading the interview below. Then look at the other ideas for action projects that follow and see what environmental issues your class could take action on.

Doing an Action Project – the Brief Guide

Why did you involve these people?
We wrote to ENFO and the local council for information on litter control. We had to ask our Principal if we could petition students at school.

Can you list the different activities/ tasks you were involved in?
We wrote on the board all our ideas for solving the litter problem
- We voted that we should petition the local council to put more bins on the road outside school
- We divided into groups for different tasks: asking the Principal to allow us to petition students; designing the petition; finally, carrying out the petition and sending it to the local council

Can you describe one thing you did?
I photocopied the petition and organised clipboards to place it on, so it was easy for students to add their names to it.

List two skills you used doing the project.
My organisation skills were needed to photocopy the petitions and arrange the clipboards. My negotiation skills were improved when I had to ask year heads for the clipboards and convince the school secretary to let me use the photocopier.

List some facts you discovered doing the project.
Ok.
- There are a lot of new laws in Ireland dealing with litter and waste
- You're breaking the law if you litter in a public place or throw rubbish from a car
- You can receive an on-the-spot fine or even end up in court if you're found littering
- It's the responsibility of the local council to put bins in their area.

Look back on your experience and tell me what you think of the topic and of doing an action project.
I realise the reason some people don't take action is because they don't know the facts. Most people who signed our petition didn't know there was only one bin near our school that was provided by the local council. Our petition showed how you can improve your area and how local councils do listen to young people.

Action Project Ideas on . . .

Your Community

1. Find out about the local clubs and organisations that young people in your community can join, and make an information leaflet that could be given out in school.
2. What does the word 'community' mean to you? You could show what it means to you in posters, paintings, photos, poetry, maps or personal writing.
3. Interview an older member of your community and find out how the area has changed.
4. Do a survey of your local community to find out how people think the area could be improved.
5. Find out if there is any action you could take to improve existing amenities, such as the local playground or swimming pool. For example, could they be made more accessible for wheelchair users?
6. Your class could volunteer to help in the Tidy Towns competition or to participate in one of the award schemes outlined in this chapter.
7. Design a poster that could be used to attract tourists to your area.

Local Government

1. Research an issue, such as a planning decision, that has caused controversy in your area. You might find local newspapers helpful. You could do a wall display highlighting the issue.
2. Invite a local councillor to give a talk to your class on the work that councillors do.

- Remember to look back over the action ideas that are suggested throughout the chapter for more topics for an action project.
- In Chapter 6 you will find advice and helpful hints on how to make posters and leaflets, and on conducting surveys, interviews, petitions and fundraising events.

STUDY 27 REVISION QUESTIONS

Section 1

Answer ALL questions in this section. (Total: 18 marks.)

1. (a) Which two of the following organisations give awards to communities in Ireland for improving their area? **(4 marks)**

(i) Tidy Towns ☐
(ii) Foróige ☐
(iii) UNICEF ☐
(iv) World Health Organisation ☐

(b) Indicate whether the following statements are true or false by placing a tick in the correct box. **(4 marks)**

(i) Being a member of a community brings with it certain rights and responsibilities.
True ☐ False ☐

(ii) Gardaí are responsible for providing amenities and services in a locality.
True ☐ False ☐

(iii) One kind of local authority is a county commission.
True ☐ False ☐

(iv) Signing a petition is a form of protest.
True ☐ False ☐

2. Fill in the missing words in the following sentences. **(4 marks)**

(a) The Minister for the ____________ ____________, ____________ and ____________ ____________ ____________ is responsible for local authorities.

(b) One of the main areas or programme groups that local authorities have responsibility for is ____________.

(c) Decisions made by councillors are reached by ____________.

(d) You must be ____________ years of age to run for office in a local election.

3. In the boxes provided below, match the letters in row X with the corresponding numbers in row Y. The first pair is completed for you. **(6 marks)**

X	A	B	C	D	E	F	G
Y	1						

X		Y	
A.	A local authority is	1.	responsible for providing accommodation for Travellers.
B.	Local councillors	2.	deals with planning applications that cause difficulty.
C.	The zoning of land is	3.	included in the area's local development plan.
D.	City/county managers	4.	are elected for a five-year term of office.
E.	Youth councils in Ireland are called	5.	carry out decisions made by councillors.
F.	Local government is	6.	Comhairle na nÓg.
G.	An Bord Pleanála	7.	the way people influence decisions in their area.

Section 2

Answer ALL questions numbered 1, 2 and 3 below. Each question carries 14 marks.

1. Examine the headlines below and answer the questions that follow.

Travellers Lobby Council for Halting Site

Local Hospital Closes

Residents Object to Speeding Traffic in their Estate

(a) What issues are these newspaper headlines concerned with? **(2)**

(b) Suggest one form of protest a community could take about an issue that concerns them. **(2)**

(c) In your opinion, why would a community group contact the media about a local issue that they are concerned with? **(2)**

(d) Name an issue of local concern that has been in the media recently. **(2)**

(e) Name a local issue that you are concerned about.
State why you are concerned and two actions you could take over the issue.
The issue **(1)**
Why you are concerned **(1)**
Action 1 **(2)**
Action 2 **(2)**

2. Examine this picture and answer the questions that follow.

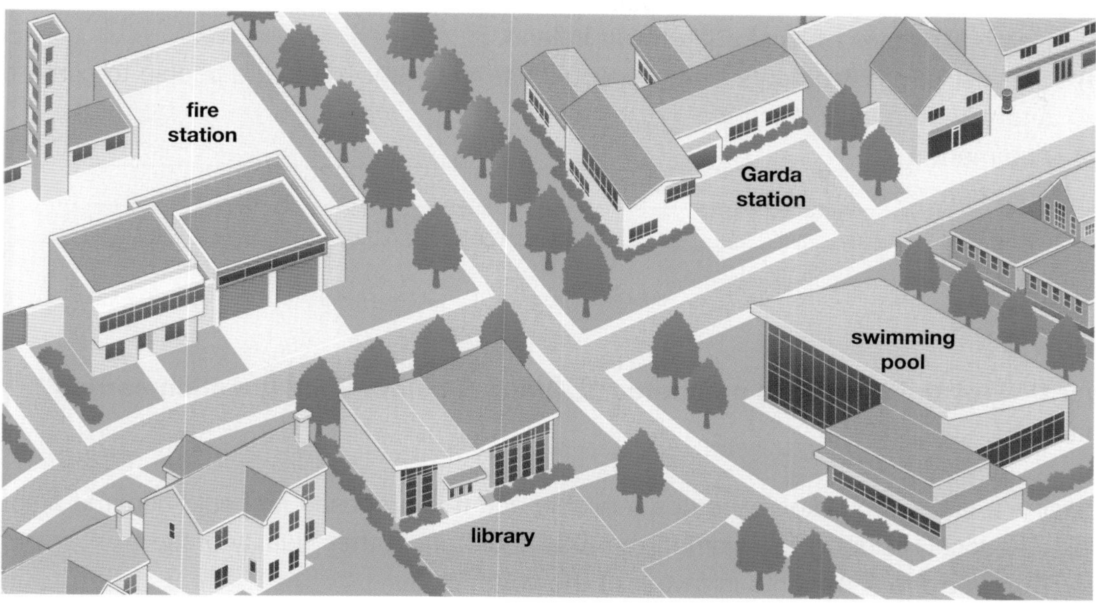

(a) What amenities and services do the people in this area have? **(2)**
(b) State one facility or service you think this community needs. **(2)**
(c) Give two reasons why you think that the facility or service that you have mentioned above would improve the area. **(2)**
(d) State how the lack of facilities, e.g. a post office, could affect the lives of the people in a community, and suggest two actions a community could take to try and get this amenity or service for their area.
Facility/amenity **(2)**
How it affects the community **(2)**
Action 1 **(2)**
Action 2 **(2)**

3. Read the text below and answer the questions on the following page.

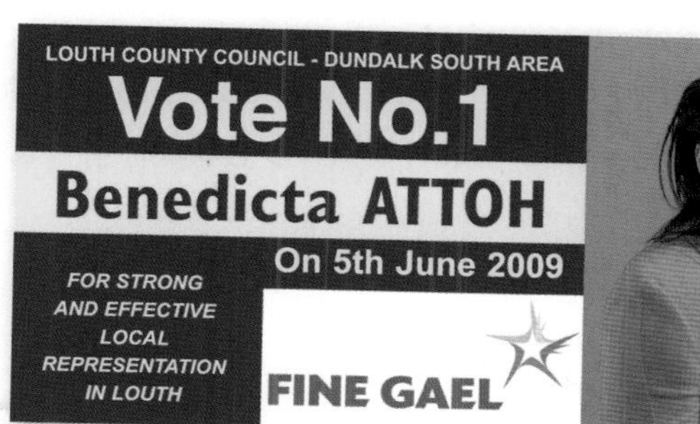

Personal profile

I was born in Nigeria and have been living with my family in Dundalk since 2000. Since coming to Dundalk, I have been working actively in the local community and nationally promoting cultural awareness and understanding by organising cross cultural events and through training of members of the Gardaí, statutory bodies, NGOs and community groups. I received the Rehabl/Louth Person of the Year Award in 2007. I also received the Edmund Rice Award in 2008 for my intercultural work in Ireland. This proves that I am here for the good of the town and will fight for you to the best of my ability if elected. I am currently working as an Independent Consultant in Training & Diversity Management.

Working for you, my priorities will include:

- Effective representation and quick response to the needs of constituents
- Intensify the call for services for people with mental health issues
- Strong commitment to the retention of full services at the Louth County Hospital
- Provision of decent and affordable childcare
- Addressing the safety needs of our senior citizens
- Access to social & affordable housing for all those in need
- Provision of facilities to engage young people and children
- Multi agency approach to eradicate anti social behaviour
- Community integration

. . . . **Vote for Change**

Benedicta Attoh, 8 Brookwood Lawns, Red Barns Rd., Dundalk. Mob: 087 - 981 7853 Email: benedicta@atthodarcy.com www.attohdarcy.com

Vote No. 1 ATTOH, Benedicta Vote No. 2 D'ARCY, Cllr. Jim

Published by the Candidate, Printed by Bellew Print, Park Street, Dundalk

(a) List two issues that are of concern to this candidate. **(2)**
(b) Which of the issues mentioned above do you think is important and why? **(4)**
(c) Name two kinds of local authority in Ireland. **(2)**
(d) Suggest three arguments that you would use to try and persuade people to come out and vote in a local election.
Argument 1: ______________________________ **(2)**
Argument 2: ______________________________ **(2)**
Argument 3: ______________________________ **(2)**

Section 3

Answer ONE of the questions numbered 1, 2 and 3 below. Each question carries 20 marks.

1. Imagine a disused building becomes available and it is proposed it should become a youth club. The local residents are worried that this could affect their quality of life.
   (a) Describe the arguments in favour of the youth club.
   (b) Describe the arguments against the youth club.
   (c) Suggest another use for the site and give reasons.

2. Imagine your local council has decided to put a halting site for Travellers in your area. A meeting has been called to discuss the proposal.
   (a) Describe the arguments for the idea.
   (b) Describe the arguments against the idea.
   (c) Describe how you would organise such a meeting in order to make sure that all sides are treated fairly and equally.

3. Imagine you have invited your community garda to talk to your CSPE class.
   (a) Name and describe two issues of concern that you would like to discuss with him/her.
   (b) Describe what actions you would take to prepare for the visit.
   (c) Suggest an action you could take following the garda's visit to inform others about the work of the community garda.

Chapter 4

The State and You

In Chapter 3 you learned what a community is and how people take part in their communities. You saw how a local community can **take action** and bring about change. But individuals or communities can also influence what happens at **national level**.

The state can be seen as a large grouping of communities. As citizens of Ireland, we are affected by what the government and the state do. We can also influence and take part in decisions. Being a citizen of Ireland means we also have certain rights and responsibilities.

STUDY 28 DEMOCRACY AND YOU

The word **democracy** comes from the Greek words **demos**, meaning people, and **kratia**, meaning to rule, so in a democracy rules and laws are made and agreed by the people of a country, for the people of a country.

The ancient Greeks were the first people to rule in this way. Because the voting population was small in ancient Greece (only freemen had the right to vote), all freemen had a chance to have a say directly in how the state was run. This was called direct democracy.

In Ireland, with a population of over four million people, it would be impossible to run a system where everyone has a say directly. What we do instead is **elect people to Dáil Éireann** to represent our views on how the country should be run. This is called **representative democracy**. The members of the Dáil represent the different views that people have on running the country. (Dáil is the Irish word for parliament.)

In a democracy, taking part in elections by voting is an important way of having your voice heard

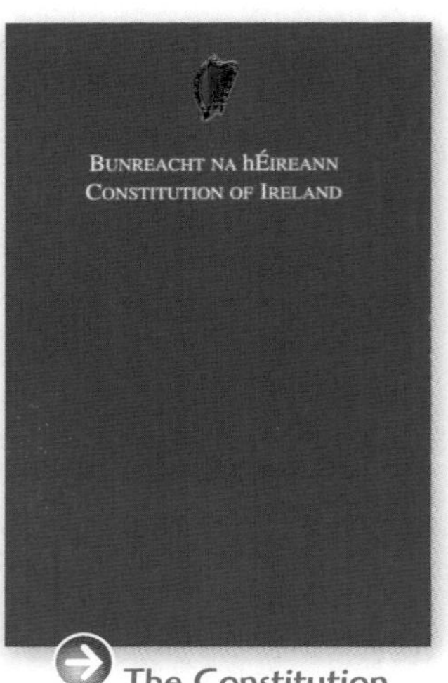

The Constitution contains the basic laws and rights of all Irish citizens

There are a number of elections a person in Ireland can vote in.

- **Local elections** – to elect members to the local authority (councils/corporations). Local elections happen every **five years**.
- **General elections** – to elect members to national government (the Dáil). A general election must be held every **five years**.
- **By-elections** – to elect a new TD if the TD of an area retires or dies.
- **European elections** – to elect members to the European Parliament (MEPs). A European election must take place every **five years**.
- **Presidential elections** – to elect a new president. This happens every **seven years**. A president can serve two terms of office, but no more than this.

You can also vote in a **referendum**. A referendum is held if we want to change any of the laws written in the **Constitution**, e.g. when people voted to remove the ban on divorce.

Steps to Voting

The voting system in Ireland is called **Proportional Representation** or **PR**.

Step 1
To vote in an election in Ireland you must be 18 years old and your name must be on the **Register of Electors**. You can register at a local post office or local authority.

Step 2
If you are registered to vote, a **polling card** will arrive in the post a few days before the election. The polling card has a number on it and this allows you to be identified when you go to vote. It also ensures that you only vote once. It is against the law to vote more than once.

Step 3
On the day of the election you go to the **polling station**. This is usually a local primary school. When you go to the polling station you must bring your polling card and other ID (such as a passport) with you.

POLLING STATION

Step 4
At the polling station you will be given a **ballot paper**.

Step 5
Voting is done in private in a polling booth, so no one can see who you are voting for. This is called a **secret ballot**. You can vote for as many people or candidates as are on the ballot paper. To do this you put:

- 1 beside the photo of the person who is your first choice
- 2 in the box beside the photo of the person of your second choice
- and so on . . .

Step 6
When you have finished marking the ballot paper you fold it in half and put it in the **ballot box**.

Step 7
At the **count**, the ballot box is opened and the ballot papers are put in a pile to be counted. Each **candidate** (person looking to be elected) is trying to reach a **quota**. A quota is the smallest number of votes needed to be elected.

Step 7
There are always more candidates than there are seats in the Dáil, etc., so counting goes on until each candidate is either **elected or eliminated**. If nobody reaches the quota on the first count, the person with the least number of votes is eliminated and their votes are transferred. This means that the vote now goes to the second choice marked on a ballot paper. This continues until someone reaches the quota and is elected.

ACTIVITIES

1. What does democracy mean?
2. Whose views do members of the Dáil represent?
3. Put these steps to voting in the correct order.
   - Fill in the ballot paper.
   - Put your name on the Register of Electors.
   - Get your polling card in the post.
   - Put your ballot paper in the ballot box.
   - Go to the polling station.
   - Go to a polling booth.
4. What four pieces of information about the candidate are there on the ballot paper?

Toghchán do Pharlaimint na hEorpa
European Parliament Election

TREORACHA

1. Scríobh an figiúr 1 sa bhosca le hais ghrianghraf an chéad iarrthóra is rogha leat, scríobh an figiúr 2 sa bhosca le hais ghrianghraf an iarrthóra do dhara rogha, agus mar sin de.
2. Fill an páipéar ionas nach bhfeicfear do vóta. Taispeáin *cúl an pháipéir* don oifigeach ceannais, agus cuir sa bhosca ballóide é.

INSTRUCTIONS

1. Write 1 in the box beside the photograph of the candidate of your first choice, write 2 in the box beside the photograph of the candidate of your second choice, and so on.
2. Fold the paper to conceal your vote. Show the *back of the paper* to the presiding officer and put it in the ballot box.

Party	Candidate	Photo	Vote
FIANNA FÁIL	**BYRNE – FIANNA FÁIL** (EIBHLIN BYRNE of Mansion House, Dawson Street, Dublin 2; Lord Mayor of Dublin) Liosta Ionaid FF Replacement List		
green party	**De BÚRCA – GREEN PARTY/ COMHAONTAS GLAS** (DÉIRDRE De BÚRCA of 11 Highland Grove, The Park, Cabinteely, Co Dublin; Public Representative (Senator)) Liosta Ionaid GP/CG Replacement List		
Labour	**De ROSSA – THE LABOUR PARTY** (PROINSIAS De ROSSA of 14th Floor, Liberty Hall, Dublin 1; M.E.P.) Liosta Ionaid LP Replacement List		
SOCIALIST Party	**HIGGINS – THE SOCIALIST PARTY** (JOE HIGGINS of 155 Briarwood Close, Dublin 15; Political Activist) Liosta Ionaid SP Replacement List		
Sinn Féin	**McDONALD – SINN FÉIN** (MARY LOU McDONALD of 23 Ashington Heath, Navan Road, Dublin 7; Public Representative) Liosta Ionaid SF Replacement List		
	McKENNA – NON PARTY (PATRICIA McKENNA of 11 Iona Road, Glasnevin, Dublin 9; Public Activist) Liosta Ionaid PMcK Replacement List		
FINE GAEL	**MITCHELL – FINE GAEL** (GAY MITCHELL of 192 Upper Rathmines Road, Dublin 6; MEP) Liosta Ionaid FG Replacement List		
FIANNA FÁIL	**RYAN – FIANNA FÁIL** (EOIN RYAN of Sussex Rd, Dublin 4; MEP) Liosta Ionaid FF Replacement List		
Libertas.eu	**SIMONS – LIBERTAS** (CAROLINE SIMONS of Denshaw House, Baggot Street, Dublin 2)		
	SWEENEY – NON PARTY (EMMANUEL SWEENEY of 23, Ormond Road, Ranelagh, Dublin 6, Ireland; Writer) Liosta Ionaid ES Replacement List		

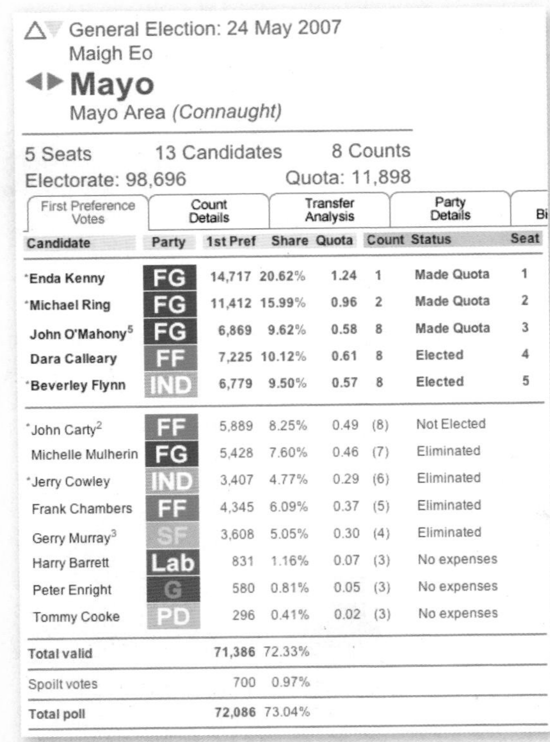

General Election: 24 May 2007
Maigh Eo
Mayo
Mayo Area *(Connaught)*

5 Seats 13 Candidates 8 Counts
Electorate: 98,696 Quota: 11,898

First Preference Votes | Count Details | Transfer Analysis | Party Details | Bi

Candidate	Party	1st Pref	Share	Quota	Count	Status	Seat
*Enda Kenny	FG	14,717	20.62%	1.24	1	Made Quota	1
*Michael Ring	FG	11,412	15.99%	0.96	2	Made Quota	2
John O'Mahony[5]	FG	6,869	9.62%	0.58	8	Made Quota	3
Dara Calleary	FF	7,225	10.12%	0.61	8	Elected	4
*Beverley Flynn	IND	6,779	9.50%	0.57	8	Elected	5
*John Carty[2]	FF	5,889	8.25%	0.49	(8)	Not Elected	
Michelle Mulherin	FG	5,428	7.60%	0.46	(7)	Eliminated	
*Jerry Cowley	IND	3,407	4.77%	0.29	(6)	Eliminated	
Frank Chambers	FF	4,345	6.09%	0.37	(5)	Eliminated	
Gerry Murray[3]	SF	3,608	5.05%	0.30	(4)	Eliminated	
Harry Barrett	Lab	831	1.16%	0.07	(3)	No expenses	
Peter Enright	G	580	0.81%	0.05	(3)	No expenses	
Tommy Cooke	PD	296	0.41%	0.02	(3)	No expenses	
Total valid		71,386	72.33%				
Spoilt votes		700	0.97%				
Total poll		72,086	73.04%				

5. What is the system of voting in Ireland called?
6. Look at the general election results from Mayo and answer the questions that follow:
   a) How many candidates were looking to be elected to the five Dáil seats in Mayo?
   b) How many votes did the candidates have to reach (i.e. the quota) before they could be elected?
   c) Which candidate was elected on the second count?

d) What independent candidate was elected?
e) How many first preference votes did the eliminated Labour Party candidate Harry Barrett get?
f) Which elected candidate got the highest number of first preference votes?
g) How many spoiled votes were there?

7. What is the Constitution?
8. Apart from elections, when else can a person vote?
9. Look at this leaflet about voting and answer the questions that follow.

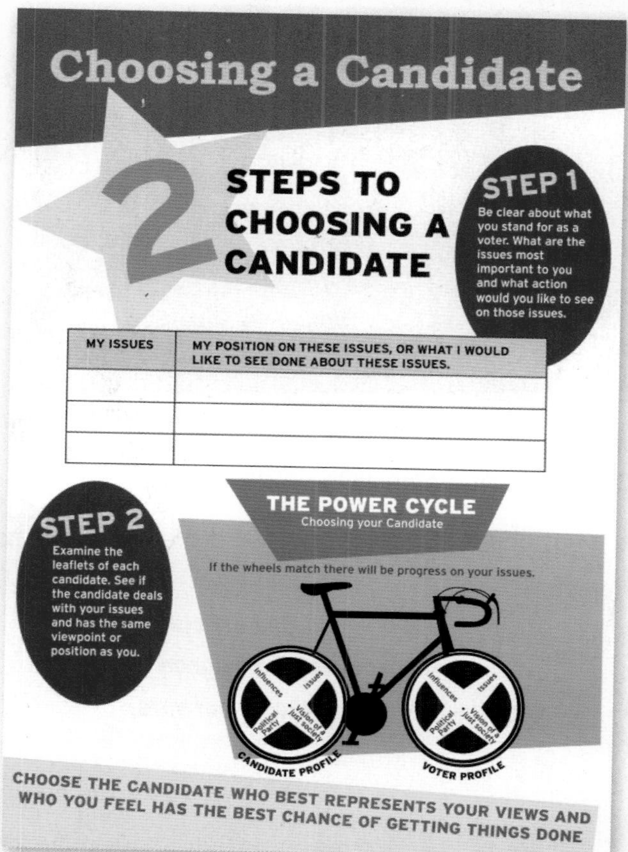

a) What did this campaign aim to do?
b) What message is the front cover of the leaflet trying to get across?
c) Design a front cover for a leaflet to encourage people to vote in your area. Make sure you come up with a slogan for the cover.
d) How can it affect an area when people do not vote?

ACTION IDEA

Survey: Carry out a school survey to see how much the members of your school community know about voting.

STUDY 29 USE YOUR VOTE

In Ireland people have the **right to vote**. Many people believe that citizens have a duty to vote in elections. In some countries (e.g. Belgium and Australia) a person can be fined for not voting. Down through history people have fought and died for the right to vote.

These women are showing the ink mark you receive when you vote in India, which is used so that no one can vote twice in the same election

In 2005 women in Kuwait were given the right to vote for the first time. In Saudi Arabia women cannot vote or stand for election.

Read what different people, past and present, have said about the importance of voting.

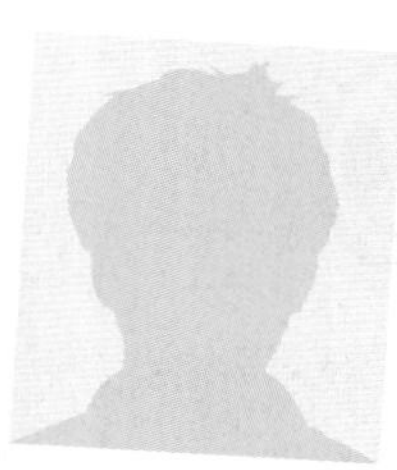

Bad officials are elected by good citizens who do not vote.

George Jean Nathan, American journalist (1882–1958)

It was my firm conviction that if the Negro achieved the ballot throughout the South, many of the problems which we faced would be solved. Once we gained the ballot we would see a new day in the South. I had come to see that one of the most decisive steps that the Negro could take was a short walk to the voting booth.

Martin Luther King (1929–68)

To make democracy work, we must be a nation of participants, not simply observers. One who does not vote has no right to complain.

Louis L'Amour, American writer (1908–88)

STUDY 30 POLITICAL PARTIES

A person may vote for a **political party** or an **independent candidate** with whose views they agree. People often vote for a political party in an election. Each political party has a different view on what kind of country we should have. Before an election each political party or independent candidate produces a **manifesto**, which states what they will do for the country and its citizens if they are elected.

Fianna Fáil

Fianna Fáil means 'Soldier of Destiny'. The party was founded in 1926 by Éamon de Valera. It believes in encouraging and developing business. One of its stated aims is 'to secure in peace and agreement the unity of Ireland and its people'. The party has been in government for periods adding up to more than 50 years.

www.fiannafail.ie

Fine Gael

Fine Gael means 'Tribes of Ireland' and was formed in 1933. Fine Gael has taken part in many coalition governments in which it has been the majority party. One of the party's stated aims is to create a just society.

www.finegael.ie

The Labour Party

The Labour Party was founded in 1912 by James Connolly, James Larkin and William O'Brien as the political wing of the Irish Trades Union Congress. The Labour Party sees poverty, homelessness and unemployment as the enemies of freedom. Its aim is a more equal division of wealth and power in society. The Labour Party has taken part in a number of coalition governments.

www.labour.ie

Green Party

The Green Party was formed in 1981 by Christopher Fettes, an Irish teacher, because of concern about increasing global and local environmental destruction. It believes that as caretakers of the planet we have the responsibility to pass it on in a fit and healthy state. Well-known TDs include Trevor Sargent and John Gormley.

www.greenparty.ie

Sinn Féin

Sinn Féin means 'We Ourselves'. The party was set up in 1905 by Arthur Griffith. It wants an end to partition, which it sees as the cause of conflict, injustice and division in Ireland. It strives towards a 32-county Ireland, and one of its aims is a more equal division of wealth and power.

www.sinnfein.ie

Socialist Party

The Socialist Party was formed in 1996 after a split with the Labour Party. It believes in promoting the rights of workers, the unemployed and women, and in social welfare rights.

www.socialistparty.net

ACTIVITIES

1. What political party (or parties) is in government now?
2. Design a logo for a political party you would like to start. Give three views your party would have on the kind of country we should have.
3. Match the name of each politician with their photo.
   a) Mary Hanafin
   b) Joe Higgins
   c) Joan Burton
   d) Olwyn Enright
   e) Caoimhghín Ó Caoláin
   f) Eamon Gilmore
   g) Enda Kenny
   h) Eamon Ryan

ACTION IDEAS

Research: Find out about the youth sections of the main Irish political parties.
Guest speaker: Invite a member of the youth section of a political party to speak to your class.

Check out www.micandidate.ie, which gives details of all candidates running in a general election in Ireland

STUDY 31 HOW IRELAND IS GOVERNED

Ireland is divided into **43 constituencies** or voting areas. In a general election the people who live in each constituency or area vote for and elect people to represent them in the Dáil. There are **166 members** of the Dáil and they are known as **TDs** (Teachtaí Dála, which in English means Deputy of the Dáil).

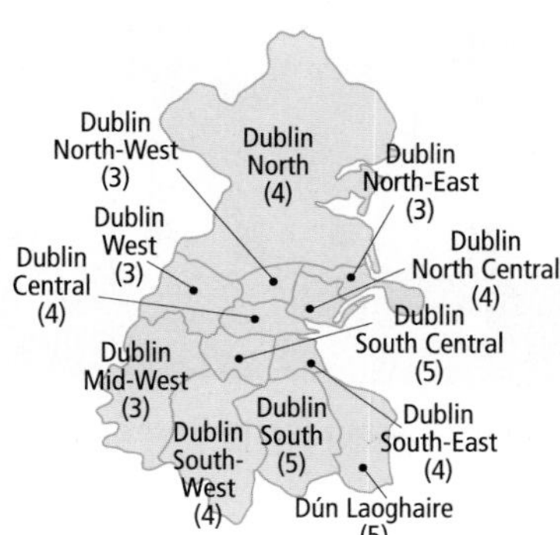

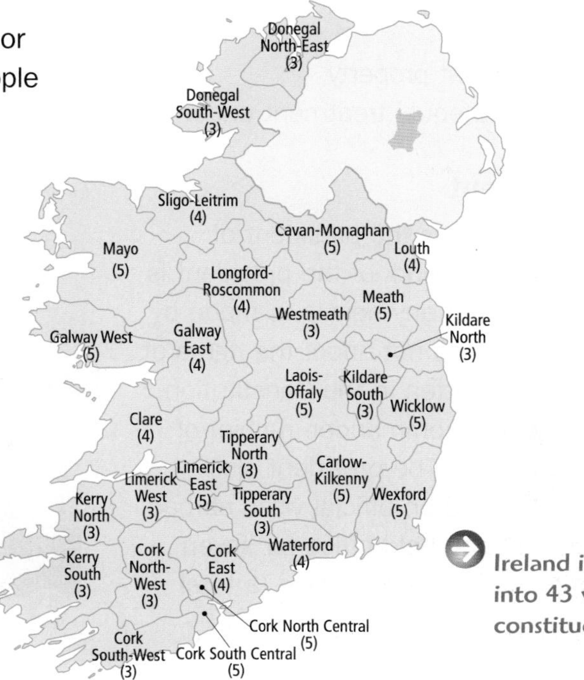

Ireland is divided into 43 voting constituencies

The government is formed when:
One single party gets the most votes = a majority government.
One party with the Independents come together = a minority government.
Two or more parties come together = a coalition government.

The government is also guided by the Constitution and the president. The TDs and political parties that are not in power (the **opposition**) make sure that the government does its job.

Dáil Éireann meets in Leinster House

The **Constitution** contains the **basic laws** of our country. It describes the powers of the president, the government and the **three houses of the Oireachtas** (the president, Dáil Éireann and Seanad Éireann). It is very important because it acts as a **safeguard against the abuse of power** and also **protects the rights of citizens**.

It states that every citizen has the right to:

- practise their religion
- education
- vote
- own and inherit property
- freedom and equal treatment under the law.

The President

The head of state is the president of Ireland. The main work of the president is to make sure that any new laws made by the government do not affect the rights of the people as written in the Constitution. He or she is the commander-in-chief of the armed forces. The president also represents Ireland on official visits abroad. The president can hold office for seven years and can be elected twice (a total of 14 years).

Áras an Uachtaráin is the home of the Irish president

The president is also responsible for:

- appointing the Taoiseach and members of the government (after an election)
- dissolving (ending) the Dáil
- appointing judges
- appointing officers of the Defence Forces (Army, Naval Service, Air Corps)
- signing bills (which then become law)
- referring these bills to the Supreme Court to make sure that they are in agreement with the Constitution.

President of Ireland 2011–
Michael D. Higgins

Mary McAleese, President 1997–2011

Mary Robinson, President 1990–97

Éamon de Valera, President 1959–73

Douglas Hyde was the first President of Ireland, 1938-45

ACTIVITIES

1. What is a constituency and how many constituencies are there in Ireland?
2. Look at the map on page 117. How many seats are there in your constituency?
3. Name a TD from your area.
4. What kind of government is in power now?
5. Who is the president of Ireland? Name one thing s/he does as part of the job.

The Dáil and the Seanad

The two **Houses of the Oireachtas** are called **Dáil Éireann** and **Seanad Éirean**. They make the laws of the country.

During Dáil sessions, TDs debate and discuss issues that affect all citizens

The Dáil

The Dáil is made up of **166 TDs**, who are voted in by the people. During Dáil meetings they **debate and discuss** issues that concern the country, such as work and unemployment. TDs also question the Taoiseach and ministers about ideas for new laws and ask them to explain any decisions made. **TDs vote on these proposals for new laws**, as well as on any changes to existing laws. They also vote on how and where money should be spent.

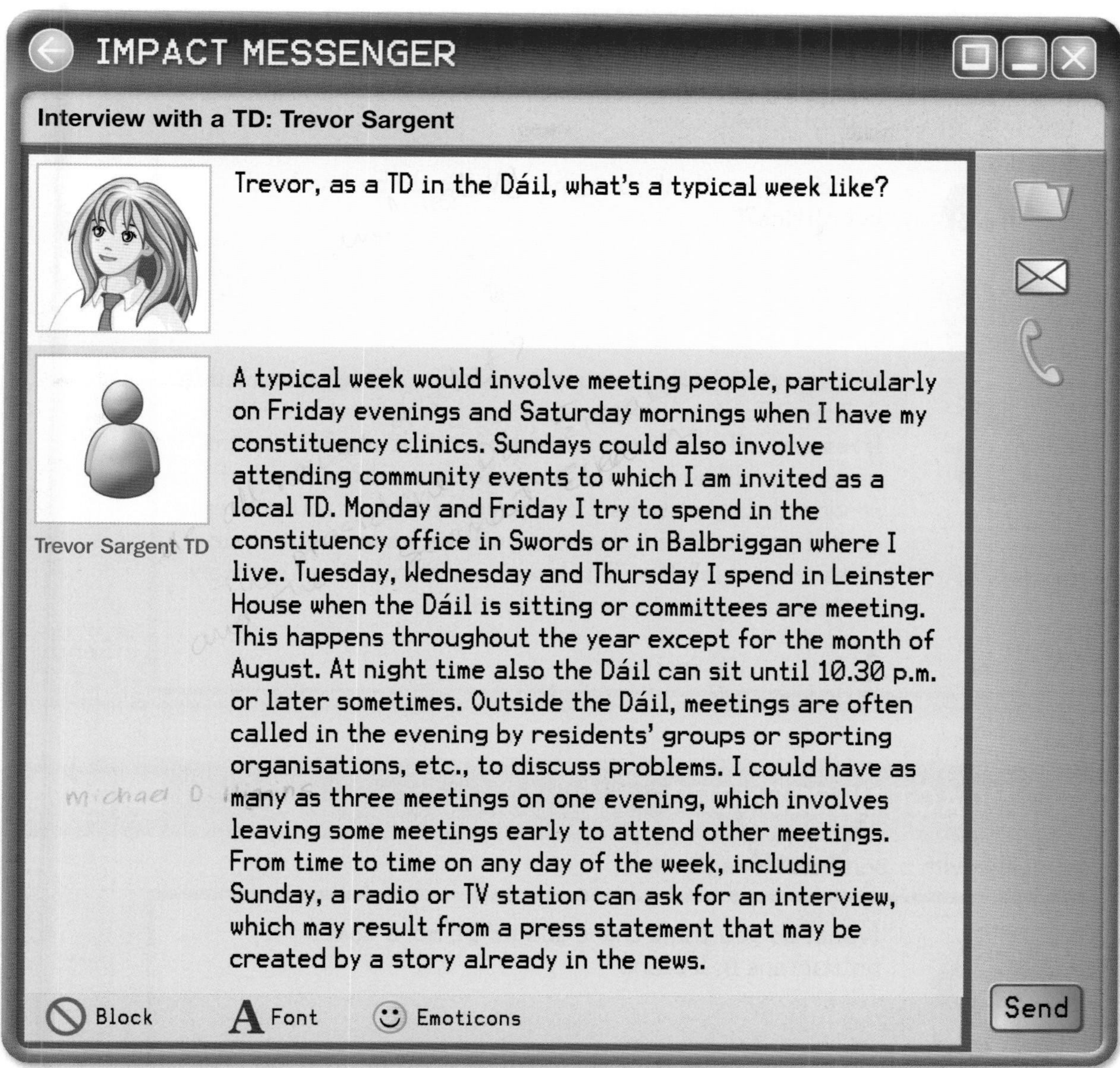

IMPACT MESSENGER
Interview with a TD: Trevor Sargent
Trevor, as a TD in the Dáil, what's a typical week like?
A typical week would involve meeting people, particularly on Friday evenings and Saturday mornings when I have my constituency clinics. Sundays could also involve attending community events to which I am invited as a local TD. Monday and Friday I try to spend in the constituency office in Swords or in Balbriggan where I live. Tuesday, Wednesday and Thursday I spend in Leinster House when the Dáil is sitting or committees are meeting. This happens throughout the year except for the month of August. At night time also the Dáil can sit until 10.30 p.m. or later sometimes. Outside the Dáil, meetings are often called in the evening by residents' groups or sporting organisations, etc., to discuss problems. I could have as many as three meetings on one evening, which involves leaving some meetings early to attend other meetings. From time to time on any day of the week, including Sunday, a radio or TV station can ask for an interview, which may result from a press statement that may be created by a story already in the news.
Trevor Sargent TD
Block
Font
Emoticons
Send

The Seanad

The Seanad is made up of **60 senators**. They are not directly elected by the people but by members of the incoming Dáil, members of the outgoing Seanad and members of the county councils and corporations. Six members of the Seanad are also elected by the universities and are voted in by graduates. The Taoiseach also nominates 11 candidates.

IMPACT MESSENGER

Interview with a Senator: David Norris

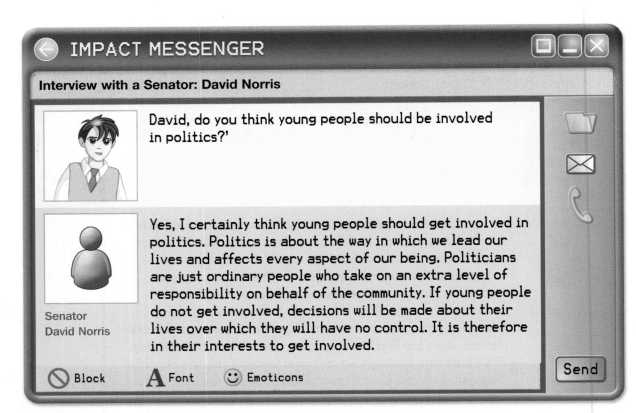

David, do you think young people should be involved in politics?'

Yes, I certainly think young people should get involved in politics. Politics is about the way in which we lead our lives and affects every aspect of our being. Politicians are just ordinary people who take on an extra level of responsibility on behalf of the community. If young people do not get involved, decisions will be made about their lives over which they will have no control. It is therefore in their interests to get involved.

Senator
David Norris

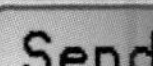

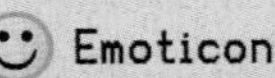

Block Font Emoticons Send

IMPACT MESSENGER

Interview with a Senator: Ivana Bacik

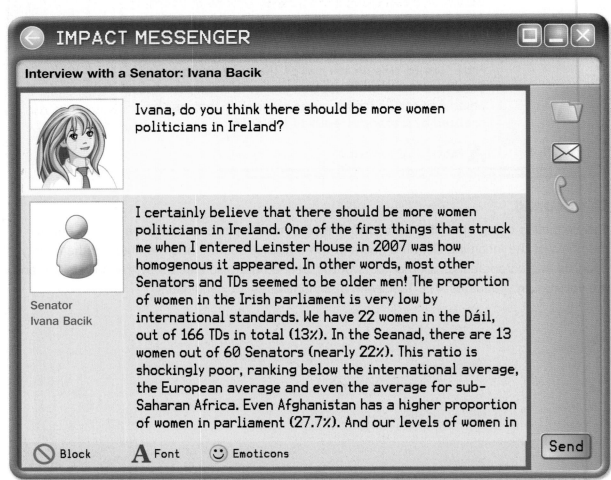

Ivana, do you think there should be more women politicians in Ireland?

I certainly believe that there should be more women politicians in Ireland. One of the first things that struck me when I entered Leinster House in 2007 was how homogenous it appeared. In other words, most other Senators and TDs seemed to be older men! The proportion of women in the Irish parliament is very low by international standards. We have 22 women in the Dáil, out of 166 TDs in total (13%). In the Seanad, there are 13 women out of 60 Senators (nearly 22%). This ratio is shockingly poor, ranking below the international average, the European average and even the average for sub-Saharan Africa. Even Afghanistan has a higher proportion of women in parliament (27.7%). And our levels of women in

Senator
Ivana Bacik

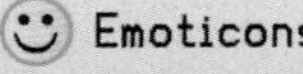

Block Font Emoticons Send

IMPACT MESSENGER

politics have not increased in recent years. The National Women's Council has estimated that at this rate it will take 370 years for the percentage of women in the Dáil to reach 50%. This is very disappointing because in any democracy the parliament should be at least broadly representative of the population – otherwise there is a flaw in the democratic process. Women make up 50% of the general population in Ireland, so they should be represented in larger numbers in the Oireachtas. I have been working to try and highlight the low numbers of women in Irish politics and to increase the numbers of women who stand for election. In December 2008, I organised an event in the Dáil to do this, by inviting all current and former living women TDs and Senators to take up seats in the Dáil Chamber. The resulting photograph illustrated how the Dáil would look if there were nearly equal numbers of women representatives elected – and it was a very colourful and vibrant gathering! I think that having more elected women in parliament can enrich the quality of debates and of policy making, and can ensure that more genuinely representative laws are passed.

Block Font Emoticons Send

This event was held to illustrate how the Dáil would look if there were nearly the same number of women representatives elected as there are men

ACTIVITIES

1. What are the two houses of the Oireachtas called?
2. What do TDs question the Taoiseach and ministers about?
3. Read the interviews with the TDs again and then answer these questions.
   a) What does Trevor Sargent do on Mondays and Fridays?
   b) Where does he spend Tuesdays, Wednesdays and Thursdays?
   c) Why do you think residents' or sporting organisations would ask a TD to come to their meetings?
4. How many senators are there in the Seanad?
5. What does Senator Norris suggest would happen if young people do not get involved in politics?
6. Are you surprised by how few TDs and senators are women? Why do you think this is?

STUDY 32 WHO IS IN CHARGE?

An Taoiseach

The head of the government is called **an Taoiseach**. S/he is elected by the Dáil following a general election. The Taoiseach is usually the leader of the political party that has the most members in the Dáil. The job of the Taoiseach includes appointing ministers to the different government departments, such as Finance and Education. S/he also tries to provide good leadership, runs government meetings and decides when a general election should be held. The Taoiseach also attends meetings with other heads of state of the European Union (EU).

A full sitting of the Dáil with all TDs present

An Tánaiste

The deputy head of the government is called **an Tánaiste**. S/he acts as head of the government when the Taoiseach is not in the country and may also be responsible for a government department.

Ministers

The members of the Cabinet are called **ministers**. The Constitution says that there must be no fewer than seven and no more than 15 ministers. Ministers are given responsibility for the working of a particular department by the Taoiseach. Besides attending government meetings, they must also answer questions in the Dáil on issues concerning their department and take part in debates about new policies or laws that they have suggested. Ministers also attend meetings of the EU.

Departments

Ministers are in charge of the following government departments:

- Agriculture and Food
- Foreign Affairs
- Arts, Sport and Tourism
- Health and Children
- Defence
- Justice, Equality and Law Reform
- Communications, Marine and Natural Resources
- Enterprise, Trade and Employment
- Education and Science
- Transport
- Social and Family Affairs
- Environment, Heritage and Local Government
- Community, Rural and Gaeltacht Affairs
- Finance.

The Civil Service

Civil servants are people who work for the state. Civil servants **advise ministers** about which policies the government should introduce and in what way this might be done. They also carry out the decisions made by the government. Civil servants have a lot of knowledge in a particular area, as they do not change when a new government comes to power. Civil servants are expected to serve equally whatever government is in power and to keep their own political views private.

ACTIVITIES

1. Who is the Taoiseach?
2. What qualities do you think the head of government should have?
3. Who is the Tánaiste?
4. Who decides who will be the ministers in the Cabinet?
5. Name the ministers for:
   - Finance
   - Health and Children
   - Education and Science.
6. What job do civil servants do?
7. The Minister for Finance decides how much each government department will get to spend on education, roads, health care, etc. He or she tells the country this on 'Budget Day'.
   Imagine a scene in which the Minister for Finance is having a meeting with some ministers before Budget Day. Can you identify from the list below which minister would say what? Example: 7 = A.

X	1	2	3	4	5	6	7
Y							A

X

1. Minister for Education and Science
2. Minister for Enterprise, Trade and Employment
3. Minister for Arts, Sport and Tourism
4. Minister for Community, Rural and Gaeltacht Affairs
5. Minister for Justice, Equality and Law Reform
6. Minister for Agriculture and Food
7. Minister for the Environment, Heritage and Local Government
8. Minister for Defence

Y

A. 'I need more money to control pollution.'
B. 'I need more money for schools.'
C. 'I need more money to help create jobs.'
D. 'I need more money for Irish-speaking areas.'
E. 'I need more money for prisons and the Gardaí.'
F. 'I need more money to help small farmers.'
G. 'I need more money for the Air Corps and Naval Service.'
H. 'I need more money to encourage more visitors to come to Ireland.'

 ACTION IDEAS 

Quiz: Design a table quiz that could be held in class. The questions could be broken up into three rounds. Below are some examples of the types of rounds and questions you could have.

Round One:

How Ireland is Governed

The type of government we have in Ireland is called:

a. democracy
b. dictatorship
c. communist

Round Two:

The head of the government in Ireland is called:

a. the President
b. the Prime minister
c. an Taoiseach

Round Three:

Local authorities are the responsibility of the Department of:

a. Education and Science
b. Environment, Heritage and Local Government
c. Finance

Information for Rounds One and Two can be found in this chapter, and information for Round Three can be found in Chapter 3.

Role-play: Imagine you have been given €300 to spend on some area of your school, e.g. improving the school grounds, developing the sports facilities, upgrading the canteen or recycling school waste.

- Elect a class member as Minister for Finance.
- Elect two class members who will act as senior civil servants to advise the minister.
- Divide the rest of the class into groups. Each of these groups decides what they would spend the money on and why, as well as how they would raise more money for their project.
- Each group presents its case to the Minister for Finance and his/her advisers.
- After hearing all the ideas and arguments the minister and the advisers decide which project should go ahead on the basis that it is the most needed in the school and also the most practical.

If you come up with a very good idea you might present it to your principal!

Check out the government website, www.irlgov.ie; or go on a tour of Leinster House, www.oireachtas.ie.

STUDY 33 OMBUDSMAN FOR CHILDREN

The word **Ombudsman** comes from Scandinavia. 'Ombuds' means defender of rights and 'man' in this case means mankind. Norway was the first country to appoint an ombudsman who would be a defender of children's rights: this was in the 1980s. Ireland has had an Ombudsman for Children since 2004. The job of the **Ombudsman for Children** in Ireland includes making sure that the government and others who make decisions about children's lives really know what is best for children and young people. The Office of the Ombudsman uses the **United Nations Convention on the Rights of the Child** as a guide, and they are concerned with the lives of all young people up to the age of 18.

Emily Logan, Ombudsman for Children. Emily was interviewed for the job by a panel that included 15 young people and children.

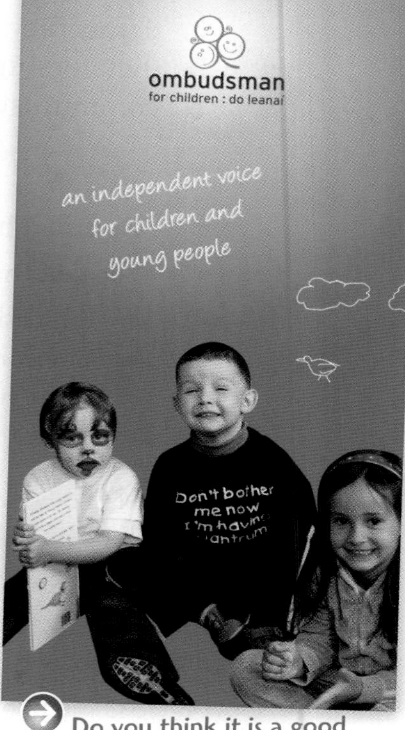

Do you think it is a good idea to have an Ombudsman for Children? Why/why not?

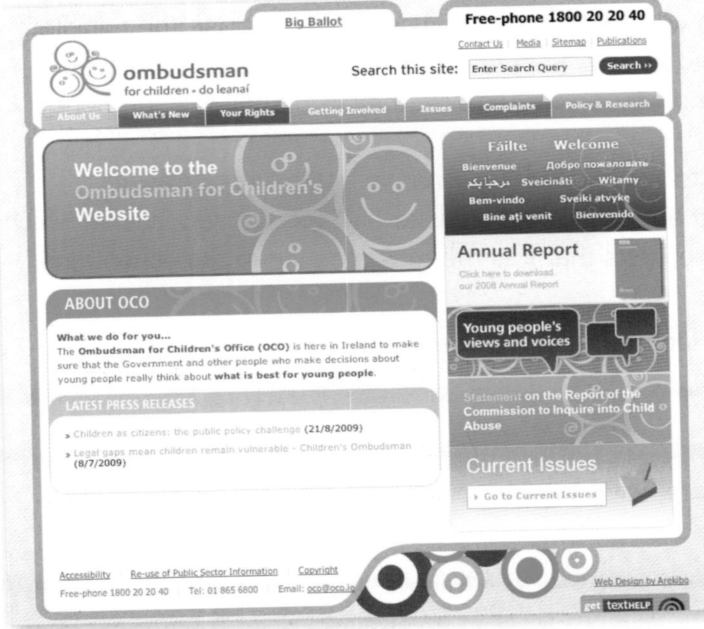

Children and young people were involved in designing the website, www.oco.ie

The Office of the Ombudsman can investigate complaints made by children (or by adults on behalf of children) if they feel they have been treated unfairly in school, in hospital, by different government departments, or by public bodies such as the Irish Sports Council, for example. They can only look at a case when all possible efforts have been made to sort out the problem with the organisation itself.

The Ombudsman's office also works to **promote children's rights**, especially to make sure that Article 12 of the United Nations Convention on the Rights of the Child, which says that young people *have the right to have their voice heard in any matter that affects them*, is respected.

The Ombudsman has a **Youth Advisory Panel** (YAP) of 25 young people aged between 12 and 17. The Ombudsman works with this panel, getting their views on what might be best for young people on issues such as education, play and recreation policies and how young people can best have a voice in Irish society.

Read about the children's right that is important to this student.

Why the Right to Education is Important to Me

'State Parties recognise the right of the child to education' – Article 28 of the UN Convention on the Rights of the Child.

Education is the key to success. Therefore, for a successful life, one has to get a good education no matter the sex, the background or the colour of the person.

Everybody has a dream of becoming somebody in the future. For this ambition to come true, the secret is education. The ability to write, to speak and to think are all helped by education.

To become somebody in the future, like a doctor, a teacher, a nurse, a president, a designer or a trader, education helps. The treasure and potential of life lies in education. Children are not to be denied their right to education because their future path depends on education. It keeps the children busy and occupies their minds. When children are not educated, they might end up on the street, which is very harmful to them, their families and to society. Children not getting an education can have a bad effect on the economic growth of the country. Schools also need to have adequate facilities to help children in their education.

Without education, life is less interesting. If we want to contribute to society, we should take our education seriously as children. We can be useful to our society and achieve our own goals only if our right to education is not denied. Children should also learn and do their homework if they are given the chance to be educated. Sometimes it is very difficult, but let's try our best to help our country.

So children, you need yourself, your loved ones need you, your society needs you, and the way to respond is to make the most of your education. Education denied is somehow life denied.

Nana, Transition Year student on work experience at OCO (www.oco.ie)

ACTIVITIES

1. Why was the Office of the Ombudsman for Children set up?
2. What does the Office of the Ombudsman for Children promote?
3. Why does Nana think education is so important?
4. What does she say about 'education denied'?
5. Do you agree with her views on the importance of education? Explain your answer.
6. Whose responsibility is it in the Irish state to see that education is provided for all young citizens?
7. If you were to meet with the Minister for Education and Science, what suggestions would you make for improving our education system?

STUDY 34 DÁIL NA NÓG

Dáil na nÓg means **youth parliament**. It provides a chance for young people in Ireland to **represent the views of all Irish children at national level**. It is held once a year.

The young people attending Dáil na nÓg have the chance to let the decision-makers in government know what they think of **issues that affect their daily lives**, for example education and play facilities.

The idea for Dáil na nÓg comes from the **National Children's Strategy**, which is a government plan of action to improve the lives of all children – everyone under the age of 18 – in Ireland over the next ten years.

At Dáil na nÓg, young people can discuss issues that are of concern to them

Making democracy work requires the participation of young people

How Do You get Involved in Dáil na nÓg?

As we saw in Chapter 3, Comhairlí (youth councils, for 12–18-year-olds) are organised by every City/County Development Board in each local area. These **youth councils give young people a voice at a community level**.

Each Comhairle na nÓg votes on the themes they would like to see discussed at the next Dáil na nÓg. The themes with the most votes are discussed at Dáil na nÓg. The representatives who will attend Dáil na nÓg are also chosen at the meetings.

Over the last number of years a huge variety of issues have been debated at Dáil na nÓg, including attitudes to young people, making changes in the education system, better facilities for young people in the Irish state, alcohol and drug misuse, bullying, stress, exercise and sport.

While Dáil na nÓg is a one-day event, a representative from each comhairle is elected to go on the **Dáil na nÓg Council**, which meets during the year to discuss the main findings from Dáil na nÓg with ministers, TDs and government officials. They then report back to the local Comhairlí about progress that has been made on issues they have raised.

Every young person in Ireland has the right to be represented at their local Comhairle na nÓg and nationally at Dáil na nÓg. There may be someone from your area, school or youth organisation who is already involved in Comhairle na nÓg, or you can find more information on their websites, www.comhairlenanog.ie and www.dailnanog.ie.

Read the following article by a delegate who took part in Dáil na nÓg.

Take Action!

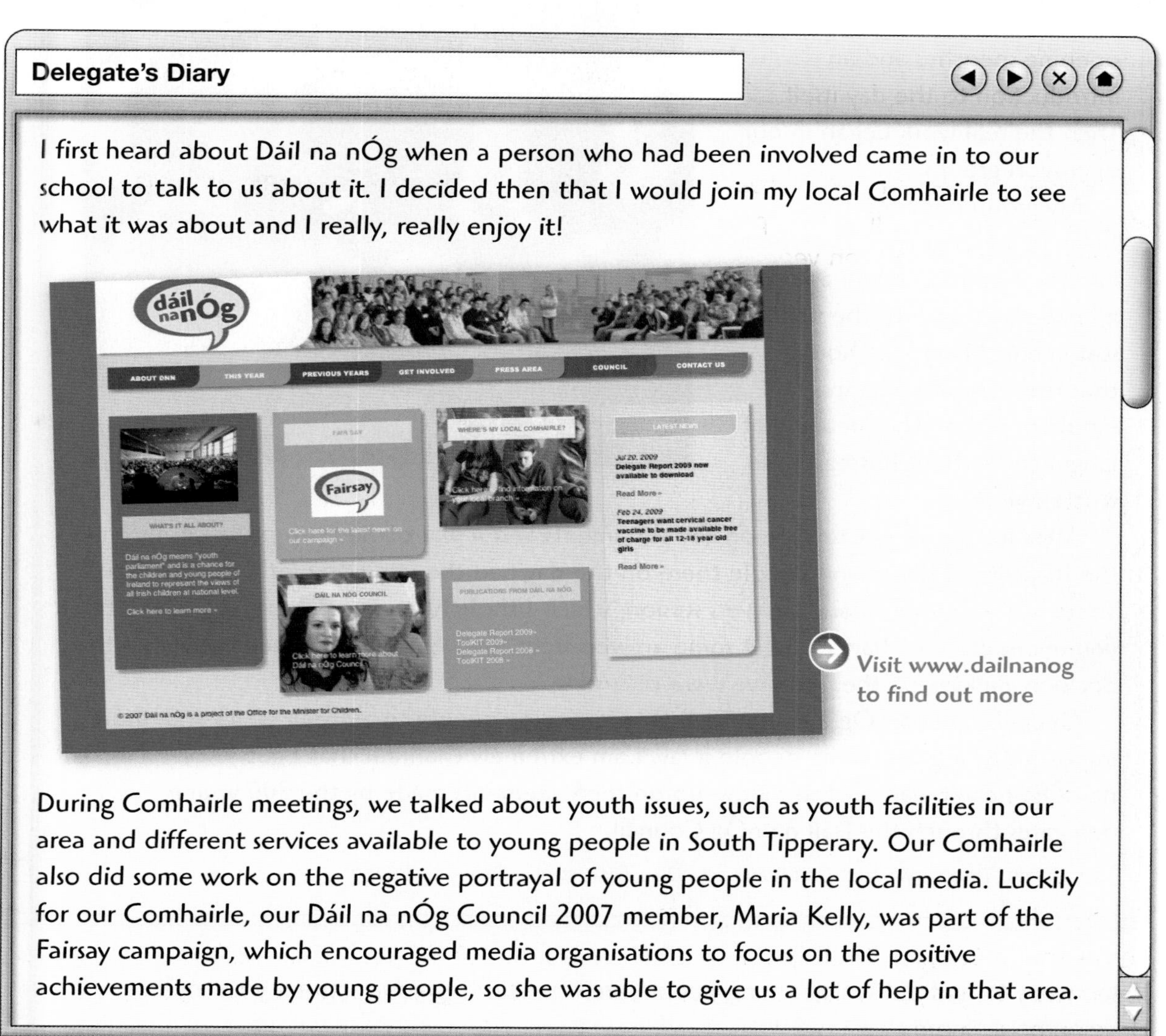

Delegate's Diary

I first heard about Dáil na nÓg when a person who had been involved came in to our school to talk to us about it. I decided then that I would join my local Comhairle to see what it was about and I really, really enjoy it!

Visit www.dailnanog to find out more

During Comhairle meetings, we talked about youth issues, such as youth facilities in our area and different services available to young people in South Tipperary. Our Comhairle also did some work on the negative portrayal of young people in the local media. Luckily for our Comhairle, our Dáil na nÓg Council 2007 member, Maria Kelly, was part of the Fairsay campaign, which encouraged media organisations to focus on the positive achievements made by young people, so she was able to give us a lot of help in that area.

Delegate's Diary

Another thing I particularly liked was how democracy is practised at Dáil na nÓg. For example, everyone who was a member of my Comhairle got a vote when an election was held to arrange delegates to represent Tipperary South at Dáil na nÓg. Luckily, I was elected and I am proud to be representing my Comhairle.

Once the delegates for Dáil na nÓg were elected, we started to prepare. We held four training sessions to discuss the topics that would be discussed at Dáil na nÓg. We got a good insight into the topics, but each of us picked one that we had an experience with or felt strongly about.

Eventually the big day came about. When we got to Croke Park, we were welcomed and given our badges. We also had time to visit some of the information stands that were there. The day began with the opening speeches and an introduction to the day itself. Then the real work began in our discussion groups.

My group discussed the teaching of languages. Everybody had their opinion heard and we all had an input into the final statement. My group thought that there should be a major emphasis put on the speaking of languages and not just based on written work.

After lunch, we got to vote on the statements and it was obvious from the voting that the majority of the young people there on the day had the same opinion on many issues. There was a Questions and Answers session, which I thought was very useful and gave the young people the chance to get some answers from the people who were involved in the decision-making on the issues we were discussing.

Overall, Dáil na nÓg is the perfect way for young people to air their views and, more importantly, it gives young people a say. I am extremely thankful that I got involved in Dáil na nÓg. I can't wait for the follow-up on the statements made by the 200 young delegates through the Dáil na nÓg Council.

Jake Walsh, Tipperary South Comhairle na nÓg – Dáil na nÓg Delegate Report

If you want to find out which young people are representing you, contact your local Development Board.

ACTIVITIES

1. Do you think Dáil na nÓg is a good idea? Why/why not?
2. If you were a member of a Comhairle na nÓg, suggest three themes you would like to see discussed at the Dáil na nÓg meeting.
3. Read what Mary Hanafin TD says about how young people can have a say on matters that affect them. What issues would you write to your local TD or councillor about?

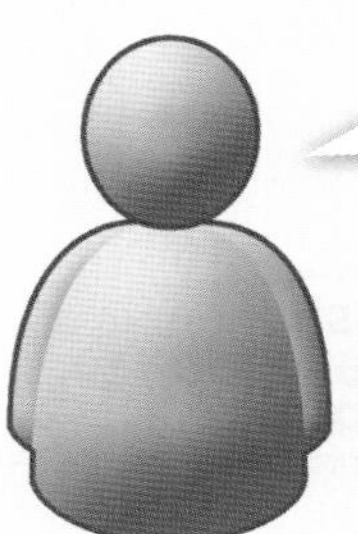

For many years children's views were not adequately taken into consideration in matters which directly affected them. This is now changing. The success of Dáil na nÓg and Comhairle na nÓg in recent times has shown that children do have a voice and are being heard by politicians, county councils, etc. Young people's opinions on a variety of issues are being taken on board at the highest level (the design of community playgrounds is just one recent example). Young people have lots of ideas and should not be shy in emailing or writing to their local TDs or anyone else.

4. What issues would you write or email your local TD about?

STUDY 35 INFLUENCING GOVERNMENT

A person does not have to be a member of a political party to influence decisions made by the government. People who want to take action on an issue often join organisations or groups that are concerned with that issue or activity.

Organisations, sometimes called **interest groups** or **pressure groups**, try to get politicians to take their ideas and concerns into account when making decisions. Some organisations, such as the **Irish Farmers' Association**, are concerned about the interests of their members, while others, such as the **Irish Society for the Prevention of Cruelty to Children**, promote a cause.

Citizens sometimes use marching as a way of protesting over an issue that concerns them

Putting on Pressure

Pressure groups try to influence the government by **lobbying**. Lobbying could include:

- writing to or emailing a local councillor or TD
- getting people to sign a petition
- organising a demonstration or protest, perhaps outside the Dáil or a local council office
- contacting the media by preparing a press release
- giving interviews on radio and television.

ACTIVITIES

1. Match the logos of these organisations with the issue that concerns them.

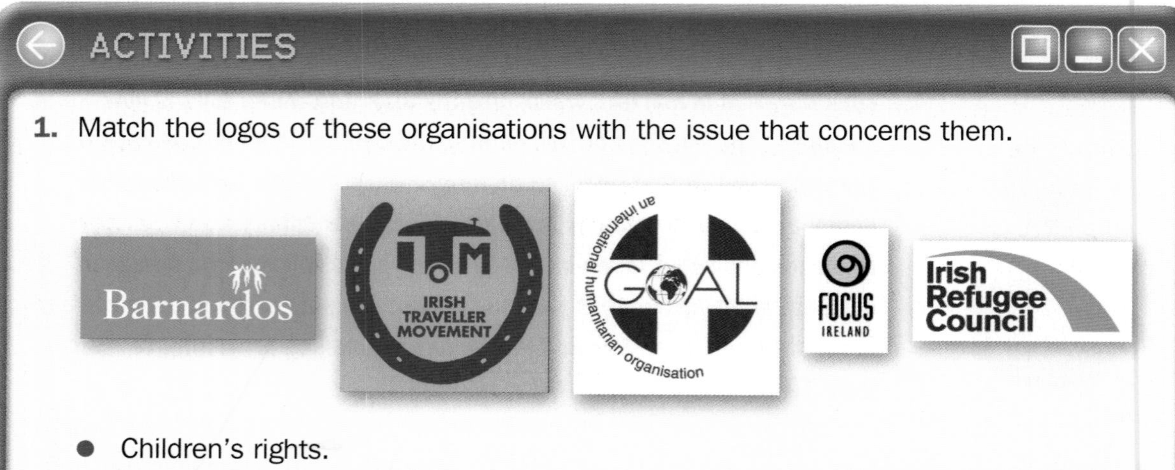

- Children's rights.
- Travellers' rights.
- Homelessness.
- Refugees' rights.
- Aid for developing countries.

2. Choose **one** of the issues that concern the organisations above and describe what steps you would take to put pressure on the government to take action.
3. What are these people protesting against? What do you think is the best way to have your views heard on an issue that concerns you?

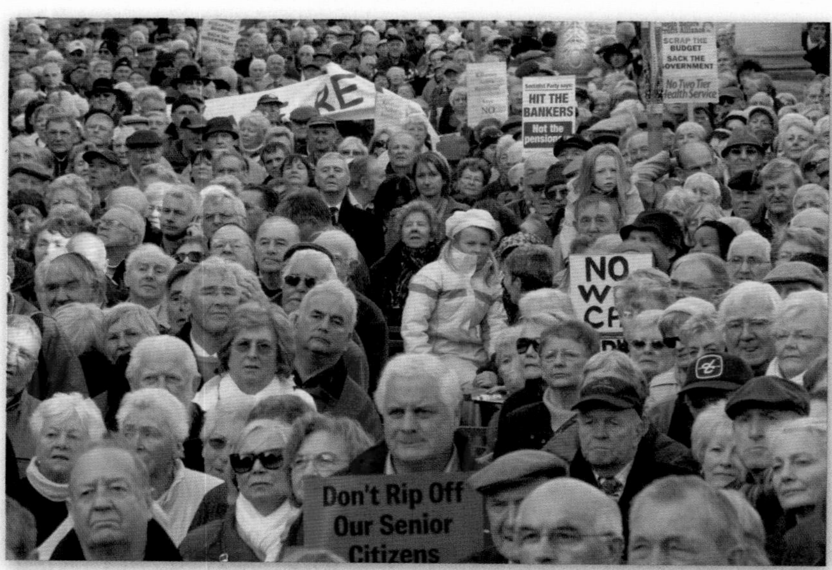

STUDY 36 IN ACTION AND THE STATE

Sometimes people do not agree with decisions made by the government, and they campaign and take action to try to get the decision changed.

Take Action!

Case Study: The M3 Motorway

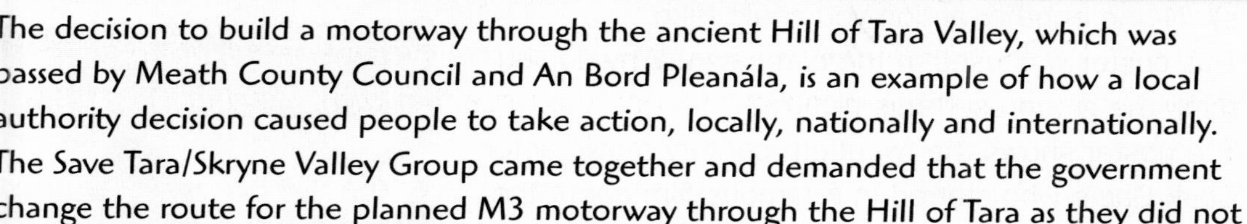

The decision to build a motorway through the ancient Hill of Tara Valley, which was passed by Meath County Council and An Bord Pleanála, is an example of how a local authority decision caused people to take action, locally, nationally and internationally. The Save Tara/Skryne Valley Group came together and demanded that the government change the route for the planned M3 motorway through the Hill of Tara as they did not want the archaeology of the Tara Valley to be destroyed.

The secretary of the Meath Archaeological Society said in a letter to the *Irish Times*, 'We do not have the right to destroy one of the richest and most important archaeological landscapes in Europe.'

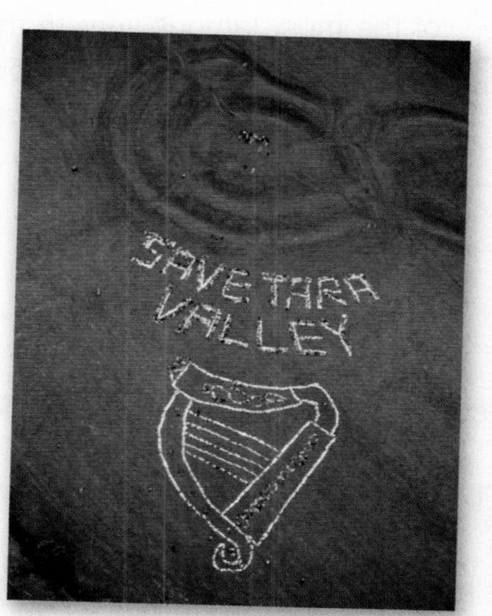

The Save Tara/Skryne Valley Group challenged the Minister for the Environment, the State, Meath County Council and the National Roads Authority (NRA) on the routing of the proposed motorway through the Tara-Skryne Valley. They lost the case, but appealed to the Supreme Court.

TaraWatch is campaigning to have the Hill of Tara and surrounding lands declared a UNESCO World Heritage Site.

ACTIVITIES

1. Why are some people concerned about the route of the motorway?
2. What do the Save Tara/Skryne Valley Group want to see happen?
3. TaraWatch suggest different ways 'anyone, anywhere', can take action:
   - signing an online petition – www.petitiononline.com/hilltara
   - sending letters to newspapers – instructions at www.hilloftara.info
   - writing to politicians – instructions at www.hilloftara.info
   - promoting the websites and the petition by sending emails and adding sites to engines and directories
   - joining the discussion group – http://groups.yahoo.com/group/hilloftara/
   - signing up to attend events when informed – groups.yahoo.com/group/litigation

ACTIVITIES

- editing websites like TaraWatch
- spreading the word
- displaying the Save Tara logo – www.hilloftara.info/images/tarabutton.gif
- donating to the litigation fund, so a professional and effective case can be made.

a) Name **four** online actions you can take.
b) Why do you think the group created a logo for the campaign?
c) Name another action you could take.

4. This poster was used in the campaign. Why do you think the group used this picture?
The poster shows the twentieth-century movie actor Clark Gable who starred in a famous film about the American Civil War called *Gone With the Wind*. One of the most famous lines in the film comes when his co-star asks what will happen to 'Tara', a big plantation house, after the war, and he replies, 'Frankly, my dear, I don't give a damn.'

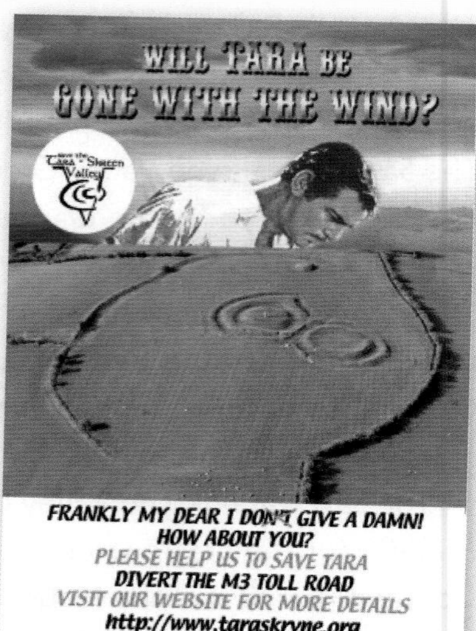

STUDY 37 MAKING LAW

The main job of government is to put laws in place that protect people's rights and improve the lives of citizens. Before a law is made it has to go through a series of stages.

A Bill's Journey to Law

1. Introduce a bill

The bill is introduced to the members of the Dáil

2. The Dáil debates

TDs give ideas for changes to the bill

3. Committee stage

The bill is examined in detail and changes discussed

4. Report stage

Changes are added to the bill

5. The Dáil and Seanad debate

The changes are discussed by both the Dáil and the Seanad. No more changes can be made.

6. Vote on the bill

Then the bill is put to a vote. Members vote by pressing the Tá or Níl button on their seats.

7. The bill becomes a law

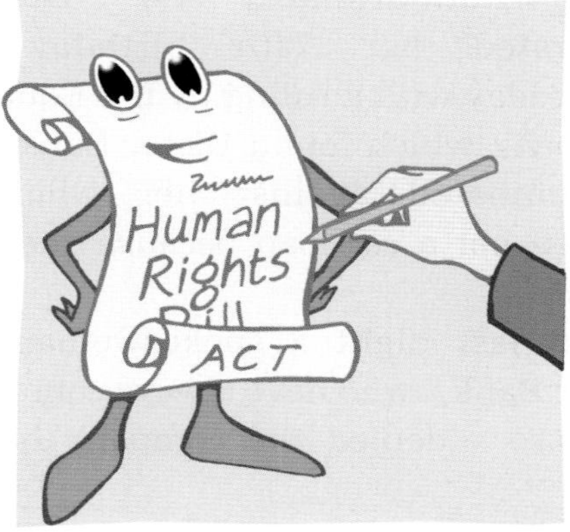

The President signs the bill into law

Equality Acts

The **Employment Equality Acts** 1998 and 2004 and the **Equal Status Acts** 2000 and 2004 are two examples of laws that went through the stages pictured above. Under the Employment Equality Acts, for example, you are guilty of **discrimination**: and you are breaking the law if you refuse to give somebody a job because of any of the following:

- age
- disability
- race
- religious beliefs
- gender
- family status
- marital status
- membership of the Traveller community
- sexual orientation.

This campaign poster was used by the Equality Authority to raise awareness of Ageism Week

Under the Equal Status Acts 2000 and 2004, if you refuse to serve someone in a shop or pub for any of the reasons listed above you are also guilty of discrimination and are breaking the law.

Take Action!

The following article shows how under the Equal Status Acts a woman was able to take a case to the Equality Tribunal after she was refused a car loan because of her age.

Delighted Grandmother Beats Bank in Age Row over Car Loan

Grandmother Phyllis Fahey spoke of her delight last night as Ireland's first senior citizen to officially take on the banks – and win. The feisty septuagenarian* from Rathfarnham, Co Dublin, celebrated her 74th birthday on Wednesday with a ruling by the Equality Authority, which found Ulster Bank had discriminated against her when it refused her a car loan because she was over 65.

But last night a spokeswoman for Ulster Bank – who have always contested the case – denied the company had a discriminatory policy. 'Ulster Bank is disappointed by the decision of the Equality Authority [and] would like to confirm that there was no upper age limit in 2005 in relation to applications for a personal loan. This remains the case.'

Ulster Bank was ordered to pay Mrs Fahey €2,000 in compensation for the upset and humiliation it caused her after a tribunal found that the bank had breached the Equal Status Act by refusing her the €6,000 loan strictly on the basis of age, despite her good credit history and ability to repay the loan.

*A septuagenarian is someone who is in their 70s.

'I feel now that I've struck a blow for older people,' she told the *Irish Independent*. 'I'm just so delighted.'

Mrs Fahey said she was stunned when she went to the bank's Maynooth branch in 2005 seeking the loan in order to trade in her car for a new Ford Fiesta and was asked her age by a bank official.

'I told her brightly and not a bit ashamed that I was 70,' she said.

But the bank official said the company had a strict policy of not giving loans to people aged 65 even though Mrs Fahey reminded her that she had been a good customer for more than a decade, owned her own home and had a healthy deposit account at the bank that would more than cover the €145 monthly repayments.

Despite this, she was flatly refused and had to go back to the car dealership and cancel her order, even though she had the car picked out and paid a deposit on it, she said.

'I rang up to cancel the car. I was too embarrassed to call round,' she said.

But she got her car after all after approaching her local credit union who gave her the loan without question. The dealership finance department also offered to finance the loan.

Mrs Fahey said she decided to take the case to the Equality Authority because of the discrimination she suffered . . .

Phyllis Fahey in her Ford Fiesta at her home in Dublin – the same car for which she was refused a bank loan because of her age

Lobby groups for the elderly applauded the decision. Age Action spokesman Eamon Timmins called the ruling a landmark decision for the elderly.

'Older people with good credit records and evidence of their ability to repay a loan are frequently refused by financial institutions. The inability to access credit can have a major impact on a person's ability to live a fulfilling life,' he said.

'Today's ruling means another obstacle has been removed for older people. We hope that all financial institutions will review their policies towards older people as a result.'

(Source: Allison Bray, *Irish Independent*)

 ACTIVITIES 

1. Below are the stages a bill goes through before it becomes law. Rearrange the stages in the correct order.
   a) Bill becomes law
   b) Bill discussed at the committee stage
   c) TDs give ideas for changes
   d) Dáil and Seanad debate bill
   e) Bill introduced in the Dáil
   f) President signs bill into law
   g) Changes added at the report stage
2. a) What law did the tribunal decide had been breached when Mrs Fahey was refused a car loan?
   b) Why did Mrs Fahey decide to take her case to the Equality Authority?
   c) What does Eamon Timmins from Age Action think that the ruling will mean for older people?

STUDY 38 YOUR RIGHTS IN LAW

Laws are the important **rules of the country**. Like school rules, they are there to **protect people's rights**. If you do not obey these rules you are breaking the law. If the Gardaí believe a person has broken the law, that person is usually taken to court. The court then decides if the law has been broken.

Ignorance of the Law is no Defence

It is important for you to know at what age it is legal for you to do certain things, e.g. when you can work full time, have a licence to drive, etc. It is also important to know when you can legally be held responsible for a crime.

- **Tipstaff/Judge's Usher**
  The tipstaff/judge's usher is the personal assistant to the judge. He/she walks ahead of the judge carrying a staff and says 'All rise' as the judge enters the room.

- **Accused**
  The accused comes before the court accused of a crime.

- **Prison Officer**
  The prison officer sits in court with the accused.

- **Members of the Public**
  Anyone can watch any court case, except where there is a sign reading 'in camera' on the door of the courtroom. This means that the case will be heard in private and that members of the public who are not involved in the case are not allowed into the courtroom to hear the evidence. The in camera rule is used to protect the privacy of the people in court mainly in family law matters and in cases before the juvenile courts.

- **Members of the Press**
  Radio, television and newspaper reporters attend to bring news of court cases to the wider public. They cannot attend 'in camera' cases. Cameras are not allowed in courtrooms.

- **The Jury**
  A jury consists of 12 men and women randomly selected from the electoral register. Most people between the ages of 18 and 70 who are registered to vote are eligible for jury duty. The jury hears the evidence and decides on the guilt or innocence of the accused in a criminal case and which party wins in a civil case.

- **Solicitor**
  Solicitors meet with clients and get instructions from them. They prepare the case for trial by getting all the papers ready and choosing/briefing a barrister to present the case.

- **The Registrar/Court Clerk**
  The registrar/court clerk assists the judge with administrative matters and is in charge of the court documents and exhibits. He/she also records the names of witnesses and the decision in the case. The registrar/court clerk also administers the oath.

- **The Judge**
  The judge is in charge of court proceedings and decides any legal issues arising in the case. If the case does not involve a jury, the judge also decides questions of fact, such as the guilt or innocence of the accused, or which party wins in a civil case.

- **The Court Reporter/Stenographer**
  The stenographer takes a note of everything said in the case and later types up the notes in the event of an appeal being lodged.

- **Witness**
  Witnesses are called by either party to prove their side of the story and may be cross-examined by the opposing party as to the accuracy of their evidence.

The Defence Forces

The Irish Defence Forces are made up of:

- the Army
- the Air Corps
- the Naval Service.

The main function of the Defence Forces is to **ensure the security of the Irish state and its citizens**. They do this in a number of ways.

- The Army often provides protection for the movement of money to and from banks.
- The Naval Service is involved in search and rescue and anti-drug patrols.
- The Air Corps is involved in many search operations.

The Irish Defence Forces are also involved in many **United Nations peacekeeping missions**. On page 183 you can read former Captain Tom Clonan's experience of such missions.

The Army often provides extra protection to banks when large sums of money are being moved

In recent years the Navy have been involved in patrolling the Irish coastline to prevent illegal drug trafficking

The Air Corp have helped deliver provisions to people stranded in the floods which occurred in Ireland in late 2009

ACTIVITIES

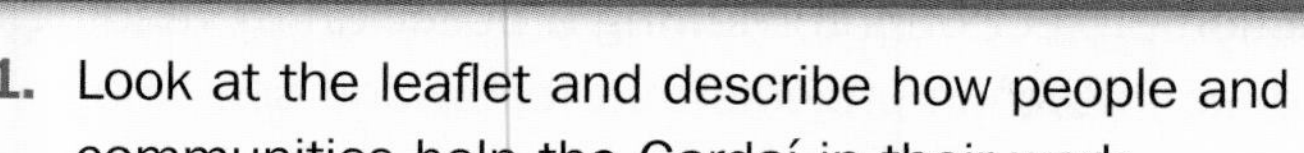

1. Look at the leaflet and describe how people and communities help the Gardaí in their work.
2. Look at the information about the workings of the court on pages 144–5 and answer the following questions.
   a) What is the main job of the judge?
   b) How many members of the jury are there?
   c) What is the barrister's job?
   d) How do the solicitor and the barrister work together?
   e) Who tells the court the judge has arrived?
   f) Who has the job of making sure that every word that is said in court is recorded properly?

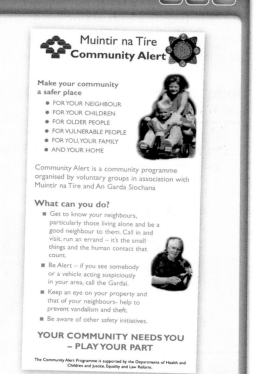

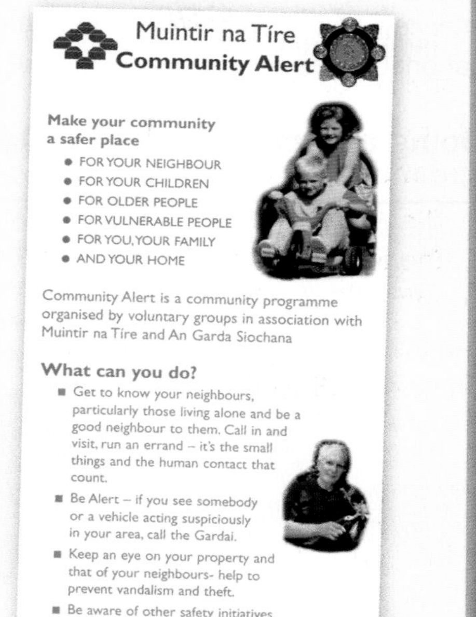

Muintir na Tíre
Community Alert

Make your community a safer place
- FOR YOUR NEIGHBOUR
- FOR YOUR CHILDREN
- FOR OLDER PEOPLE
- FOR VULNERABLE PEOPLE
- FOR YOU, YOUR FAMILY
- AND YOUR HOME

Community Alert is a community programme organised by voluntary groups in association with Muintir na Tíre and An Garda Síochana

What can you do?
- Get to know your neighbours, particularly those living alone and be a good neighbour to them. Call in and visit, run an errand – it's the small things and the human contact that count.
- Be Alert – if you see somebody or a vehicle acting suspiciously in your area, call the Gardaí.
- Keep an eye on your property and that of your neighbours- help to prevent vandalism and theft.
- Be aware of other safety initiatives.

YOUR COMMUNITY NEEDS YOU – PLAY YOUR PART

The Community Alert Programme is supported by the Departments of Health and Children and Justice, Equality and Law Reform.

ACTION IDEAS

Survey: Do a survey of people your age to find out their views on crime. You could ask questions like:

- Do you know what crimes are most common in your area?
- Have you or has anyone you know been a victim of crime?
- Do you feel safe in your home and locality?
- How do you think crime could be reduced?

Your classmates or students from another class could answer the questions in your survey. You could present the findings of your survey as a wall chart or newspaper article.

Issue Tracking: Look through local or national newspapers and see what types of crime are most frequently reported. You could invite a solicitor/barrister/garda/army representative to your class to explain their work.

Viewing: There are lots of famous films that are based on court cases, including *12 Angry Men*, *To Kill a Mockingbird* and *Evelyn*. After viewing any of these films you could have a debate in class on the issues that came up in the film.

Check out the courts – www.courts.ie.

STUDY 39 IDEAS FOR ACTION PROJECTS

See how you might go about doing an action project on interviewing a politician by reading the interview below. Then look at the other ideas for action projects that follow and see what national issues your class could take action on.

Doing an Action Project – The Brief Guide

How were these people involved in the action project?
We emailed political parties to send us information on their policies. Different groups in class gave presentations on what different parties stood for. We contacted our local TD to see if we could visit the Dáil.

Tell me some of the different activities you were involved in.
Ok:
- We divided into groups and each group found out about a different political party.
- We gave presentations on each party in class.
- We contacted a TD.
- We visited the Dáil and interviewed the TD.

Can you describe one thing you did?
I recorded the questions and answers session with the TD in the Dáil and I made a summary of the main points of the interview.

List two skills you used doing this project.
Technical recording skills and listening skills – picking out the main points from the interview.

Tell me five facts you discovered doing the project.
Sure:
- Fianna Fáil was founded by Éamon de Valera
- The Labour Party wants a more equal society
- Ireland has never had a woman Taoiseach and there are far more men than women in the Dáil
- The Green Party is concerned with the environment
- Fine Gael means 'Tribes of Ireland' and was formed in 1933

Look back now on your experience and tell me what you think about the topic and about carrying out an action project.
The most exciting part of the project was our visit to the Dáil and the Seanad – seeing all those familiar faces from TV! They cared about the issues they were discussing and I know more now about what different parties stand for. When my time comes to vote at least I'll know what I'm doing.

Action Project Ideas on . . .

Democracy

1. Invite a TD or senator to visit your class to explain how s/he became involved in politics.
2. Do an interview with a young member of a political party.
3. Arrange a visit to the Dáil or the Seanad.
4. In groups, form your own political parties, presenting your main policies to your classmates. You could run an election in your year group.
5. Hold an inter-class table quiz based on how Ireland is governed.
6. Survey schoolmates or family and friends on their knowledge of Irish politics.
7. Hold an election or referendum in class or school.

National Issues

1. Find out about a national issue you feel strongly about and design an information poster to raise awareness of the issue.
2. Organise a debate about a national issue.
3. Choose an issue and contact political parties to find out what their policy is regarding this issue.
4. Carry out a survey in your area to find out about attitudes towards unemployment or poverty.
5. Conduct a survey in your school to find out how many of your schoolfriends' brothers and sisters have left the area to find work and where they went.
6. Contact an organisation like Alone to find out what changes they'd like to see the government make on issues that concern them.
7. Fundraise for an organisation that you feel strongly about.
8. Invite a member from a local community group into class and find out about their work and how they link with the government.

- See what other action ideas you and your classmates can come up with!
- Remember to look back over the action ideas that are suggested throughout the chapter for more topics for an action project.
- In Chapter 6 you will find advice and helpful hints on how to make posters and leaflets, and on conducting surveys, interviews, petitions and fundraising events.

STUDY 40 REVISION QUESTIONS

Section 1

Answer ALL questions. (Total: 18 marks.)

1. Which two of the following politicians are or have been leaders of political parties? Put a tick in the boxes opposite the correct names. **(4 marks)**

(a) Joan Bruton ☐
(b) Enda Kenny ☑
(c) Mary Coughlan ☐
(d) Eamon Gilmore ☑

2. Indicate whether the following statements are true or false by placing a tick in the correct boxes. **(4 marks)**

(a) The ancient Romans were the first people to rule by democracy.
True ☐ False ☑

(b) The system of voting we use in Ireland is called proportional representation.
True ☑ False ☐

(c) A quota is the smallest number of votes needed to be elected.
True ☑ False ☐

(d) In Ireland you can be fined if you don't vote.
True ☑ False ☐

3. Fill in the missing words in the following sentences. **(4 marks)**

(a) If a person is registered to vote they will receive a voting card in the post a few days before an election.

(b) People who work for the state are called civil servants. They are expected to serve equally whichever government is in power.

(c) The head of the government in Ireland is called __________ __________ .

(d) The Department of __________, __________ and __________ __________ is responsible for the Gardaí.

4. In the boxes provided below match all the letters in row X with the corresponding numbers in row Y. The first pair has been done for you. **(6 marks)**

X	A	B	C	D	E	F	G
Y	3	4	6	2	1	7	5

X		Y	
A.	A manifesto is	1.	built on the principle of socialism.
B.	Fianna Fáil was	2.	made up of 60 members.
C.	The Constitution is	3.	a document produced by political parties saying what they will do if elected.
D.	The Seanad is	4.	founded in 1926.
E.	The Labour Party is	5.	made up of 166 members.
F.	A pressure group	6.	a book containing all the basic laws of the country.
G.	The Dáil is	7.	tries to influence the government by lobbying.

Section 2

Answer ALL questions numbered 1, 2 and 3 below. Each question carries 14 marks.

1. Read the following description of the work of a TD and answer the questions that follow.

> At weekends most TDs meet the people of the area they have been elected to represent. The meetings are called clinics; the TD meets people to discuss problems or issues which they think the TD can help them with.
>
> During the week a TD might contact a local authority, which could help solve some of the problems that have been raised at the clinics.
>
> A TD spends most of his/her time in the Dáil dealing with the issues that might have been raised at clinics, and taking part in debates on national issues and proposed new laws. If a TD wants to raise an issue that is important in his/her constituency, s/he usually does this at Question Time in the Dáil.

(a) Name two things a TD does in a working week. **(2)**

(b) List two ways in which a TD might deal with problems raised at his/her clinic. **(2)**

(c) Describe an issue you could contact a TD about. **(2)**

(d) Suggest two actions you would take in a campaign to raise awareness of the importance of voting in a general election.

Action 1 **(4)**

Action 2 **(4)**

2. Read these explanations of poverty and answer the questions that follow.

The biggest cause of poverty is that wealth is not shared equally

We have poverty because there are not enough jobs

Poverty needs to be solved by better training and education for young people and adults

We need to give people skills so that they can enter the workforce with confidence

(a) List the causes of poverty mentioned in the above statements. **(6)**

(b) Choose one statement you agree with, explain it in your own words and say why you agree with it. **(2)**

(c) Choose another issue that you think is a national issue and explain why you think it is important. (*Hints:* transport/housing.)

Issue **(2)**

Why it is important **(2)**

(d) What action would you take over the issue mentioned above? **(2)**

3. Look at this photo and answer the questions that follow.

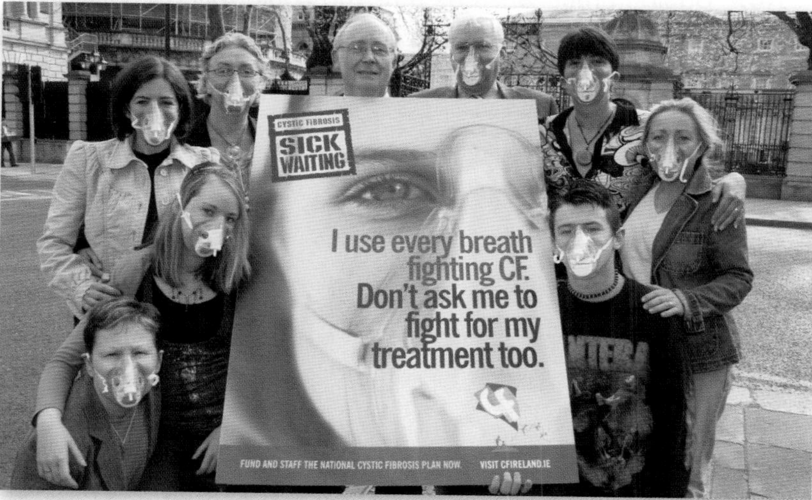

(a) What are these people protesting about? **(2)**

(b) Name two other methods of protest this group could have used. **(2)**

(c) In your own words, explain what a pressure group is. **(2)**

(d) Name an issue that has featured in the news about which people have protested. **(2)**

(e) Name an issue that you feel is important and suggest two actions you would take over this issue.

Issue **(2)**

Action 1 **(2)**

Action 2 **(2)**

Section 3

Answer ONE of the questions numbered 1, 2 and 3 below.
Each question carries 20 marks.

1. Imagine that you are part of a local development group. A government agency wants to know why your group should get money for a festival in your area. Write a report that includes the following:
   (a) the sort of events you would hold
   (b) an explanation of how your area would benefit from the festival
   (c) a list of the forms of advertising you will use to attract people to the festival.

2. Imagine you are the Taoiseach. Prepare a speech you would give on your first day in the Dáil outlining changes that you would like to see made in Irish society.
   Hints:
   - changes in education/the transport system/the environment/young people working
   - solving the problem of homelessness
   - how to create more jobs.

3. Imagine your CSPE class has decided to invite a TD to your class to outline his/her work.
   (a) Write a letter of invitation explaining to the speaker why s/he is being invited.
   (b) Make a list of all arrangements that would have to be made to ensure a pleasant visit for the speaker.
   (c) Outline practical steps that you could take to share with the wider school community the new information you have about the work your TD does.

Chapter 5

Ireland and the Wider World

In Chapter 4 you saw how as citizens of Ireland we take part in and influence what happens at a national level. As citizens of Ireland we are also members of **international groups** such as the **European Union** (EU) and the **United Nations** (UN). As a member of international organisations, Ireland takes part in, influences and is affected by what happens in the wider world. As a **global citizen**, a member of the world community, each of us can **influence what happens outside Ireland**. As global citizens we also have certain rights and responsibilities that go beyond our local and national communities.

STUDY 41 CONNECTED

We do not have to look very far to see some of our connections with the wider world.

Think about the food you eat and where it comes from. The cereals you eat were probably grown in the United States, your jam might have come from Belgium, your fruit from Latin America and your tea from India. The T-shirts you wear may have been made in Bangladesh and the jeans in America. Some of the clothes we wear do not carry a label stating the country of origin because they are made for large chain stores in Europe.

From the moment you wake up in the morning you rely on and are linked to the wider world.

How has Your Morning Connected You to the Global Village?

This morning you could have got out of a bed made of wood from Norway, thrown back sheets made of cotton grown in India and pulled back curtains that were sewn in a factory in China.

Your breakfast may have been made up of cereals grown in the US, oranges from Spain and coffee from Brazil. The TV you might have watched before you got ready for school was probably made in Japan.

The jumper you pulled on as you got ready for school could have been made with Australian wool, the school shirt sewn in a factory in Taiwan and washed by a detergent made in Germany.

ACTIVITIES

1. Fill in the following chart and see how you are connected to the world. Remember to name the country you are connected to for each item.

	Item/country
Name a type of music, a band or a singer you like from another country.	e.g. rap (USA)  Ellie Goulding (UK)
What TV programme do you watch from another country?	e.g. *X Factor* (UK)  How I met your mother (USA)
Name a famous person you admire who is not from Ireland.	e.g. Cristiano Ronaldo (Portugal)  Nelson Mandela (South Africa)
What fast food restaurants have you eaten in?	e.g. Burger King (USA)  McDonald's (USA)
A food you like that is a dish of another country.	e.g. pizza (Italy)  Croissant (France)
Find something you are wearing from another country.	Tights (Bangladesh) 
Find something in your school bag made in another country.	Pencil case (china)
Name a car you like and say where it is made.	

ACTIVITIES

2. Many of the English words we use every day come from other languages. Match these words to the language they first came from.

Words	Languages
Karate	Finnish
Pasta	Italian
Sauna	Japanese
Patio	Turkish
Kebab	Australian Aboriginal language
Kangaroo	Spanish
Ambulance	French

3. Music and dance from other countries is also something we all enjoy. Match each type of music or dance with the country it first came from.

Music or dance	Countries
Reggae	Italy
Rap	Russia
Opera	Jamaica
Ballet	USA
Céilí	Brazil
Samba	Ireland

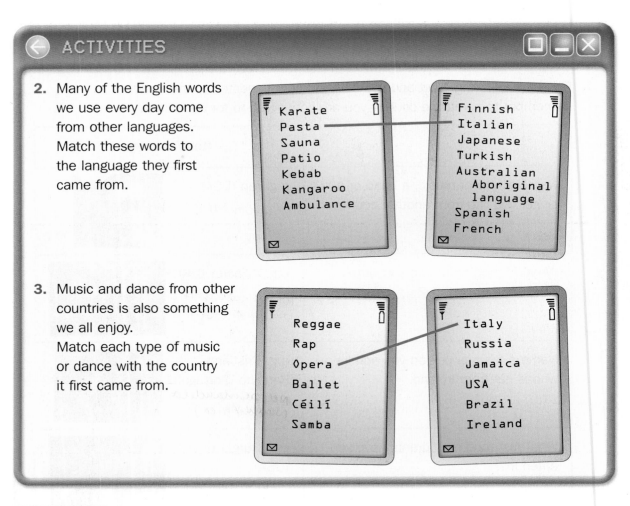

STUDY 42 THE EU AND YOU

Another way we are connected to the wider world is by being a member of international groups like the **European Union** (EU).

It was CSPE class again ... and the subject was Europe
Anybody know anything about Europe?
Yeah, my passport has 'European Union' printed on it.
And now there's the euro in most EU countries.
My brother Paul has worked in lots of different EU countries with his company. I visited him in Germany once. No matter where he works he doesn't need a work visa because we're all in the EU.
My brother Seán is studying in university in Paris as part of the EU Erasmus Programme and I'd like to do that, too... when I get out of here!

And on our holidays last year we took the car and drove through France – your driving licence is valid in all European countries.
I've an aunt who lives in Spain and she can vote in the elections there to elect members to the European Parliament.

Sir, aren't loads of those bypasses and big roads built with EU money? You always see the sign beside the roadworks.
That's right.

My dad is a farmer and he gets payments from the EU. And my granddad got a grant from the EU to clean up his farm – it's called REPS, the Rural Environmental Protection Scheme.
Don't the EU have lots of laws about the environment and stuff that we have to keep, too, or else we get fined?

Who needs the textbook when I have such geniuses in my class?!

ACTIVITIES

1. Work out from the cartoon **three** ways in which travelling in Europe is made easier by our membership of the EU.
2. If you were living in another EU country, what elections could you vote in?
3. Name **three** ways mentioned in the cartoon in which Ireland gained from being a member of the EU.
4. What can happen if Ireland breaks EU law?

MEPs Have their Say

IMPACT MESSENGER

File Edit View Actions Help

Would you describe yourself as an Irish citizen or a European citizen?

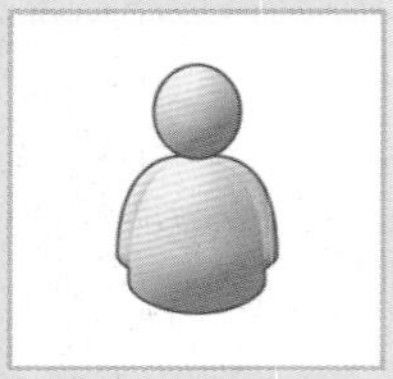

Proinsias De Rossa MEP: I have a two-sided citizenship. I am a citizen of Ireland and of the European Union. Each 'side' of my citizenship is linked to the other and each one gives me rights and responsibilities.

Mairead McGuinness MEP: I am both! I consider myself to be an Irish citizen, but also to be a European citizen. It is possible to have multiple loyalties. For example, I was born in Ardee, Co. Louth, but now live in Co. Meath – however, I regard myself as being from Co. Louth, but being very much part of Co. Meath, too.

Block Font Emoticons Send

ACTIVITIES

Use the interviews to answer the following questions:

a) According to Proinsias De Rossa, how is each side of his citizenship linked?

b) What rights and responsibilities do you think he is talking about?

c) What do you think Mairead McGuinness means when she talks about 'multiple loyalties' and being both an Irish and a European citizen?

d) Do you consider yourself an Irish citizen or a European citizen? Give three reasons for your answer.

ACTION IDEAS

Interview: Find out from a local farmer how EU grants and policies have affected his/her profession and way of life. (*Hints:* REPS scheme, CAP.)

STUDY 43 ABOUT THE EU

Why a European Union?

Jean Monnet, French statesman

Robert Schuman, French statesman

After **World War II** people in Europe lived in fear of something similar happening again. Many people thought that the best way to **prevent war** between European nations was to create strong economies, more employment and a higher standard of living. Leading statesmen, in particular **Jean Monnet** and **Robert Schuman**, felt that if the economies of European countries were linked closer together there would be less chance of war. But how could small European states compete against huge markets like the USA and Russia? A **United States of Europe** was their answer.

A Brief History of the European Union

Step 1: 1951

Six European countries signed the **Treaty of Paris** and formed the **European Coal and Steel Community** (ECSC). Coal and steel were very important in rebuilding Europe after World War II. It was felt that if countries co-operated in the production of these resources it would be difficult for one country to plan a war in secret. The six states were Belgium, the Federal Republic of Germany, France, Italy, Luxembourg and the Netherlands.

Step 2: 1957

The same countries signed the **Treaty of Rome**, which set up the **European Economic Community** (EEC). This meant that a 'common market' was created in Europe. Now goods could be traded freely among EEC members.

The Treaty of Rome got its name because it was signed in Rome – all major European treaties are called after the European city where they were signed

Step 3: 1973

Ireland, the **UK** and **Denmark** joined the EEC in 1973.

Step 4: 1979

The European Parliament in Strasbourg

The European Parliament was elected directly by the citizens of the EEC for the first time in 1979.

Step 5: 1981

Greece joined the EEC in 1981.

Step 6: 1986

Spain and **Portugal** joined the EEC in 1986.

Step 7: 1987

The EEC became known as the **European Community**, or **EC**, in 1987.

Step 8: 1993

Under the **Maastricht Treaty**, countries agreed to:

- introduce a **single currency** (the euro) by 1 January 1999
- change the name of the EC to the **European Union** (EU).

Step 9: 1995

Austria, **Finland** and **Sweden** joined the EU in 1995.

Step 10: 1999

On 1 January 1999, **11 EU countries introduced the euro**. The **Amsterdam Treaty** meant that for the first time the EU became involved in peacekeeping missions.

Step 11: 2000

The **Nice Treaty** prepared the EU for more countries joining (enlargement). The EU charter of **fundamental rights** of all EU residents was also signed.

Step 12: 2001

A **referendum** was held in Ireland and the people of Ireland voted **against** the Nice Treaty.

Step 12: 2002

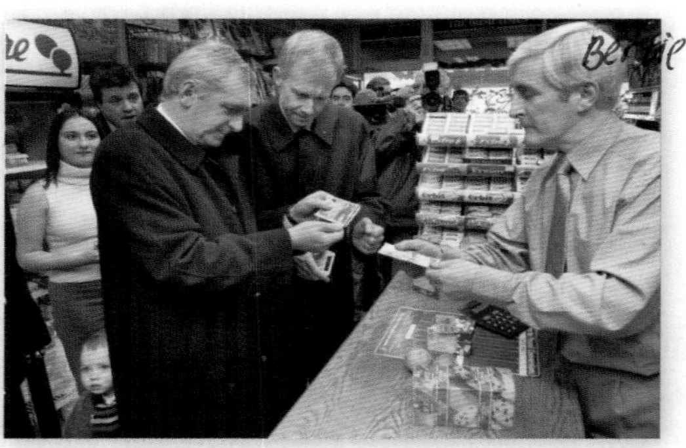

On 1 January 2002 **euro notes and coins** were used for the first time.

A **second referendum** was held in Ireland and this time the Nice Treaty was **accepted**.

Step 13: 2004

Ten new countries joined the EU in 2004 – Cyprus, Czech Republic, Estonia, Hungary, Latvia, Lithuania, Malta, Poland, Slovakia and Slovenia.

Step 14: 2007

Bulgaria and **Romania** joined the EU in 2007, bringing the total number of EU states to **27**. The Lisbon Treaty was signed by leaders of EU countries.

Step 15: 2009

Elections were held for a new European Parliament and Ireland signed the Lisbon Treaty.

How do Countries Join the EU and Who will be Next?

Any European country can join the EU if it can show that it is a democracy that **respects the rule of law and human rights**. Countries wanting to join must also be able to show that their economy is up to a certain standard, and that the country has a civil service that can make sure that EU laws are carried out.

Currently **Turkey**, **Croatia** and the former Yugoslav Republic of **Macedonia** are hoping to join the EU, and there will be more countries hoping to join in the future.

The EU Symbols

The European Flag

The flag shows 12 stars in a circle, which symbolises the ideas of **unity, solidarity and harmony** between the peoples of Europe.

What ideas are the 12 stars of the EU flag trying to get across?

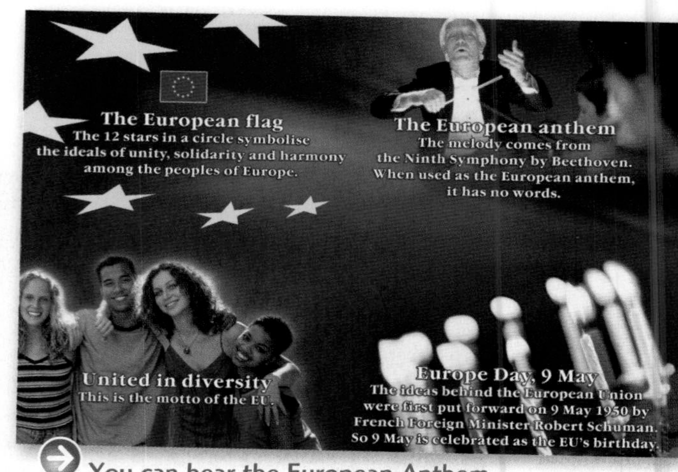

You can hear the European Anthem on the internet at http://europa.eu/abc/symbols/anthem/index_en.htm.

The European Anthem

The European Anthem is taken from Beethoven's ninth symphony. The original words are in German, but when the tune is used as the European anthem, it has no words.

Europe Day

The idea of a Europe Day came from one of the founders of what is now the European Union, Robert Schuman, and 9 May every year is celebrated as the EU's birthday.

The EU Motto

The motto of the EU is **United in Diversity**, which tries to suggest that, even though there are differences in language and culture in the different European nations, we are united in common aims.

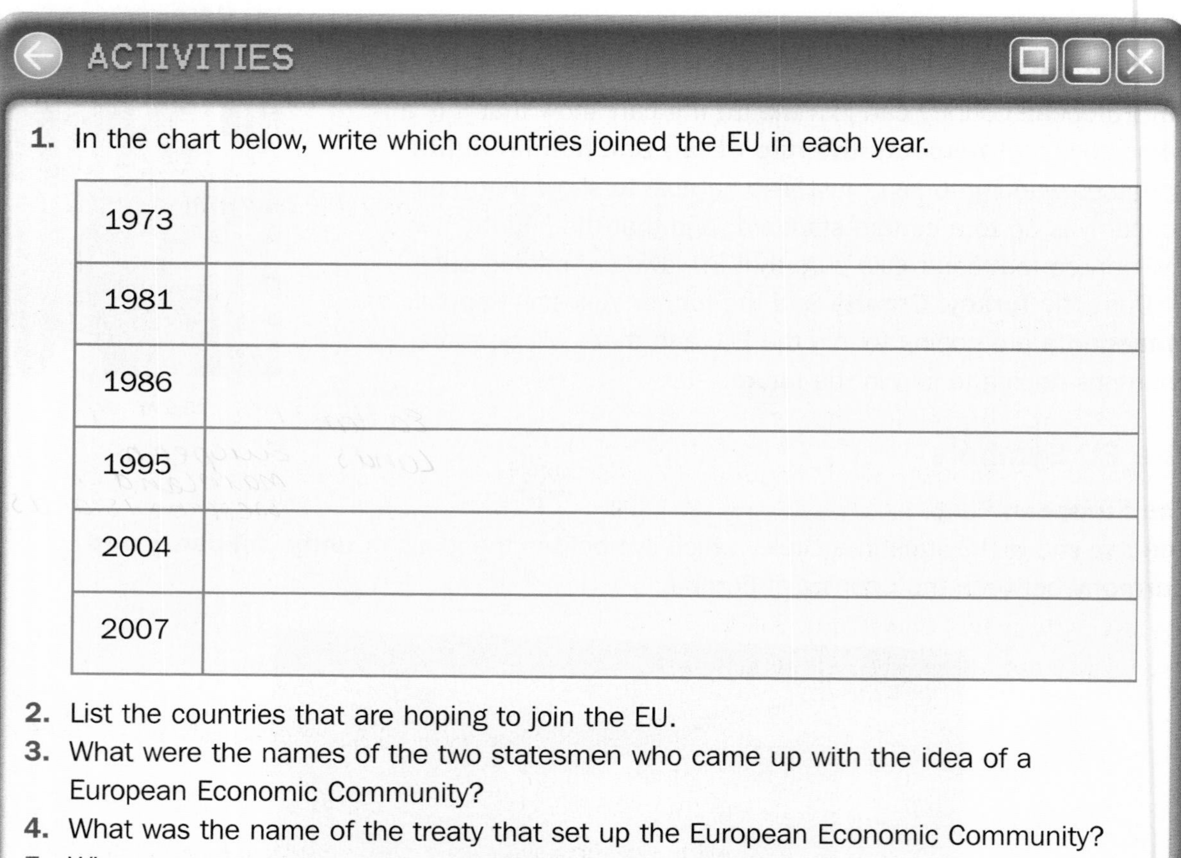

ACTIVITIES

1. In the chart below, write which countries joined the EU in each year.

1973	
1981	
1986	
1995	
2004	
2007	

2. List the countries that are hoping to join the EU.
3. What were the names of the two statesmen who came up with the idea of a European Economic Community?
4. What was the name of the treaty that set up the European Economic Community?
5. When were euro notes and coins used for the first time?
6. What was the largest number of countries to join the EU at the same time?

STUDY 44 CLOSE-UP ON THE EU

Being a member of the EU allows you to live, work and study in any of the other EU countries. However, there are lots of other benefits of being part of the EU. Read below how the EU's laws, rules, decisions and ideas are working to make the lives of EU citizens better and easier.

Travelling in the EU

EU countries have rules about the rights of airplane passengers. If your flight has been delayed by more than a few hours, or cancelled without letting you know beforehand, or overbooked, it is the airline's responsibility to get you home or to your final destination.

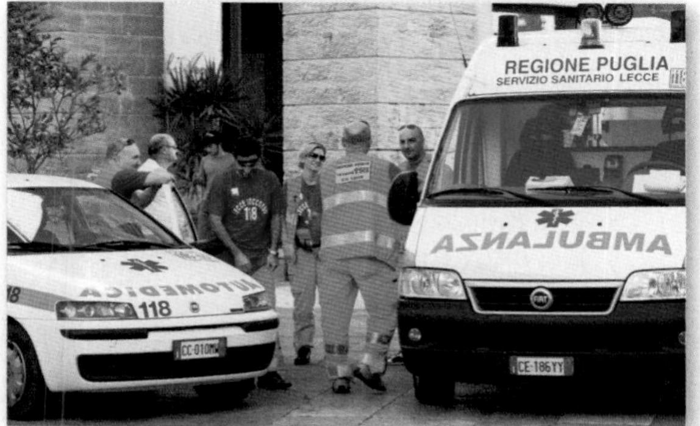

Getting Emergency Help

There is now a single European Emergency number – **112** – that you can call in any EU country if you have an accident and need an ambulance, police or any of the emergency services.

European Health Card

You can get a European health insurance card, which can be used in any EU country, that will allow you to get medical help if you get sick. Each country's card has the same design, which means that doctors and nurses will recognise it even if you can't speak the same language.

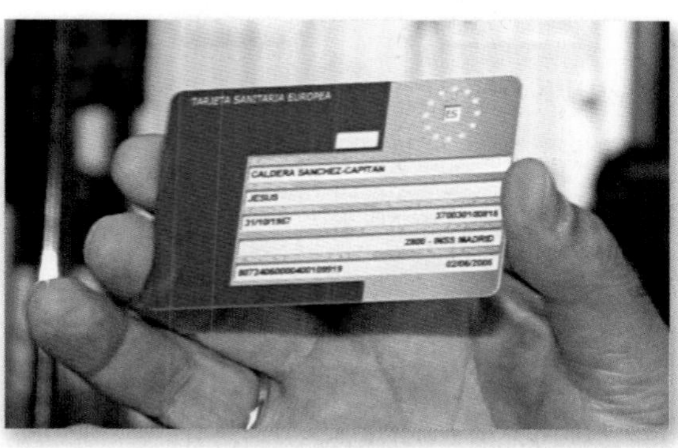

Making the Food you Eat Safer

EU rules and laws mean that we can see where all our foodstuffs come from and they can be traced through the 'farm to fork' policy. If, for example, a person got sick from eating bad meat it is possible to find out from what farm the animal was brought, and who processed the meat from the animal. This happened in Ireland in 2008 when there was a scare about pork.

Jobs

The EU wants to create new and better jobs for its citizens. It does this by helping people to set up new businesses and gives money to train people and give them new skills under the Leonardo Programme.

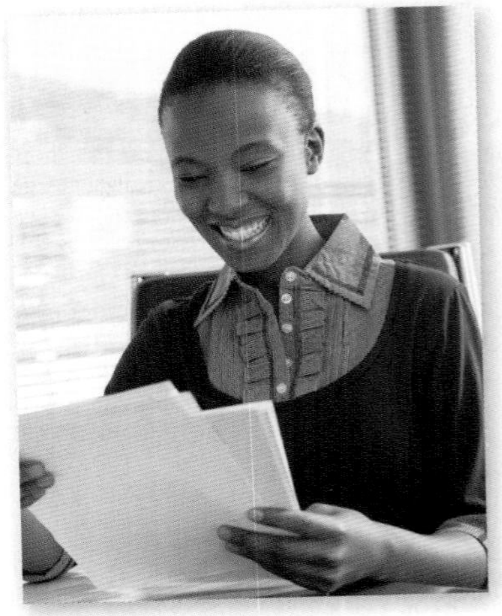

Equal Rights for Men and Women in Work

It is because of EU laws that in Ireland men and women must have the same pay if they are doing the same work. In most EU countries a new dad is entitled to time off work to look after a newborn baby, if he chooses to do so.

Helping Regions or Areas of the EU in Difficulty

The EU also helps countries to improve by giving money for new roads and rail links so that they can attract more businesses and create more jobs. In the past Ireland was given a lot of money by the EU to do this and we are still being helped out with big projects.

Fighting Crime

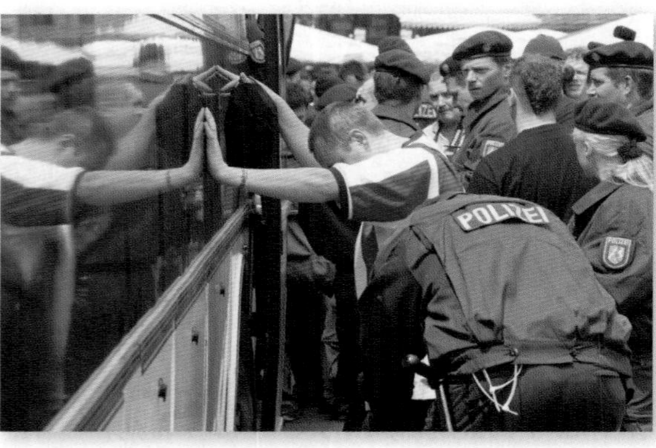

Europol is the name of the force that helps police officers in all EU countries to fight against drug trafficking, human trafficking, terrorism, etc. by sharing information on criminal gangs who may have operations in a number of countries. There is a European Arrest Warrant that makes it easier to take suspected criminals from the country where they have been arrested to the country where they are wanted by police for questioning.

Making Europe Greener

The **European Climate Change Programme** has taken a lot of steps to protect the environment, because pollution crosses all country borders. One such step is a scheme to reduce carbon emissions by big polluters in the EU, such as power plants, steel and cement plants. These plants account for almost half of the EU's CO_2 emissions. Each country is allowed to emit a certain amount of carbon. If a plant releases less carbon dioxide than they are allowed to they can sell the unused amounts to other companies that are going over their quota. This is what is meant by **carbon trading**.

EU Help to Developing Countries

The European Humanitarian Office (ECHO) is the world's largest donor of aid in the world. Many Irish NGOs get funds from ECHO to help them in their work. ECHO supports programmes like the ones shown in these pictures.

It is sometimes very difficult to reach the victims of humanitarian crises. One of ECHO's key objectives is to ensure that aid is safely delivered to the people who need it. Check out www.europa.eu.int.

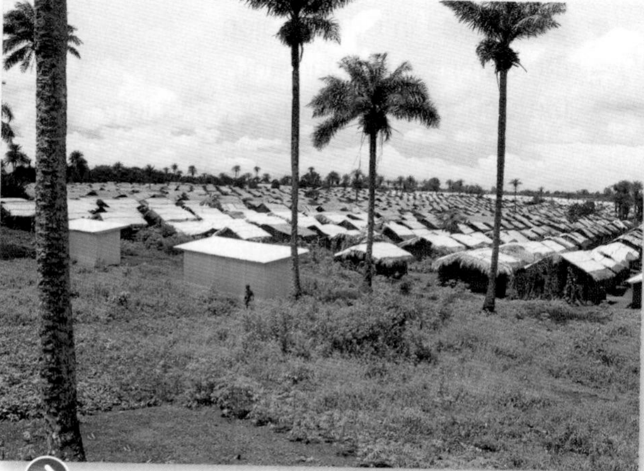

Providing shelter is one of the first priorities when people are displaced. It is then necessary to organise the co-ordinated distribution of clean water, food, medical aid, etc. ECHO also finances aid co-ordination efforts.

The legacy of conflict includes an estimated 110 million anti-personnel mines scattered in more than 70 countries. The European Commission finances humanitarian de-mining projects – mainly to enable the return of refugees and displaced people to their home regions.

There are 840 million people in the world who do not have enough to eat. The European Commission supports food distribution programmes in humanitarian crises.

ACTIVITIES

1. Explain how being a member of the European Union makes it easier to get medical care.
2. What is the EU 'farm to fork' policy?
3. How does membership of the EU mean greater equality for men and women at work?
4. What work does Europol do?
5. What kind of work does ECHO do?

STUDY 45 THE EU AND HOW IT WORKS

The three **main institutions** of the European Union are:

- the European Commission
- the European Parliament
- the Council of the European Union.

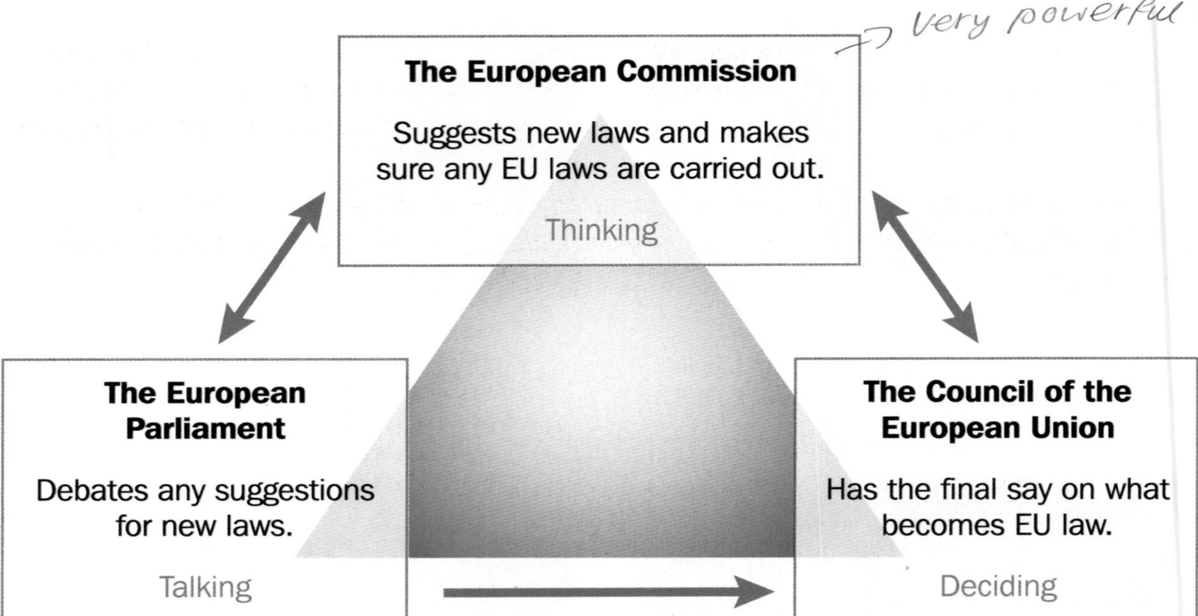
very powerful
The European Commission
Suggests new laws and makes sure any EU laws are carried out.
Thinking
The European Parliament
Debates any suggestions for new laws.
Talking
The Council of the European Union
Has the final say on what becomes EU law.
Deciding

EU Commission, Brussels

There are **27 commissioners**, one from each EU country. The job of the commissioners is to think about what is best for all the citizens in the EU. If you are made a commissioner from Ireland, for example, it would not be your job to look out for Irish interests, but to put what is good for all of the EU first. The commissioners get together in Brussels every week to **suggest new laws**, which they send on to the Parliament.

The European Commission also makes sure that any laws passed by the Parliament and the Council of Ministers are carried out. The Commission can take any country that breaks EU law to the European Court of Justice if needed.

A meeting of the European Commissioners in Brussels

EU Parliament, Strasbourg – The Voice of the People

The **citizens of Europe elect members** to the EU Parliament. The parliament could be called the voice of the people. The number of **MEPs** you have depends on how big your population is. There are 13 Irish MEPs.

MEPs are elected every five years. They meet every month in Strasbourg to **discuss and debate the ideas for laws** that come from the Commission. They can ask for changes to be made. They also help decide on the EU budget. The parliament works in all 23 official EU languages.

The members elected from each country do not sit together in blocks (e.g. the Irish MEPs, the Spanish MEPs, the French MEPs, etc.), but in one of the **seven Europe-wide political groups**. The seven groups include the Christian Democrats, the Socialists, the Liberals and the Greens.

As you can't be an expert on everything, smaller groups of MEPs meet in different committees (20 of them) in Brussels for three weeks every month to discuss details of the Commission's ideas in areas like education, the environment, etc.

A meeting of the European parliament in Strasbourg

The Council of the European Union, Brussels – The Voice of the Member States

The Council of the European Union is made up of **ministers from the different member states** who meet to make **final decisions about suggestions for new laws** that have come first from the European Commission and have been debated in the European Parliament.

Which ministers meet in the Council of Ministers depends on what topic is being discussed. If they are deciding on a new environment law, the Minister of the Environment from each EU country will be there. If the topic is education, all the education ministers will be there. The laws are passed when the Council and the Parliament agree.

Changes in the EU under the Lisbon Treaty

At present, every six months a different EU country takes over the job of the presidency of the Council of the EU. There are big meetings called summits to decide what the EU should do next.

Changes under the Lisbon Treaty mean that:

- The Parliament can have no more than 751 members.
- There is now a job called **'President of the European Council'**. This means that a **person, not a country**, will hold the Presidency of the Council of the EU. It is expected that we will be as familiar with this person as we are with the President of Ireland or the President of the United States.
- One person is in charge of foreign affairs. This makes it easier for the EU to speak with one voice and respond to threats of war or terrorism around the world.

ACTIVITIES

1. Match the names with the pictures of Irish MEPs below.

   a) Gay Mitchell
   b) Mairead McGuinness
   c) Jim Higgins
   d) Nessa Childers
   e) Sean Kelly

2. These are posters advertising Europe Day. Design a poster for this year's Europe Day.

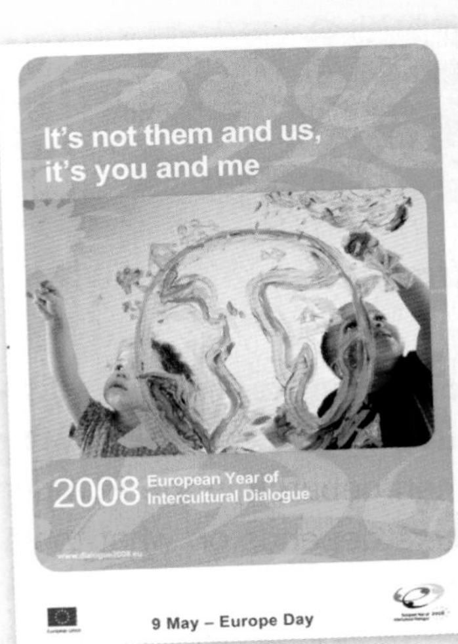

It's not them and us,
it's you and me
2008 European Year of Intercultural Dialogue
9 May – Europe Day

Your Europe:
Democracy
Dialogue
Debate
9 May – Europe Day

3. Read about what a typical month is like for Brian Crowley MEP and then answer the questions below.

What would a typical month be like for you?

Each month is divided into the four weeks. Monday to Thursday of each week I am abroad as part of my work in the European Parliament. Three weeks are spent in Brussels where the committees of the Parliament meet and the fourth week in Strasbourg where the plenary sessions take place. That is, all the members of the European Parliament meet to take the final debates and votes on issues which were dealt with in the committees in the previous weeks in Brussels. Also, I deal with the European Commission and the Presidency of the Council, putting questions to them on urgent topical issues at international, national or local levels. Each Friday, Saturday and Sunday I am back home in my constituency of Munster meeting with different groups of people and dealing with their problems as well as talking with them and discussing Europe and issues that they have concerns about.

a) Why does Brian spend three weeks of each month working in Brussels and Strasbourg?

b) What work is he involved in at weekends?

4. It would be impossible for one MEP to be expert in all the issues that come up in the EU Parliament. So they join one or more of the 20 committees set up to discuss issues like education, the environment, etc.
Read the article below about a decision taken by the European Parliament's Transport Committee and answer the questions:

MEP Drives Safety Issues On and Off the Road

In the future every road-going vehicle will be fitted with seat belts as a result of a vote by the European Parliament's transport committee. The measure means that seat belts will have to be installed in new minibuses, coaches, buses, light commercial vehicles and even lorries. The Parliament is also drawing up plans to make road signs similar throughout the EU as a way to reduce accidents.

MEPs in Brussels held talks with the Fédération Internationale de l'Automobile – a body which represents more than 200 motoring organisations and associations in over 120 countries. At the moment there is a bewildering array of different signs for speed limits, parking and other road instructions depending on which EU country or even which region of a country is in question. Over 90 per cent of European drivers in a recent survey responded that they felt a standard signage system would improve road safety and reduce accidents.

(*Source:* taken from *Life Times*)

ACTIVITIES

a) As a result of the vote by this committee, what will happen in the future?
b) What else is the Parliament drawing up plans for?
c) Why does the Parliament think this action is necessary?
d) What other actions could the Parliament take to improve road safety?

5. Look at this diagram and answer the questions that follow.

GOING IN
Every member state has to give money to the EU every year.

GOING OUT
Spent on agriculture, environment, training, technology, etc.

The EU cannot go into debt. A special body called the European Court of Auditors makes sure that the money is spent properly.

a) Where does the EU get its money?
b) What is the job of the auditors?

6. Do you think it is a good idea to have a person as the President of the EU? Give reasons for your answer.

ACTION IDEA

Research: Do a survey to find out how much your friends and family know about the European Union. You could use the information in this chapter to decide what questions should be asked; 10–20 questions should be enough. You could then present your findings as a report or a graph.

Sample question: What is the term of office of a MEP?

a) 5 years
b) 7 years
c) 10 years

Discussion/Essay: 'The idea of a European superstate is a good one.'

Research: Investigate the countries that joined the EU since 2004.

- You could present your findings in map form.
- Present a brief history/profile of these countries – language, capital, food, dance, music, famous people, famous places, etc.

You can find out more interesting information about all things European at: www.youtube.com/eutube, www.europa.eu, www.europarl.eu.

STUDY 46 HOW YOU CAN INFLUENCE THE EU

There are many ways in which citizens of the EU can influence events in Europe.

1. You can **petition the European Parliament** by sending a written request or complaint. For example, the Parliament has received many petitions about human rights and environmental protection.
2. You can **contact your local MEP** to raise issues that concern you.
3. Once you are 18 you can **vote in European Parliament elections**. If you decide to live in another EU country, you will have the right to vote in their local and European elections. You would also be able to stand for the European Parliament in another EU country.
4. You could **bring a case to the European Court of Justice** if a national law that affects you contradicts an EU law.

The Petitions Committee

The petitions committee of the European Parliament receives thousands of petitions each year. See how EU citizens have been using the right to petition the European Parliament:

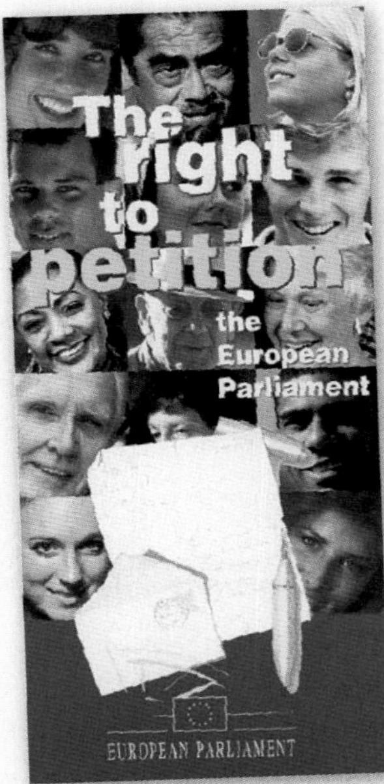

The right to petition is used by many different lobby groups to bring about change in EU laws

Illegal Trade in Bushmeat

More than 1.9 million people have signed a petition to the European Parliament calling for the EU to take action to protect great apes and other species endangered by the illegal trade in bushmeat. This trade is carried on mainly in Africa but is also on the increase in Asia and Latin America, and is leading to a loss of wildlife in forests – some species even face extinction. Dublin MEP Proinsias de Rossa (Labour) has called on the EU to adopt an action plan in this area.

Young People and the EU

The European MEP Proinsias de Rossa answers the question about how young people can influence what happens in the EU.

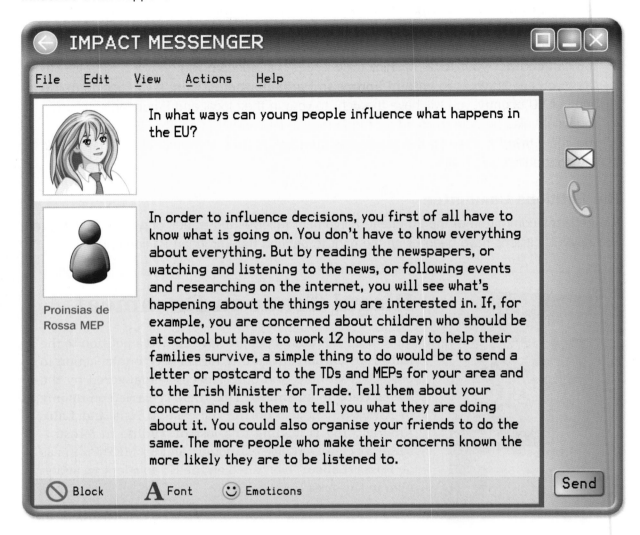

IMPACT MESSENGER

File Edit View Actions Help

In what ways can young people influence what happens in the EU?

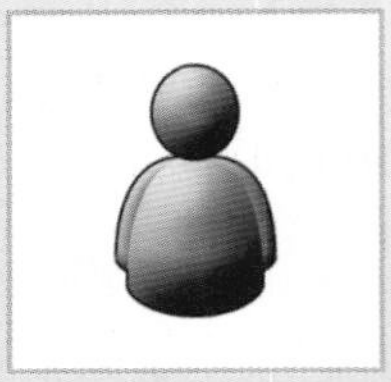

Proinsias de Rossa MEP

In order to influence decisions, you first of all have to know what is going on. You don't have to know everything about everything. But by reading the newspapers, or watching and listening to the news, or following events and researching on the internet, you will see what's happening about the things you are interested in. If, for example, you are concerned about children who should be at school but have to work 12 hours a day to help their families survive, a simple thing to do would be to send a letter or postcard to the TDs and MEPs for your area and to the Irish Minister for Trade. Tell them about your concern and ask them to tell you what they are doing about it. You could also organise your friends to do the same. The more people who make their concerns known the more likely they are to be listened to.

Block Font Emoticons Send

Europe Direct

To help citizens understand the rights and opportunities that come with being of a member of the EU a website called **Europe Direct** has been set up. People often need advice about what it might be like to live in another EU country and to find out if there are any particular things they need to know, or maybe they want to complain about some EU rule that affects them. You can check out this website at http://ec.europa.eu/europedirect/index_en.htm, or use the free phone number 00 800 6789 1011 from anywhere in Europe.

You can also find out more interesting information about all things European at www.youtube.com/eutube, or you can visit Europe Direct Information Centres throughout the country.

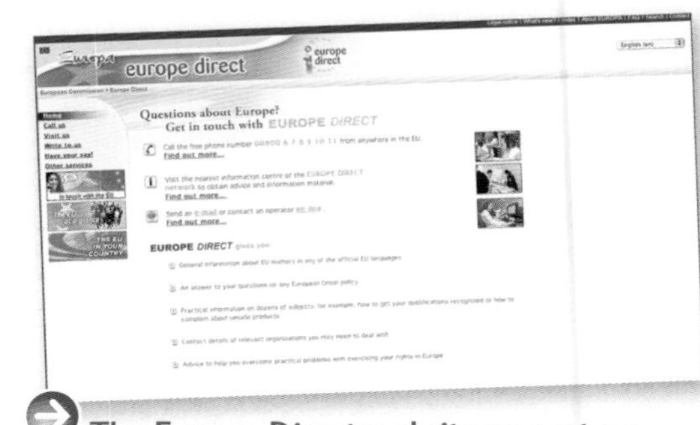

The Europe Direct website was set up to help and advise European citizens

ACTIVITIES

1. List **four** ways in which you can influence events in Europe.
2. How many EU citizens signed the petition on the illegal trade in bushmeat?
3. Why do you think EU citizens saw this as an important issue?
4. How does Proinsias de Rossa think young people can influence what happens in the EU?
5. What kind of information can Europe Direct give you about EU matters?

STUDY 47 EU RIGHTS AND LAWS

The European Court of Justice

The European Court of Justice sits in Luxembourg and is made up of 27 judges appointed for a six-year term. **Any individual, company or EU country can bring a case to the court.**

The court is important because **its decisions are final** and take priority over, or are more important than, the decisions of national courts. The court has the **power to make a member state change any law that is not in keeping with EU law** and to impose a fine on any member state that fails to do so.

The European Court of Justice, Luxembourg

Keeping an Eye on Europe

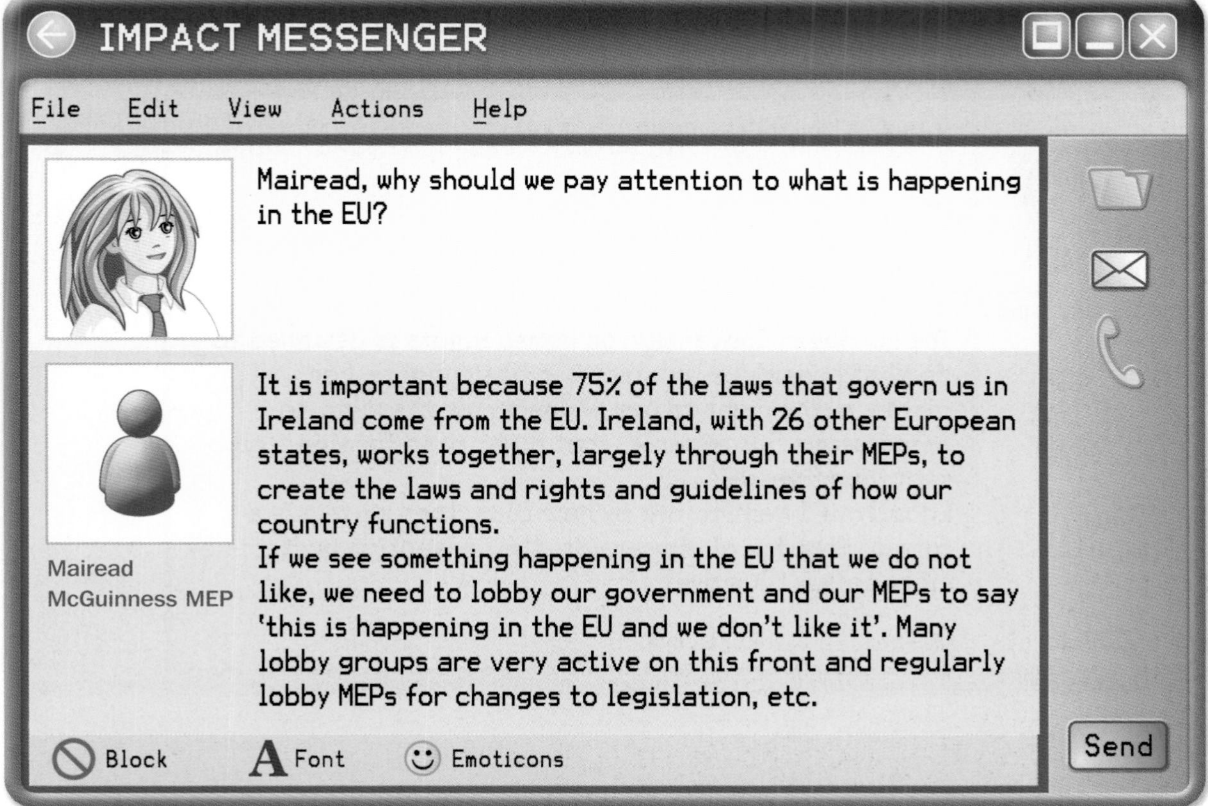

IMPACT MESSENGER
File Edit View Actions Help
Mairead, why should we pay attention to what is happening in the EU?
It is important because 75% of the laws that govern us in Ireland come from the EU. Ireland, with 26 other European states, works together, largely through their MEPs, to create the laws and rights and guidelines of how our country functions.
If we see something happening in the EU that we do not like, we need to lobby our government and our MEPs to say 'this is happening in the EU and we don't like it'. Many lobby groups are very active on this front and regularly lobby MEPs for changes to legislation, etc.
Mairead McGuinness MEP
Block
Font
Emoticons
Send

The European Convention on Human Rights (ECHR)

The **European Convention on Human Rights** (ECHR) contains a lot of the same rights that are in the UN Declaration of Human Rights (see page 15). In 2003 the ECHR was passed into Irish law. It means that you can take a case to court in Ireland if you think your rights are not being upheld.

European Convention on Human Rights

Article 2: Right to life

Article 3: Prohibition of torture

Article 4: Prohibition of slavery and forced labour

Article 6: Right to a fair trial

Article 7: Right to respect for private and family life

Article 9: Freedom of thought, conscience and religion

Article 10: Freedom of expression

Article 11: Freedom of assembly and association

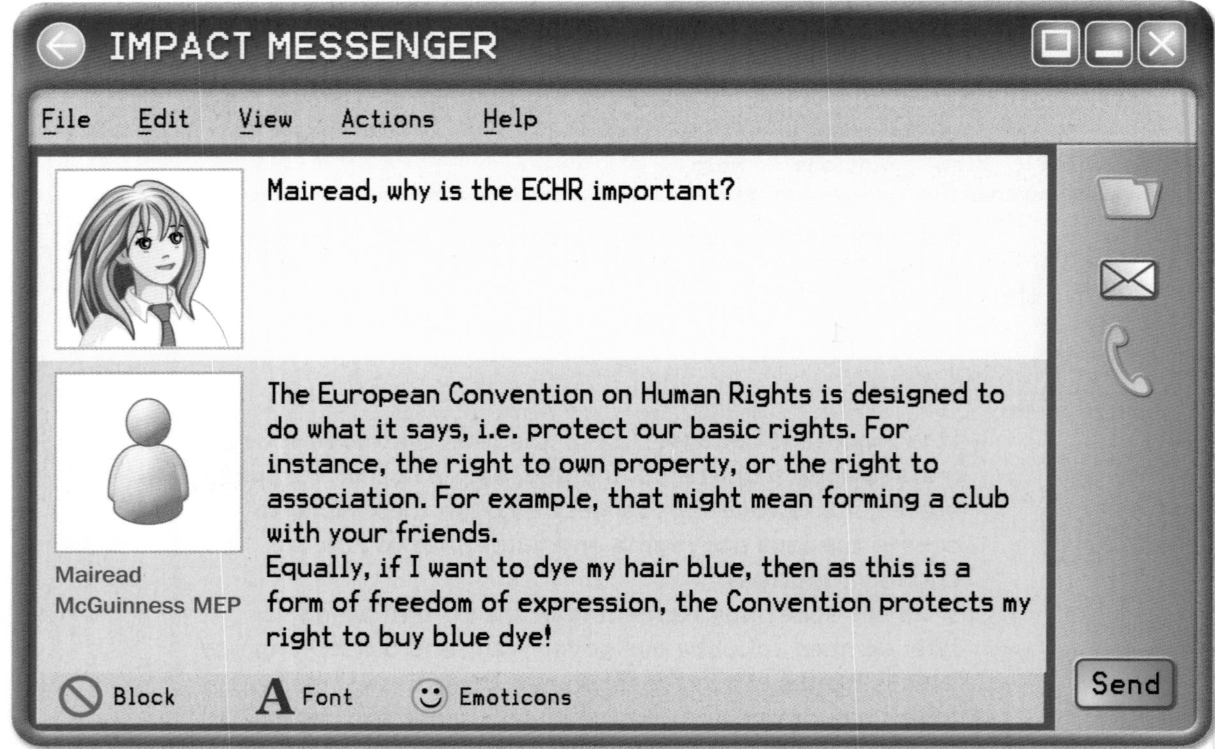

IMPACT MESSENGER
File
Edit
View
Actions
Help
Mairead, why is the ECHR important?
The European Convention on Human Rights is designed to do what it says, i.e. protect our basic rights. For instance, the right to own property, or the right to association. For example, that might mean forming a club with your friends.
Equally, if I want to dye my hair blue, then as this is a form of freedom of expression, the Convention protects my right to buy blue dye!
Mairead McGuinness MEP
Block
Font
Emoticons
Send

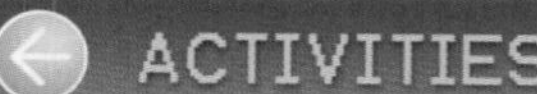

ACTIVITIES

1. What power does the European Court of Justice have over countries that are members of the EU?
2. According to Mairead McGuinness MEP, what should we do if we see something happening in the EU that we don't like?
3. What does the European Convention on Human Rights (ECHR) protect?
4. How does the ECHR effect Irish law?
5. Take the quiz below and see how much you know about the EU. Underline the correct answers.

a) How many MEPs does Ireland have?
25 13 15

b) In which European city is the EU Parliament?
Brussels Berlin Strasbourg

c) How many stars are there on the EU flag?
6 15 12

d) In which European city is the EU Commission?
Antwerp Paris Brussels

e) What day of the year is Europe Day?
6 June 9 May 4 July

f) Which of these countries has applied for membership of the European Union?
Switzerland Iceland Croatia

g) When did Ireland join the EU?
1973 1981 2000

h) The music of the European Anthem was written by:
Mozart Beethoven Schubert

i) Under the Lisbon Treaty, what will be the maximum number in the European Parliament ?
550 340 751

j) The motto of the EU is:
'All for One' 'United in Diversity' 'Together we Stand'

STUDY 48 THE UNITED NATIONS

The headquarters of the UN is in New York

The United Nations was set up on **24 October 1945**, after World War II. This day is now celebrated around the world as **United Nations Day**.

The main aims of the UN are:

- to keep **peace** throughout the world
- to develop **friendly relations** between nations
- to encourage r**espect for each other's rights** and freedoms
- to help people live better lives by **solving the problems** of poverty, disease and illiteracy in the world, as well as trying to put a stop to environmental destruction.

All actions by the UN depend on the will of member states to accept, fund or carry them out.

How the UN Functions

The Security Council

- The main aim of the Security Council is to **keep international peace**.
- It meets in **New York**.
- It has **15 members**. Five of these are permanent: France, China, Russia, the UK and the USA. The other ten are elected by the General Assembly on a rotating basis.
- It has the power to take decisions that member states then carry out. However, any of the five permanent members can stop an action or decision happening, even if the other 14 are in favour. This is called the **power of veto**. For this reason the Security Council has not always been successful in taking action in crisis situations.

A meeting of the Security Council at the UN

Secretary-General

- The Secretary-General **acts as the head** of the United Nations.
- S/he carries out the decisions made by the Security Council.
- S/he acts as a **mediator** (go-between) in conflict situations.
- S/he is the head of the civil service of the UN (secretariat).
- The term of office of a Secretary-General of the UN is five years, after which s/he can be re-elected.

Ban Ki-moon of the Republic of Korea, the eighth Secretary-General of the United Nations

The General Assembly of the UN

The General Assembly

- The General Assembly is the closest thing there is to a **world Parliament**; nearly every nation of the world is a member (**192 members** at present).
- This is where the member states can **discuss any matter of global concern**.
- Every member has **one vote**, regardless of the size of the country.
- It encourages **co-operation** between different countries and the protection of **human rights**.
- When the General Assembly agrees on an issue it is known as a **resolution**. However, these resolutions, or decisions, **cannot be enforced**.

United Nations Headquarters

The United Nations Headquarters is in New York City but the land and buildings are international territory. The United Nations has its own flag, its own post office and its own postage stamps. Six official languages are used at the United Nations – Arabic, Chinese, English, French, Russian and Spanish.

United Nations Headquarters in Geneva

United Nations flag

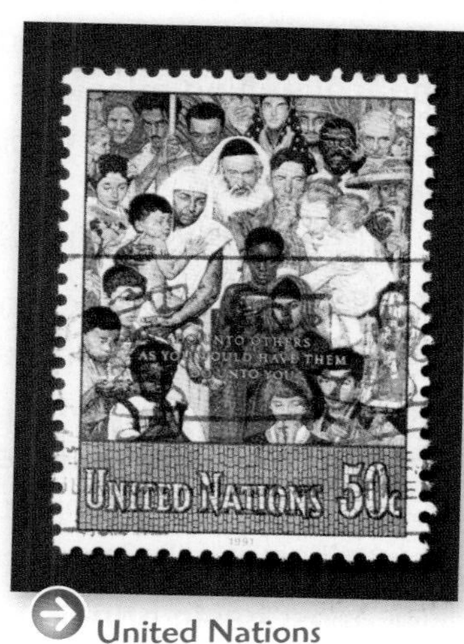

United Nations postage stamp

United Nations Special Agencies

The United Nations organisation has a number of special agencies that try to help find solutions to global problems.

Special programmes include:

- UNICEF – United Nations Children's Fund

- UNHCR – United Nations High Commissioner for Refugees

- UNEP – United Nations Environment Programme

- UNAIDS – United Nations Agency dealing with the Aids epidemic.

United Nations Peacekeeping Missions

The **Irish army** is involved not only in the security of the State but also in **United Nations peacekeeping missions**. Irish Defence Forces have been involved in UN peacekeeping missions since 1958 in places such as Lebanon, Somalia, Bosnia, Kosovo, East Timor and Chad.

The differences between UN peacekeeping forces and other armed forces are:

- UN peacekeepers cannot take sides
- countries involved must agree to the presence of peacekeepers
- UN peacekeepers are generally lightly armed and only use arms in self-defence
- UN peacekeepers are also involved in clearing mines, providing humanitarian aid to local people, investigating human rights abuses, and observing and reporting on a situation as well as monitoring elections when necessary.

The most **basic principle** is that **using arms and force is not the best way of solving a conflict**. Peace will last only when there is some form of agreement.

The Defence Forces and the UN

Tom Clonan, formerly a captain in the Irish Army, served on a number of peacekeeping missions.

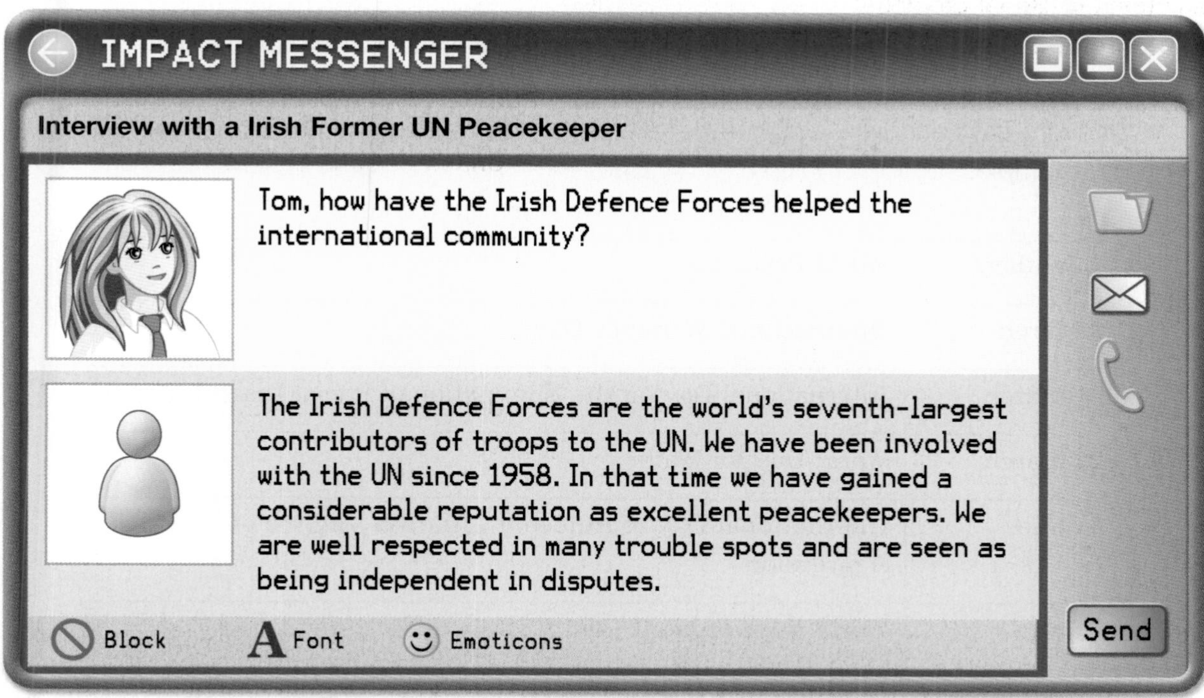

IMPACT MESSENGER
Interview with a Irish Former UN Peacekeeper
Tom, how have the Irish Defence Forces helped the international community?
The Irish Defence Forces are the world's seventh-largest contributors of troops to the UN. We have been involved with the UN since 1958. In that time we have gained a considerable reputation as excellent peacekeepers. We are well respected in many trouble spots and are seen as being independent in disputes.
Block
Font
Emoticons
Send

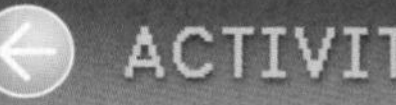

ACTIVITIES

1. What are the main aims of the UN?
2. What is the main aim of the Security Council?
3. Why is the Security Council sometimes not successful in taking action?
4. What is the General Assembly?
5. What does the job of Secretary-General involve?
6. Name some of the UN's special programmes and explain what they do.
7. *There are no islands in the world today, and there are no domestic and international diseases. We live in a global village. We live in a shrinking world. And there are many contacts between us. No one is isolated, no one can be smug and sit in his or her corner and say, 'I'm safe because it is somewhere else.'*

   Kofi Annan, former Secretary-General of the United Nations 1997–2007

   a) According to Kofi Annan, how is our world 'a global village'?
   b) Why can we not be 'smug'?
   c) Name four ways in which you rely on the rest of the world.
   d) How, as 'global citizens', are we responsible for what happens outside Ireland?
8. Give two differences between a UN peacekeeping force and other armed forces.
9. According to Captain Clonan, why are Irish peacekeeping forces well respected?

ACTION IDEAS

Research: Find out more information about the United Nations. Here are some examples to help you:

- Different days and weeks of the year are dedicated to issues of concern to the UN. For example:

1 January	World Peace Day
8 March	International Women's Day
21 March	International Day for the Elimination of Racial Discrimination
22 March	World Day for Water
4 June	International Day of Innocent Children Victims of Aggression
5 June	World Environment Day
8 September	International Literacy Day
21 September	International Day of Peace (Opening of UN General Assembly)
1 October	International Day of Older Persons
16 October	World Food Day
24 October	United Nations Day
24–30 October	Disarmament Week
20 November	Universal Children's Day
1 December	World Aids Day
3 December	International Day of Disabled Persons
10 December	Human Rights Day

- You could base an action project around one of these days.
- You could find out more about the work of a UN special programme such as UNICEF.
- You can check out the biography and the daily schedule of the Secretary-General of the UN at www.un.org/sg/.

Interview: You could invite a member of the Defence Forces who has served abroad to speak to your class about their experience of a UN peacekeeping mission.

UN Goodwill Ambassadors

Goodwill Ambassadors are chosen by various UN agencies.

Some Goodwill Ambassadors are Angelina Jolie, Geri Halliwell, Seamus Heaney, Magic Johnson, Muhammad Ali and David Beckham.

Former Secretary-General of the UN, Kofi Annan, has said: 'The Goodwill Ambassadors have the power to inform people about the hardships of others and do something about it . . . putting their names to a message could break through the barriers of indifference and lack of news coverage . . . they could explain how the UN changed people's lives, strengthened peace and ensured human rights.'

David Beckman is one of approximately a hundred Goodwill Ambassadors working with various UN agencies

Angelina Jolie is a Goodwill Ambassador for the UN refugee agency

Model United Nations Conferences for Secondary Students

In order to help young people understand how the UN works, a number of Model United Nations Conferences take place around the world each year.

Model UN Conferences

In Ireland, St Andrew's College in Booterstown, Dublin hosts a conference every Easter with up to 800 Irish and foreign students taking part.

Each group of four to six students takes on the role of a country and becomes an expert on that country and its different policies. Each student delegate joins different committees in which questions relating to the environment, human rights, etc. are discussed. In these discussions the student delegate puts forward the viewpoint of the country they represent.

The aim of the conference is to get as many resolutions (recommendations for actions to be taken) as possible passed in the model General Assembly. Part of the process is that student delegates have to lobby other student delegates in order to persuade them of their point of view.

Irish students at the Model United Nations Conference run by St Andrew's College, Booterstown, County Dublin

 ACTIVITIES 

1. According to Kofi Annan, how can the UN Goodwill Ambassadors help the work of the United Nations?
2. The majority of the ambassadors are celebrities. How can they draw attention to the work of the UN?
3. How does the Model United Nations Conference help students understand the workings of the United Nations?

 ACTION IDEA 

Research: Check out www.un.org/cyberschoolbus/, where you can learn about global issues and the UN. You can check out statistics and interesting information on all the UN member states, look at webcasts of UN meetings and events or play a number of interactive online games to increase awareness of refugee situations, or how to respond in different disaster situations.

STUDY 49 UN DEVELOPMENT GOALS

In 2001 192 members of the United Nations signed the **Millennium Development Goals** (MDGs). These goals are about **ending world poverty**. The aim is that by 2015, 500 million people will no longer be living in poverty. By signing up to the goals the governments of both developing and developed countries have agreed to **work together towards a better future for everyone**. By 2015 the governments of the world have promised to:

Change the World in 8 Steps

Goal 1: Reduce Poverty

About 1.2 billion people live on less than $1 a day. Millions of people do not have basic needs like access to clean water. Eight hundred million people do not have enough to eat.

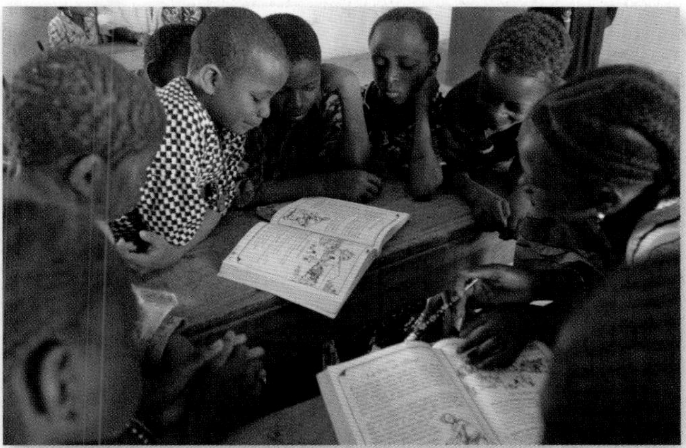

Goal 2: Educate every child

One hundred and fifteen million children of primary school age are not in school: 97 per cent of them are in developing countries.

Goal 3: Provide equal chances for girls and women

Sixty-four per cent of the world's adults who cannot read and write are women. Only in nine countries in the world are at least one-third of the seats in parliament held by women.

Goal 4: Reduce the number of babies and children who die

Every year more than ten million children die. That is 30,000 children a day who die from diseases that can be prevented by immunisation and medicine.

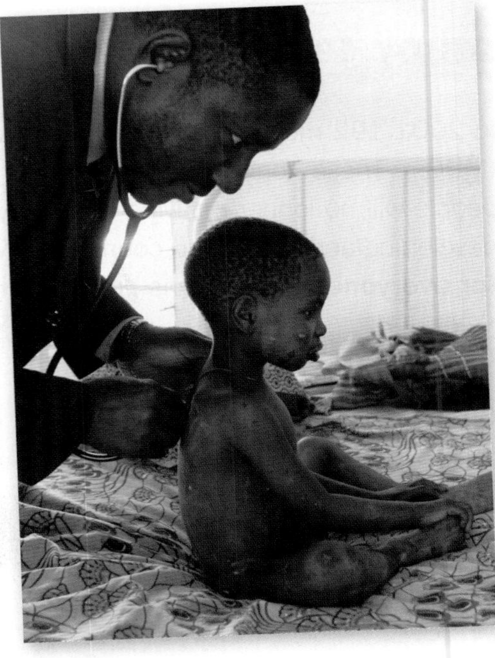

Goal 5: Ensure safe and healthy motherhood

Every year 500,000 women die during pregnancy and childbirth.

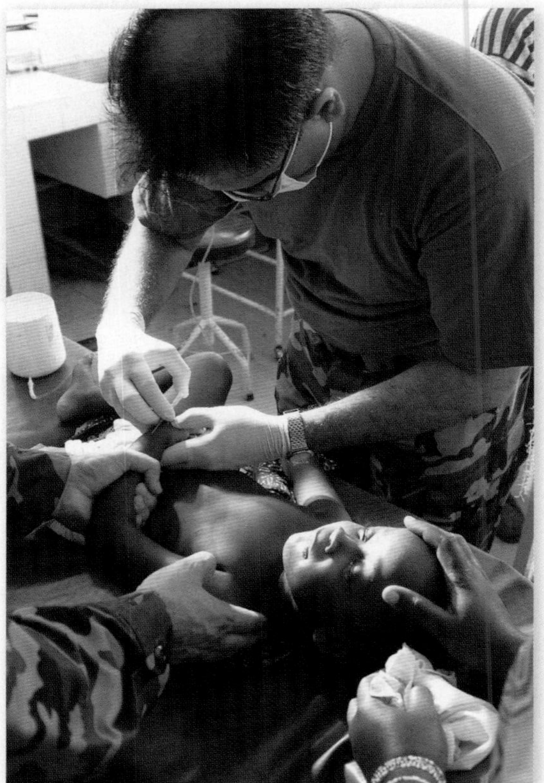

Goal 6: Fight infectious diseases

Every minute of every day, a child dies because of Aids and another four children lose a parent to Aids-related causes. Malaria kills more than one million people each year, mostly children.

Goal 7: Clean up the environment

More than one billion people in developing countries (one person in every five) do not have access to safe, clean drinking water.

Goal 8: Share responsibility for making the world a better place
The eighth goal is about rich countries and the wider 'global community' working together to do things like reduce debt, give more and better aid and make trade fairer. Many campaigns have been set up to put pressure on governments to meet the goals and end world poverty.

The Millennium Campaign

The Millennium Campaign was launched by the United Nations to **encourage citizens around the world to get their governments to keep their promise of ending world poverty**. The campaign calls on all organisations that work for a fairer and better world (such as UNICEF, Trócaire, Concern, Goal, Oxfam, etc.) to come together and bring world attention to achieving the goals. The campaign also looks for youth groups, politicians, the media, celebrities and every citizen to promote the goals and end world poverty, by reminding government leaders in both rich and poor countries of their promise.

The symbol of the white band, saying 'Make Poverty History', is worn by people across the world

A Closer look at Millennium Goal 6

Aids Orphans – a Tragedy of the 21st Century

By 2010 it is expected that more than 20 million children will have become orphans because of HIV/Aids. The majority of these orphans are in countries in Africa.

Being an Aids orphan often means being at increased risk of poverty, hunger and homelessness. It also means suffering discrimination and stigma, and being less protected as you may not have a caring adult to look out for you. Aids orphans often have to leave school in order to work as there is no adult to help to provide basic food and shelter. In addition to all of this is the loneliness and stress of losing your loved ones.

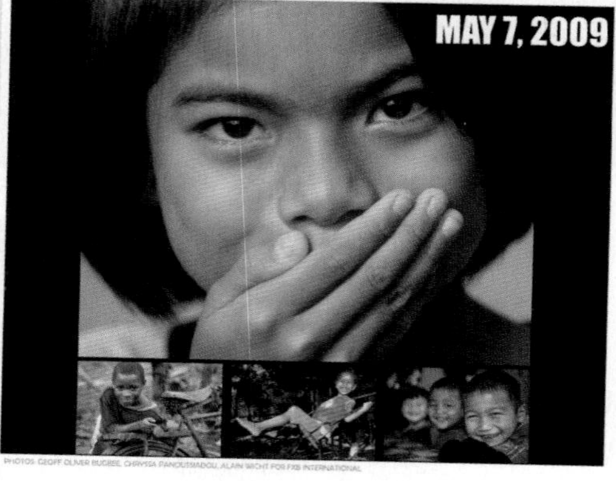

8th ANNUAL WORLD AIDS ORPHANS' DAY
MAY 7, 2009
YOUR VOICE IS THEIR FUTURE
Contact FXB International
Phone: +41 (0) 79 221 13 50
82 rue de Lausanne - 1202 Geneva
Contact FXB France
Phone: +33 (6) 09 221 332
20 Rue Vignon – 75009 Paris

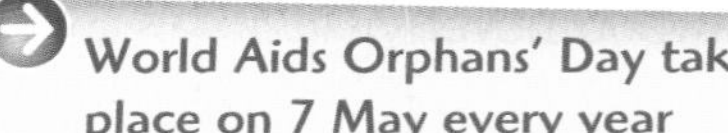
World Aids Orphans' Day takes place on 7 May every year

Number of orphaned children due to Aids in a sample of nine African countries	
South Africa	1,400,000
Uganda	1,200,000
Nigeria	1,200,000
Zimbabwe	1,000,000
Tanzania	970,000
Ethiopia	650,000
Zambia	600,000
Malawi	560,000
Côte d'Ivoire	420,000

(*Source:* www.avert.org – 2007 figures)

Aids Orphans – a Tragedy of the 21st Century

In Africa, children who were orphaned were traditionally most often cared for by their grandparents, aunts, uncles or some member of the extended family. However, the sheer number of orphans has in some cases made this impossible. For example, in Zambia, 20 per cent of all children were orphans in 2005, leaving a population of 11.7 million to support more than 1.2 million orphans. This has meant that children have had to take on a huge burden of responsibility by themselves, having to become the head of their household, often looking after younger brothers and sisters. In other cases it has meant trying to survive on the streets.

The huge problems facing children led to the **Unite for Children, Unite against Aids** global campaign launched in 2005 in the hope of increasing the chances of meeting Millennium Goal 6 – to halt and begin to reverse the spread of the disease by 2015. UN special agencies like **UNICEF** and **UNAIDS** have, through this campaign, been trying to help children affected by Aids through supporting health and education programmes. Coupled with poverty, the Aids epidemic is one of the biggest threats to development in this region, especially in the way it is affecting the lives of so many children who will find it difficult to realise their life's dreams of perhaps becoming a nurse or a doctor or a teacher, as the circumstances of their lives are so difficult.

UNITE FOR CHILDREN
UNITE AGAINST AIDS

ACTIVITIES

1. Below are pictures used by the UN that stand for the different Millennium Development Goals (MDGs). Match each picture to the development goal.

   a) Fight infectious diseases.
   b) Educate every child.
   c) Reduce poverty.
   d) Ensure safe and healthy motherhood.
   e) Provide equal chances for girls and women.
   f) Reduce the number of babies and children who die.
   g) Share responsibility for making the world a better place.
   h) Clean up the environment.
2. In what way are all the goals linked?
3. One of the slogans of the UN Millennium Campaign is 'Your voice can change the world'. Explain what you think is meant by this.
4. This is Trócaire's campaign poster to raise awareness of the Millennium Goals. What do you think the slogan 'Keep our word' is referring to?

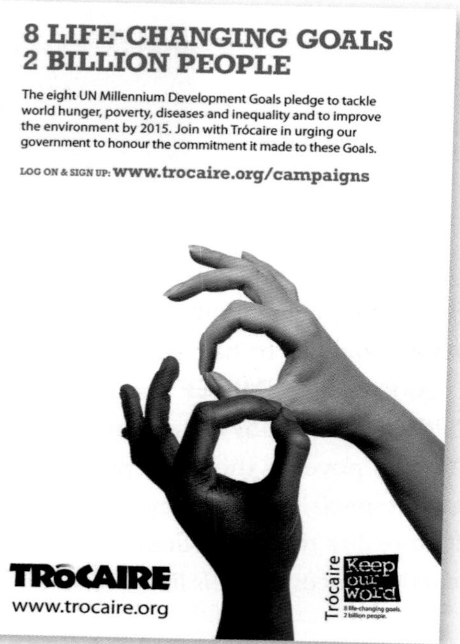

8 LIFE-CHANGING GOALS
2 BILLION PEOPLE
The eight UN Millennium Development Goals pledge to tackle world hunger, poverty, diseases and inequality and to improve the environment by 2015. Join with Trócaire in urging our government to honour the commitment it made to these Goals.
LOG ON & SIGN UP: www.trocaire.org/campaigns
TRÓCAIRE
www.trocaire.org
Trócaire
Keep our word

5. Design a poster and slogan for your school to let people know about the Millennium Goals.
6. In what ways does being orphaned due to the Aids epidemic affect the lives of children?
7. What UN agencies have been trying to help children affected by the Aids epidemic?

Check out:

www.makepovertyhistory.org
www.oxfam.org
www.trocaire.ie
www.concern.net
www.unicef.org
www.goal.ie.

STUDY 50 CHILD LABOUR

Children who are forced to work are **denied their basic rights**. They have little time to play. They cannot go to school. As a result they will not be able to find better jobs when they grow up and so their children will also have to work to survive.

In total there are about **218 million children** between the ages of four and 15 **who are working**. Many are leather workers, carpet weavers, tea pickers, brick makers, farm workers, football stitchers and workers in garment and toy factories, who produce many of the products that end up in our shops.

Many of these children work because their families are poor. Their parents may be out of work or so badly paid that the family needs all the extra money the children can earn. Sometimes, because families need money for basics like food and clothes, parents sell their children into **bonded labour**, which means that they get a sum of money and the child must work to pay off the loan. This can go on for life.

A World Cup football costs $91; the stitcher, often a child, gets 17¢

Take Action!

Iqbal Masih, a Child Labourer

Iqbal Masih lived in the village of Muridke in Pakistan. His family was extremely poor and lived in a two-roomed hut. When Iqbal was four years old, his family was given a loan of 800 rupees (about €13) in return for putting Iqbal to work in the village carpet factory. About 500,000 children aged between four and 14 work in carpet factories in Pakistan. They work for 14 hours a day. These children are considered good workers because their small hands are good at tying the knots of expensive hand-knotted carpets.

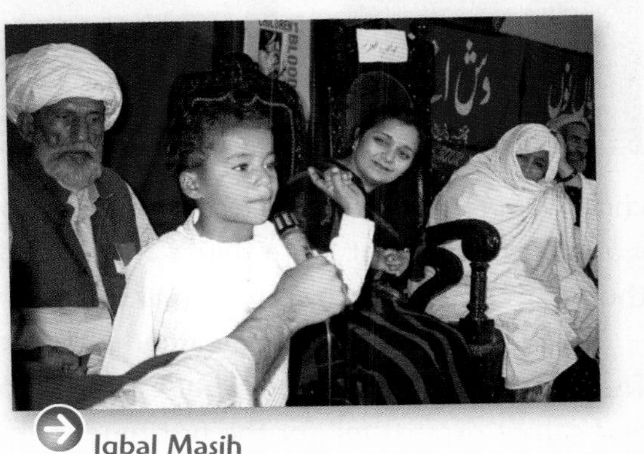

Iqbal Masih

These child workers get no formal education. When working they are not allowed to speak in case they make mistakes in the patterns. They have one 30-minute lunch break per day and are often forced to work overtime without extra pay. Complaints result in punishments such as beatings or having their hands plunged into boiling water.

Iqbal Masih, a Child Labourer

Iqbal was extremely unhappy at the carpet factory but his parents could not afford to have him set free. One day Iqbal heard the founder of the Bonded Labour Liberation Front (BLLF) speak about their work in freeing bonded labourers and about new laws that forbade child labour. Iqbal asked how he could be set free. He knew the factory owner claimed that his parents now owed 16,000 rupees. He was afraid that his entire life would be spent repaying the debt.

Iqbal told the owner of the factory about his rights and said that he would no longer work as a slave. The factory owner was furious and punished him severely, but Iqbal refused to work. Iqbal said, 'I am not afraid of the carpet master. He should be afraid of me.' The factory owner demanded his worker or his money. The family could not persuade Iqbal to work and so the factory owner threatened them.

The family had to flee from the village. Iqbal was taken by the BLLF to a school. He was ten years old and worked very hard, quickly learning to read and write. He hoped that one day he could become a lawyer helping to free child labourers.

When he was 11 years old, Iqbal began to work with the BLLF. He sneaked into factories to see where the child labourers were kept. He began to make speeches at the factory gates telling the workers of their rights. As a result, 3,000 child labourers broke away from their masters and thousands of adults began to demand improved working conditions.

People in other countries learned about Iqbal's work. They began to ask questions about carpet production in Pakistan, and carpet exports fell for the first time in three decades. The manufacturers and exporters blamed Iqbal Masih for these problems. Iqbal was given a number of human rights awards around the world.

goodweave

The GoodWeave label is a consumer's best assurance that no child labour was used

When Iqbal was on a visit to Muridke to see some members of his family, a shot rang out and Iqbal Masih fell dead. A poor labourer confessed to the killing but later withdrew his confession. International pressure has failed to get any satisfactory answer as to why Iqbal Masih, aged 13, died.

It is widely believed that he was killed for his work fighting child slavery.

Taking Action

Free the Children

Craig Kielburger, a Canadian, read an article in a magazine that told the story of Iqbal Masih. He had never heard of child labour and was shocked to learn that there were 250 million child labourers in the world. He and his friends, all 12 years of age, set up a group called Free the Children. His organisation has helped build more than 500 primary schools in Asia, Africa and Latin America, providing education for over 50,000 children.

You can find out more about Free the Children on their website

Craig Kielburger

The organisation has groups in over 35 countries. Besides education, they work on campaigns to protect children's rights and believe that children can help change the world. Free the Children believes that all young people should have a voice and the chance to take part in issues that affect them in their communities, their country and their world. For his work Craig has received the **World's Children's Prize for the Rights of the Child** (this is often called the Children's Nobel Prize). You can see videos of Craig and the work of his organisation on YouTube.

Check out:
www.stopchildlabour.net www.concern.net www.freethechildren.com.
www.goodweave.org

ACTIVITIES

Iqbal's story

1. What happened to Iqbal as a result of his family's poverty?
2. What kind of conditions did the children work in?
3. Why did Iqbal begin to think about being set free?
4. What do you think Iqbal meant when he said, 'I am not afraid of the carpet master. He should be afraid of me'?
5. What were Iqbal's hopes for the future?
6. What effects did Iqbal's speeches at the factory gates have on the workers?
7. What did people in the West do when they heard Iqbal's story?
8. Why do you think Iqbal was killed?
9. What does the GoodWeave label mean?
10. Look at the pie charts below and answer the questions.

Where and how do children work?

While the figure of 218 million child labourers is used in official calculations, the actual number of children working is probably much higher. This is due to the invisible and informal nature of child labour and the fact that many children have not been registered because they have no birth certificate and they do not appear on any school or employment records.

GLOBAL ESTIMATES ON CHILD LABOUR

218 million – total number of children working Source: ILO 2006

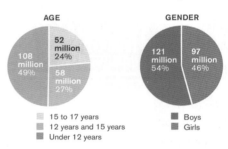

AGE
52 million 24%
58 million 27%
108 million 49%
15 to 17 years
12 years and 15 years
Under 12 years

GENDER
121 million 54%
97 million 46%
Boys
Girls

WHERE?
122 million
49.3 million
5.7 million
41 million
Asian-Pacific
sub-Saharan Africa
Latin America & Caribbean
Rest of world

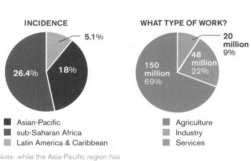

INCIDENCE
18%
26.4%
5.1%
Asian-Pacific
sub-Saharan Africa
Latin America & Caribbean

Note: while the Asia-Pacific region has the highest number of child labourers, the incidence is highest in sub-Saharan Africa.

WHAT TYPE OF WORK?
150 million 69%
48 million 22%
20 million 9%
Agriculture
Industry
Services

Source: Concern Labour Campaign Toolkit

a) What part of the world do most child labourers come from?
b) What action could you take to highlight the issue of child labourers?
c) Name three rights child labourers are being denied.

11. Name **three ways** in which organisations like Concern Worldwide highlight issues like Stop Child Labour.
12. What are the main beliefs and campaigns of the Free the Children organisation?

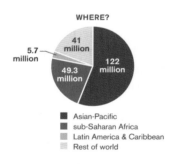

ACTION IDEAS

Guest Speaker: Invite a speaker from Concern to your class to tell you about child labour.
Research: Find out what people/organisations have won the World's Children's Prize for the Rights of the Child at www.childensworld.org. You can nominate a person or organisation to win this prize for their work in helping improve the lives of children around the world.

STUDY 51 THE DEBT CRISIS

The **developing world** consists of much of Asia, Africa and South America. It is also referred to as the **South**, the **Third World** or the **Majority World**. The poverty experienced in many countries in the developing world, where the basic needs and rights of people are not met, is due in part to the debt these countries owe.

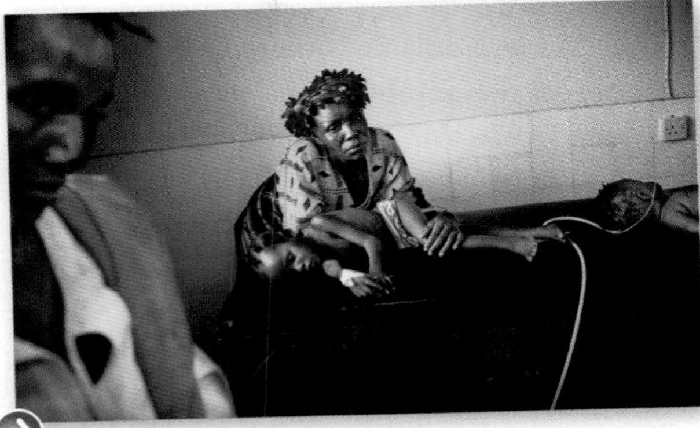
The cost of debt in some countries means that often the basic needs of citizens are not met and good healthcare and education are not available

How the developing world has huge debts that they have to repay has a history dating back to the 1970s, when massive loans were given to countries in South America and Africa, some of which were run by military dictatorships. A lot of these loans never reached the people they were intended to help because of corruption. However, international organisations like the World Bank insisted that these countries cut back on government spending in order to repay their debts.

This meant that health clinics and hospitals often had no medicine, and primary school children had to pay to go to school, as these governments had to keep money to repay the loans instead of using it to improve the lives of their citizens. This has kept ordinary people, who had no part in the arrangement of these loans, in poverty.

While banks were willing to give enormous loans to sometimes corrupt governments, many of the ordinary citizens could never get even a tiny loan from a bank.

New Solutions to Old Problems

One person who was determined to come up with solutions to the question of poverty in the developing world was **Dr Muhammad Yunus**, one of the **Global Elders** mentioned in Chapter 1.

Dr Muhammad Yunus, who has often been called 'the world's banker to the poor'

Helping those in Poverty to Help Themselves: Dr Muhammad Yunus and the Grameen Bank

One of the great difficulties facing people in the developing world has been that most poor people have been unable to borrow money from ordinary banks. They are often refused on the basis that they could not provide any guarantees and the belief that they would be unable to repay their loans. People were often forced to use money lenders who charge very, very high rates of interest, which means that even if borrowers manage to set up a small business, any money that they make has to be used to repay money lenders rather than to send their children to school, or provide a better standard of living for their families. It has also traditionally been very difficult for women to get loans.

These problems bothered Mr Muhammad Yunus, an economist from Bangladesh, one of the poorest countries on the planet.

In 1976, Mr Yunus decided to use $27 of his own money to give a loan to 42 women in the village of Jobra in Bangladesh to help them with their furniture-making businesses. From there he started the Grameen (Village) Bank to help give small loans, or what has been called 'micro-credit', to the poorest of the poor. His bank has since given small loans (less than $100) to over seven million Bangladeshis, 97 per cent of whom are women.

This means that a woman with one sewing machine might be able to borrow the money to buy two or three sewing machines to make more clothes, to increase her business and employ more people. Mr Yunus's scheme has now been copied in over 40 countries worldwide.

Dr Yunus and the Grameen Bank won the Nobel Prize for Peace in 2006. Peace often depends on development in society, when people have the means to feed themselves and send their children to school.

ACTIVITIES

1. How has Third World debt affected the lives of many ordinary citizens?
2. What problems was Dr Yunus concerned about in Bangladesh?
3. What action did he take to try and solve these problems?
4. Name **two** developments that giving loans brought about.
5. What rights can be denied to those who live in extreme poverty?
6. What do you think is being said about the 'Progress of Man' in this cartoon?

7. Name **three actions** you could take to draw attention to the debt crisis in developing countries.

ACTION IDEA

View a documentary about Muhammad Yunus and prepare a PowerPoint presentation about the Grameen Bank. See http://nobelprize.org/mediaplayer/index.php?id=146

STUDY 52 FAIR TRADE

Fair trade is an important way of making sure that **producers in developing countries get a better deal**. Fair trade allows us to **take more responsibility** for the goods we buy from people in the developing world.

For many producers in developing countries, the price they receive for the goods we buy from them is often not enough to cover their basic costs of food, healthcare and education. Millions of people in developing countries produce goods like coffee, tea, cocoa, bananas and other foods.

A Better Deal

Before we leave the breakfast table we've already depended on half the world, we're not going to have peace on earth until we realise that.

I AM YOU
BE FAIR TO ME
10 May 2008
World Fair Trade Day 2008
World Fair Trade Organization (WFTO)

Fairtrade began over 30 years ago, and many Fairtrade Mark products are in Irish supermarkets. The main products that carry the Fairtrade Mark are coffee, tea, bananas, fruit juices, snacks and biscuits, chocolate, honey, sugar, footballs, cotton and wine. If the Fairtrade Mark is shown on a product it guarantees that more money is received by the producers.
In return, the producers have to meet certain standards about how they are organised. For example, people working on tea or banana plantations must be free to join a trade union and must have decent employment conditions.

During Fairtrade Fortnight, the first two weeks in March every year, individuals and organisations run coffee mornings, tastings, leafleting promotions and other events that raise the profile of Fairtrade.

A Better Deal

The **Fairtrade Towns** project is another way people get involved. There are now 38 towns and cities around Ireland involved in this project. One of the six criteria that Fairtrade Towns have to meet is to involve schools in their area in their work. Schools can get involved by doing the Fairtrade education pack for the Civil, Social and Political Education (CSPE) curriculum, by organising activities during Fairtrade Fortnight, by converting the staff and restaurant canteen to Fairtrade coffee and tea, and by having Fairtrade products for sale in the school.

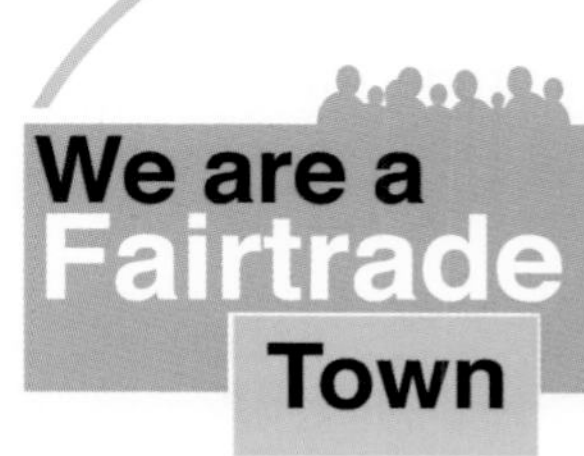

(Thanks to Peter Gaynor, Co-ordinator, Fairtrade Mark Ireland for this article.)

ACTIVITIES

1. Explain in your own words what Martin Luther King was saying.
2. Look at the diagram and answer the questions.

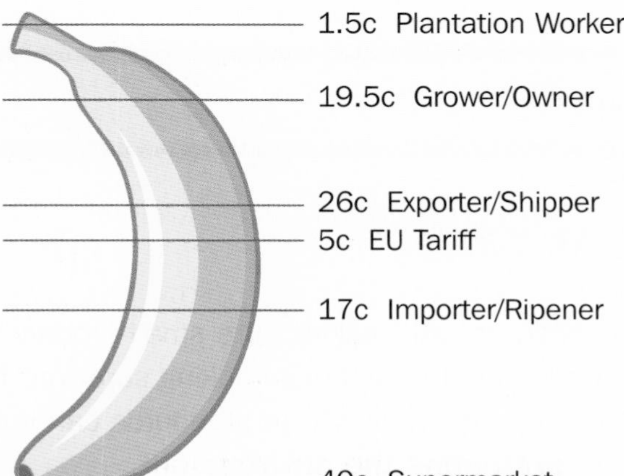

   a) Who makes the most money?
   b) How much more does the supermarket get compared to the plantation worker?
   c) After the supermarket, who gets the most money?

ACTIVITIES

3. What message is this poster trying to get across?
4. a) Imagine you have been asked to design a poster for your local café letting people know they serve Fairtrade coffee. Design the poster and come up with a slogan.
   b) Suggest two ways the staff and students in your school could use Fairtrade goods in the school.
   c) Write a letter to your town council telling them about Fairtrade and why you think your town should try to become a Fairtrade Town.

ACTION IDEA

Survey: Conduct a survey in your area to find out what type of coffee people drink and how much of it they drink. Find out if they know about Fairtrade coffee and whether or not they'd buy it.

Check out www.fairtrade.ie

STUDY 53 ETHICAL TRADE

While fair trade is mostly concerned with making sure small producers in the developing world get a fair deal, **ethical trade** is about companies making sure that they meet certain **standards** in the production of their goods. These standards can relate to **protecting workers' human rights** and **protecting the environment**.

Behind many brands are large **multinational companies**. Multinational companies control over 70 per cent of world trade. Some multinational companies can move the production of their goods to countries with the lowest wages, lowest taxes or lowest standards of care for the workers and then return the profits to the home country. This is often called the 'race to the bottom'.

Most of the world's refugees – 80 per cent – live in the developing world. Twenty million are in Asia and Africa, most in refugee camps bordering their own country. The **poorest countries in the world look after the most refugees**. Europe receives only five per cent of the world's refugees.

People fleeing their home in search of safety

In recent times, because of conflict and civil wars, many people do not make it across borders even into neighbouring countries but are nonetheless forced to move to another, safer part of their own country. People who move away from violence in their own states are called '**internally displaced**'.

Becoming a refugee, or becoming internally displaced, has major effects on your life. In a report called *Will You Listen? Young Voices from Conflict Zones*, children from countries like Afghanistan, Somalia, Sudan, Kosovo and Sri Lanka explained how being caught up in a conflict affects their lives.

Will You Listen?

For many of us, war came to our towns and villages before we knew what was happening. We had to run, often with little more than the clothes on our backs. We were forced to flee so suddenly that we became separated from our families and neighbours, sometimes for ever.

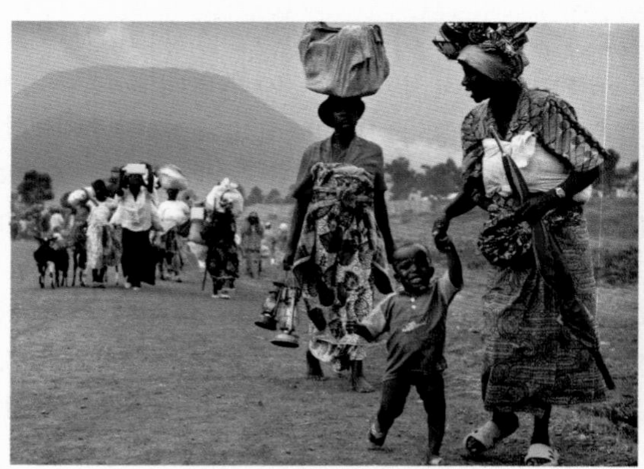

Can you imagine what it would be like to suddenly lose everything – to be uprooted from your home, your livelihood, your friends and maybe even your family? To start again in a new place is not easy. We miss our teachers and our friends. We miss relatives and neighbours and other people we loved and looked up to for guidance.

Some of us walk across barren deserts or risk our lives to reach another country, in hopes of finding a better life, free of violence and poverty and fear.

For some of us, the problem is not being forced to move. It is being unable to move.

But others of us are forced to seek refuge in a strange country without knowing if we will ever go home again.

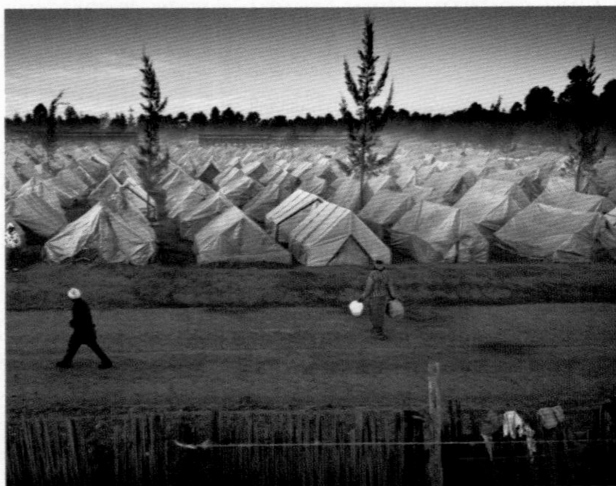

Those of us who remain displaced within our own countries sometimes have it even worse. The armed forces can still come after us and we can't reach a safe place. We are sometimes haunted by the memories of brutal atrocities committed before our eyes. We are not adults yet but our childhoods have ended very abruptly. We must suddenly fend for ourselves and sometimes our families, even if we lack the skills and means to do so.

Those of us who make it to refugee camps and other settlements often find ourselves treated without any respect. We sometimes lose hope and wonder why the world fails to understand or accept us. Those of us who try to live in a new culture feel unwelcome. People in the host communities sometimes say we are not fit to play with their children. Even the teachers in the schools sometimes refuse to teach us or to treat us the same as the local kids. Some of us even feel like going back to our communities to join the fighting forces, just to feel like we belong somewhere.

Source: *Will You Listen? Young Voices from Conflict Zones*, Unicef 2007

Ireland and Refugees

If a refugee comes to Ireland, and asks the Irish government for the right to live and work here because of persecution in their own country, the government has a legal obligation to hear that person's case. If the government decides that the person's human rights will be abused if they are forced to return to their country of origin, the person will be given **refugee status**, which allows them to live and work here legally.

In 1992 only 39 people asked for refugee status in Ireland. That figure increased to a high of 11,634 in 2002, but has decreased every year since, down to 3,866 at the end of 2008. The rules regarding who will be given refugee status are very strict. You have to show proof that your human rights are at risk if you are returned home. Only about nine per cent of those who apply for refugee status in Ireland get it.

ACTIVITIES

1. Where are most of the world's refugees?
2. Why do people become refugees?
3. Look at the poster and answer the questions below.

SPOT THE REFUGEE
There he is. Fourth row, second from the left. The one with the moustache. Obvious really.
Maybe not. The unsavoury-looking character you're looking at is more likely to be your average neighbourhood slob with a grubby vest and a weekend's stubble on his chin.
And the real refugee could just as easily be the clean-cut fellow on his left.
You see, refugees are just like you and me.
Except for one thing.
Everything they once had has been left behind. Home, family, possessions, all gone. They have nothing.
And nothing is all they'll ever have unless we all extend a helping hand.
We know you can't give them back the things that others have taken away.
We're not even asking for money (though every penny certainly helps).
But we are asking that you keep an open mind. And a smile of welcome.
It may not seem much. But to a refugee it can mean everything.
UNHCR is a strictly humanitarian organization funded only by voluntary contributions. Currently it is responsible for more than 26 million people around the world.
UNHCR Public Information
P.O. Box 2500
1211 Geneva 2, Switzerland
Models courtesy of The LEGO Group.

   a) What is the message of this poster?
   b) What does the poster ask people to do?
   c) Why do you think a poster like this is needed? Give three reasons for your answer.
4. What does 'internally displaced' mean?
5. Name five rights the children in the story on pages 207–8 are being denied.

ACTION IDEA

Interview: Contact an organisation that is concerned with refugees and invite a representative to speak to the class.

Check out the UNHCR's school kit and DVD *Not Just Numbers,* available in English and Irish. Contact the Irish UNHCR office (01 631 4614) or go to the UNHCR's website, www.unhcr/org/numbers-toolkit/unhcr_en.html.

STUDY 56 KNOW RACISM

Racism is a form of **discrimination faced by ethnic minority groups**.* Racism is based on the false belief that some 'races' are superior to others. **Racism denies people basic human rights, dignity and respect**.

The Show Racism the Red Card organisation uses footballers to send an anti-racist message

What is Racist Behaviour?

Racist behaviour can take many forms. For example:

- leaving a person out or snubbing them because of their race, colour, national or ethnic origins
- making jokes or hurtful remarks or insults about a person
- physically hurting or threatening a person.

What does this poster ask you to 'pass on'?

What Can You do about Racism?

We all have a responsibility to tackle racism. Here are some ways in which you can do this.

- Treat people from minority groups with the same respect you show to everyone else.
- Challenge racist remarks and insults.
- Report racist incidents to the Gardaí.
- If you see a racist incident happening in a public place, such as a shop, cinema, restaurant, etc., tell the management.
- Offer the hand of friendship to persons of different cultural backgrounds.
- Do not prejudge or label people because of their cultural or ethnic origin.
- Respect different cultures.
- Make your school a comfortable place for everyone.

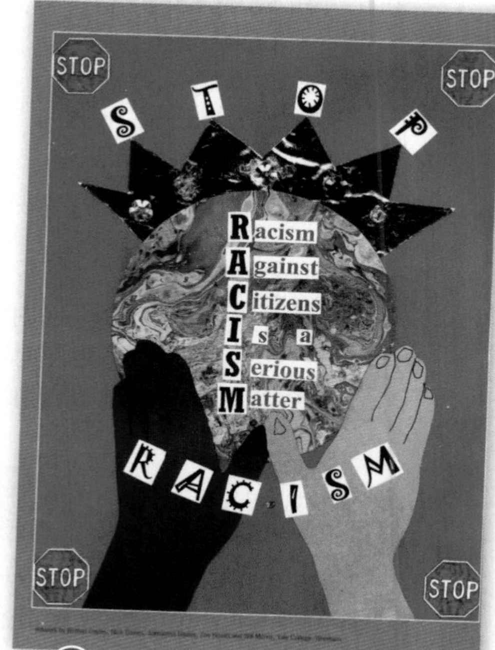

What message is this poster trying to get across?

*An ethnic minority group is a group of people whose skin colour, religion or culture is different from the majority of people living in the same place.

 ACTIVITIES 

1. What does racism mean?
2. Describe different forms of racist behaviour.
3. List five things you could do about racism.
4. Read what Thierry Henry says about racism and suggest **three ways** football fans can help 'drown out racists'.

Racism is one of the biggest problems facing football across Europe. People may think the problem has disappeared, but it hasn't. The players on the pitch need the help of all fans to help drown out the racists and tell them their actions aren't acceptable.

 ACTION IDEA 

Design an anti-racism poster or anti-racism charter for your school.

Check out:
Football Against Racism – www.farenet.org
Show Racism the Red Card: www.theredcard.ie
Sport Against Racism Ireland (SARi) – www.sari.ie.

STUDY 57 IDEAS FOR ACTION PROJECTS

See how you might go about doing an action project on refugees by reading the interview below. Then look at the other ideas for action projects that follow and see what issues related to the wider world your class could take action on.

Doing an Action Project – The Brief Guide

So what's the title of your action project?

'Raising Awareness about Refugees in our School'.

And what action did you take?

We investigated what life was like for refugees in Ireland. We got a guest speaker into school. We organised a campaign through the school to raise awareness.

What CSPE concepts did that link to?

Rights and responsibilities, human dignity and interdependence.

How is the action based on these concepts?

Refugees are people like us – they have rights and should be treated with dignity. We have a responsibility to see that their rights are protected. And we're all interdependent because there's only one race – the human race!

Why did you choose this action project?

We were talking in class about different groups in Ireland and around the world that don't always have their rights respected. Everyone mentioned refugees.

Who did you communicate with?

Students in our class, organisations that work with refugees and the whole school community.

How were these people involved in the action project?
We wrote to groups concerned about refugees, like Amnesty. We had a guest speaker from the Irish Refugee Council. We had to get permission for our wall display from our Principal. We had to ask year heads for permission to talk about the issue of refugees at different year assemblies.

Can you list the different activities?
We looked at the Universal Declaration of Human Rights and we watched a video about why refugees have to leave their homes. We wrote to organisations like Amnesty and we invited a guest speaker from the Irish Refugee Council to our class.
We did a role play to explore what it would be like to have to suddenly leave your home. We also made a wall display and we talked about the issue to different year groups.

Can you describe one thing you did?
I'm good at art so I made all the posters and images that were used for the wall display.

Can you list two skills you used?
I improved my computer skills, learning loads about how to get better graphics using an Apple Mac. I also improved my negotiating skills in asking the art teacher to lend us art materials for our wall display.

Can you list five things you discovered?
Ok:
- There are 20 million refugees in the world.
- 80% of refugees are women and children.
- The number of asylum seekers in Ireland is decreasing.
- I learned that we've legal responsibilities not to send a person back to a country where their life would be in danger.
- A person asking to stay and live in Ireland is not allowed work while their case is being decided.

Can you think back over your action project and tell me what you know now?
Doing the role play I had only five minutes to decide what I'd take with me if I'd to leave home. It was so hard – I could take just two things. It helped me understand what it might be like to be a refugee. None of us thought about bringing a passport. I learned it's very difficult to stay in Ireland if you look for refugee status.

- See what other action ideas you and your classmates can come up with!
- Remember to look back over the action ideas that are suggested throughout the chapter for more topics for an action project.
- In Chapter 6 you will find advice and helpful hints on how to make posters and leaflets, and on conducting surveys, interviews, petitions and fundraising events.

STUDY 58 REVISION QUESTIONS

Section 1

Answer ALL questions. (Total: 18 marks.)

1. Which two of the following politicians are Irish MEPs? **(4 marks)**
   (a) Proinsias de Rossa ☐
   (b) Mary Coughlan ☐
   (c) Mairead McGuinness ☐
   (d) Noel Dempsey ☐

2. Indicate whether the following statements are true or false by placing a tick in the correct boxes. **(4 marks)**
   (a) Ireland has 21 MEPs.
   True ☐ False ☐
   (b) The Treaty of Rome set up the European Economic Community.
   True ☐ False ☐
   (c) Irish MEPs sit together as a national group in the European Parliament.
   True ☐ False ☐
   (d) Europol helps police officers in all EU countries to fight against drug trafficking.
   True ☐ False ☐

3. In the boxes provided below, match all the letters in row X with the corresponding numbers in row Y. The first pair has been done for you. **(6 marks)**

X	A	B	C	D	E	F	G
Y	2						

X
A. The European Commission
B. Developing countries
C. The European Court of Justice
D. The Council of the European Union
E. An NGO is
F. The European Parliament
G. Dr Muhammad Yunus

Y
1. has the final say on what becomes EU law.
2. suggests/proposes new laws.
3. debates suggestions/proposals for new laws.
4. decides if a national law that affects you contradicts an EU law.
5. started the Grameen Bank to help give loans to the poor in Bangladesh.
6. are sometimes called the South or Third World.
7. a voluntary organisation like Trócaire, Goal and Oxfam.

4. Fill in the missing words in the following sentences. **(4 marks)**
   (a) In 1957 six European states signed the Treaty of __________, which set up the European Economic Community (EEC).
   (b) In 1973, the UK, Denmark and _____________ joined the EEC.
   (c) In 2004 a large group of _________ countries joined the EU.
   (d) You can find out information about the EU on a website called ___________________.

Section 2

Answer ALL questions numbered 1, 2 and 3 below. Each question carries 14 marks.

1. The following information on trainers (running shoes) is adapted from the Trócaire CSPE website. Study the information carefully and answer the questions that follow.

Trainers

Made up of dozens of different man-made materials, my trainers were assembled in a Korean-owned factory in Indonesia. The leather for the upper came from Texan cows whose hides were sent for tanning in South Korea, where wages are not high. Tanning is the process in which the hides are turned into leather and can involve very strong chemicals.

The Indonesian woman who made my €64 shoes earned €2 a day and worked in temperatures nearing 40 degrees Celsius.

Tiger Woods, the golfer, is sponsored by trainer manufacturer Nike. They pay him nearly €38 million a year to wear their emblem on his cap and jumper.

The price of a pair of trainers is divided up between the main groups involved in its production and distribution in the following way:

Groups involved	Percentage take
Nike	33%
Shops	50%
Factories (owners/managers)	11.5%
Factories (workers)	0.5%

(a) Of the groups involved in the production and distribution of trainers, which one of these is getting:
the highest percentage take? **(2)**
the lowest percentage take? **(2)**

(b) Why do you think Nike are prepared to pay Tiger Woods nearly €38 million a year to wear its emblem on his cap and jumper? **(2)**

(c) The production of trainers is an example of global interdependence. Using information ONLY from the passage above, explain what this means. **(4)**

(d) Nike is an example of a multinational company. What does this mean?
A multinational company is ____
____ **(2)**

(e) Give an example of TWO different multinational industries working in Ireland, and give an example of what each produces.
Examples of multinational industries in Ireland:
Example 1 ________________________________.
This industry produces ____________________________.
Example 2 ________________________________.
This industry produces ____________________________. **(2)**
(Taken from the 2002 JC CSPE exam.)

2. Examine the headlines below and answer the questions that follow.

Colombian boys as young as 7 are being abducted and used as child soldiers

Access to primary education especially difficult for girls in Niger

Emergency accommodation not enough for growing number of internally displaced in Sudan and Chad

(a) From information given in the headlines, what rights do you think are being denied in each case?
Group 1 ________________________________ **(2)**
Group 2 ________________________________ **(2)**
Group 3 ________________________________ **(2)**
(b) Take one group above and name an NGO or voluntary organisation concerned with their plight. **(2)**
(c) Describe the work of the organisation you mentioned in part (b) above. **(4)**
(d) What day of the year is chosen/designated as International Human Rights Day? **(2)**

3. Examine the postcard and answer the questions that follow.

MISSING: PEACE
Somalia's displaced are a forgotten people, in a forgotten conflict.
TROCAIRE

(a) What is the name of the organisation that produced this postcard? **(1)**
(b) What does the organisation say they are working for? **(1)**
(c) What does the organisation claim is missing in Somalia? **(1)**
(d) Who do they claim are the forgotten people in Somalia? **(1)**
(e) Would you consider the design of this postcard effective? Explain your answer. **(2)**
(f) Name two areas of a child's life that you think would be affected if they suddenly had to leave their home because of conflict.
Area 1 ______________________________ **(2)**
Area 2 ______________________________ **(2)**
(g) Name two actions that your class could take to highlight the plight of displaced peoples in countries like Somalia.
Action 1 ______________________________ **(2)**
Action 2 ______________________________ **(2)**

Section 3

Answer ONE of the questions numbered 1, 2 and 3 below.
Each question carries 20 marks.

1. Your CSPE class has decided to find out more about the UN and the part Ireland plays in UN peacekeeping missions.
   (a) Write a letter to an army representative outlining the purpose of such a visit.
   (b) Outline three questions you would like to ask and why you think they are important.
   (c) Describe how you would let the rest of the school community know about the role that Irish soldiers play as part of UN peacekeeping missions.

2. You are writing an article for your school newsletter about major issues that young people in the Third World are faced with in the twenty-first century.
   (a) Outline three major issues that you have identified for your article.
   (b) Describe or suggest two ideas that would highlight these problems more effectively.
   (c) Suggest what kind of photo/illustration or slogan would draw students' attention to such an article.

3. You have been invited to design an information leaflet to inform young people about Ireland and the EU.
   (a) Briefly outline the main EU institutions.
   (b) Explain how Ireland has benefited from membership of the EU.
   (c) Name and describe a major issue facing the EU.

Chapter 6

Action Projects

In this chapter you will find out about action projects and the **steps to an action project**. You'll also look at the **skills** you need when taking action. As part of your Junior Certificate examination you have to write up a **report on an action project** (RAP) and you can see an example of a completed RAP in this chapter.

STUDY 59 STEPS AND SKILLS

As part of your CSPE course, you and your classmates will do an **action project**. You will have seen examples of action project ideas throughout the book.

What is an Action Project?

An action project means being **actively involved in developing an issue or topic** that has come up in class. It involves finding out more about the topic or issue by taking action. Reading your textbook is not an action!

You can be involved in an action project as part of a group or on your own.

Action projects must:

- be based on one of the seven CSPE concepts
- be in keeping with the human rights and social responsibility focus of CSPE
- have an action element that is more than looking up information
- have an involvement with other people or communities about the issue
- develop your knowledge and understanding of the issue or topic
- develop and use the skills linked to CSPE.

Step 1
Agree on an issue or topic
Step 2
Form teams or committees
Step 3
Plan team tasks or jobs
Step 4
The action happens!
Step 5
Think back on your action
Step 6
Report on the action

Step 1: Agree on an Issue or Topic

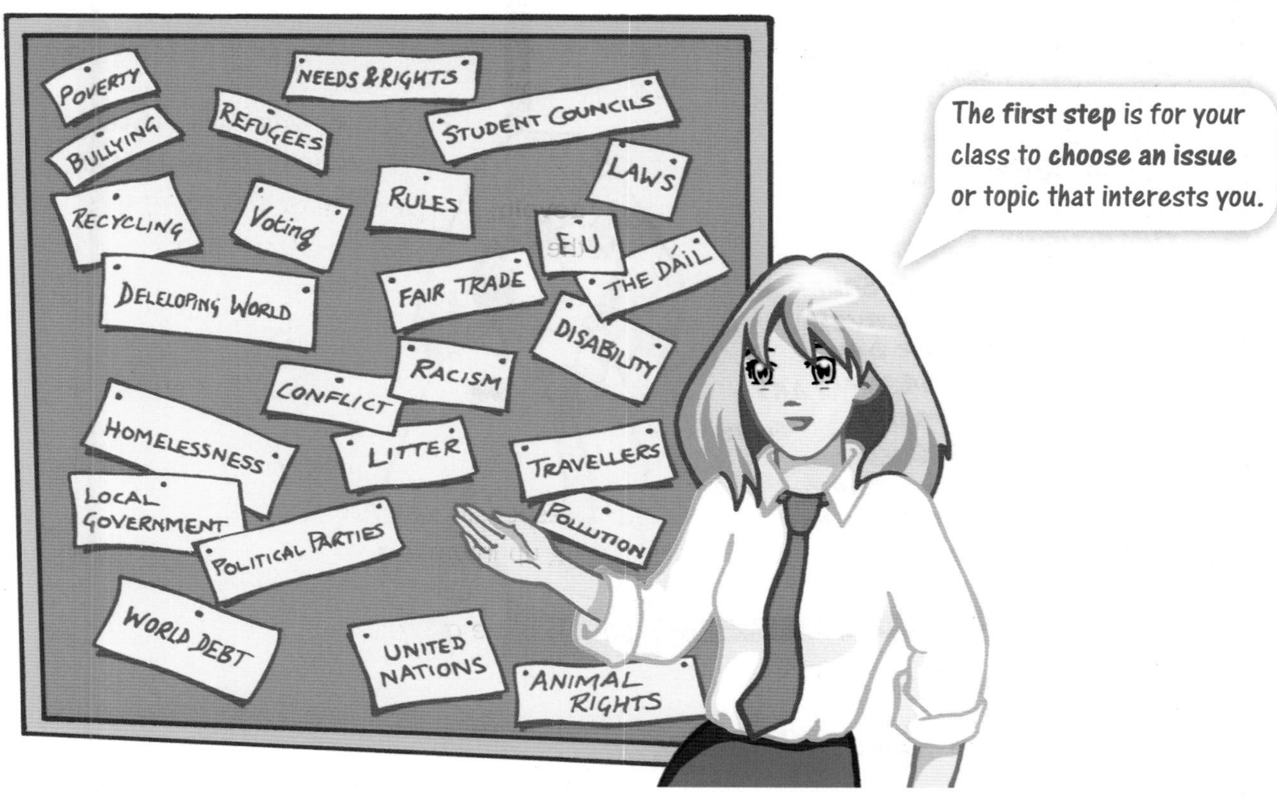

Step 2: Form Teams or Committees

This step involves deciding what you want to do about the issue – what action you will take. After the action is decided you can form teams to do the jobs needed so the action can happen.
Let's design a survey
What about a poster and wall display?
We could fundraise

INFORMATION POSTERS
FUNDRAISING
ORGANISING A VISIT
HOLDING A MOCK ELECTION
MAKING FACT SHEETS
LETTER WRITING CAMPAIGN
CREATING A WALL DISPLAY
ORGANISING A PETITION
INVITING A GUEST SPEAKER
CARRYING OUT A SURVEY
A LITTER CLEAN-UP DAY
HOLDING AN AWARENESS DAY
PRODUCING INFORMATION LEAFLETS
CARRYING OUT A QUESTIONNAIRE
CARRYING OUT AN INTERVIEW
HOLDING A DESIGNATED DAY
GOING ON A VISIT

Your action could involve you and your classmates doing...

Step 3: Plan Team Tasks or Jobs

You've decided on the issue and the kind of action you'll take. Now you must **plan all the jobs that need to be done** to make the action happen. When you've made a list of all the jobs, each job is allocated to a team or committee.

Committee Tasks

These are examples of the different types of committee or team and the jobs each might have to do for a class action that involves inviting a guest speaker (e.g. a TD).

The Permission Committee – Actions:

- asks school principal for permission to invite guest speaker into the school
- informs principal of the date and time the speaker will be in
- asks permission to put announcement of visit in the day events/intercom notices
- invites principal to the talk
- invites other teachers and tutors to the talk.

The Inviting Committee – Actions:

- finds name of organisation and person to contact for visit
- phones or writes to speaker asking them to visit
- forwards questions that will be asked
- greets speaker on arrival at school
- introduces speaker to the rest of the class
- thanks speaker at end of interview/talk
- sends thank-you letter from class to the speaker.

The Questions Committee – Actions:

- brainstorms questions with all students
- selects questions to be asked on the day
- prepares questions on cards
- nominates students to ask the different questions
- arranges back-up people in case of absences on the day.

The Recording Committee – Actions:

- decides how the answers to the questions will be recorded
- organises who will record what
- decides what will be done after the talk with the information gathered
- suggests possible follow-up events or actions.

The Room-Organising Committee – Actions:

- arranges chairs in room for students
- arranges chair and table for speaker
- organises tea/coffee/water for speaker
- puts room back in order after visit
- returns any borrowed items such as glasses, etc.

It is important that during the action project you keep a log or diary of the jobs you were involved in, and what others did too. This will help you later when you have to write your individual report on the action project for your CSPE Junior Cert exam.

The next study has lot of examples of how to plan, organise, design and carry out the different actions that might be involved in your project, e.g. survey design, letter writing, poster design, etc.

Step 4: The Action Happens

This step **could take a day or a number of weeks** depending on the action you have chosen. For example, a visit to the courts would take place on one day and a petition could take a number of days to carry out.

Step 5: Think Back on your Action Project

When you finish the action, you need to spend some time **thinking back (reflecting)** on it and you must also think about **what went well and what you would do differently (evaluating)**. Write this in your diary or log – you'll need it for the next step.

What went well and what would we do differently?

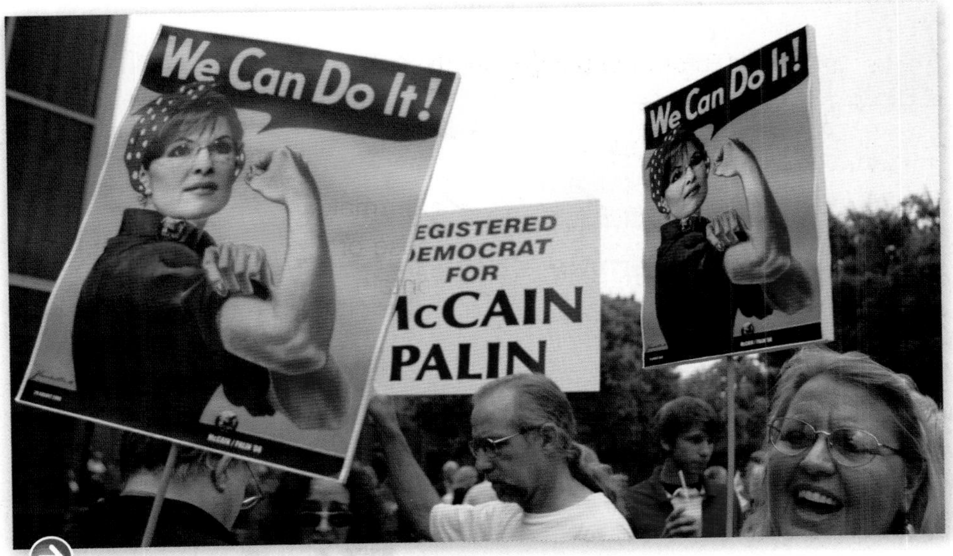

A well-designed poster can be read from a distance. Don't use too much text.

Surveys

As part of an action project you could use a survey to find out and gather information on a topic or issue. Remember to:

- decide on the questions you want to ask – use closed questions that require a yes/no answer, e.g.

  'Do you know the name of the Taoiseach?' Yes ☐ No ☐

  You could also ask questions that give a number of answers, e.g.

  'How many TDs are in the Dáil?'

  a. 166 b. 110 c. 121
- keep the survey short
- write out what your introduction will be, e.g. 'Hello. We are doing a survey about . . . Would you answer some questions, please?' To see if any changes are needed, practise your introduction and questions on your classmates beforehand
- decide on how many people you want to survey and photocopy that number of sheets
- decide when and where you will carry out the survey
- plan what you will do with the results of the survey, e.g. create a wall display; publish them in the school newsletter; make a leaflet with the findings; tell other students about the findings at assembly, etc.

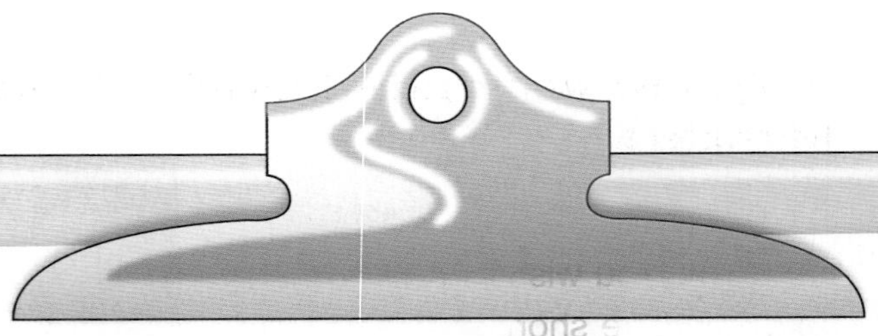

Sample - Bullying Survey

1. Which sex are you?
   Male [ ] Female [x]
2. Have you ever been bullied?
   Yes [x] No [ ]
3. Have you ever witnessed anyone being bullied?
   Yes [ ] No [x]
4. When was the last time you were bullied?
   - Today [ ]
   - In the last week [ ]
   - Within the last month [ ]
   - Within the last 6 months [ ]
   - A year or more ago [x]
5. How often were you bullied?
   - Once [ ]
   - Several times [x]
   - Almost every day [ ]
   - Several times a day [ ]
6. Where were you bullied?
   - Going to or from school [ ]
   - In the school yard [ ]
   - At lunch time [ ]
   - In the toilets [x]
   - In the classroom [ ]
   - In the changing rooms [ ]
7. If you were bullied, what sort of bullying was it?
   - Physical [ ]
   - Verbal [x]
   - Online [ ]
8. Do you consider bullying to be:
   - No problem [ ]
   - Worrying [x]
   - Frightening [ ]
9. If you were bullied, what effects did it have?
   - No effects [ ]
   - Some bad effects [x]
   - Terrible effects [ ]
10. Who do you think is responsible when bullying continues to go on?
    - The bully [x]
    - The bully's parents [ ]
    - Teachers [ ]
    - The victim [ ]
    - The principal [ ]
    - Students who witness the bullying but do nothing [ ]

Questionnaires

As part of an action project you may want to gather information. One way of doing this is by using a questionnaire. Remember to:

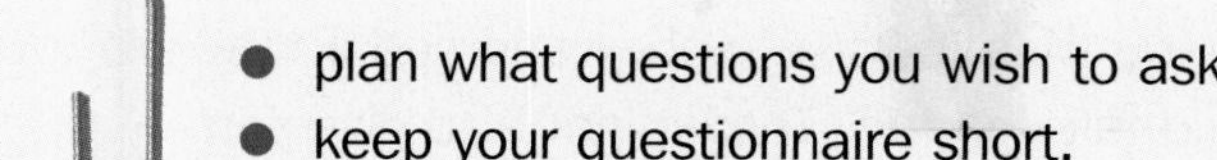

- plan what questions you wish to ask
- keep your questionnaire short.

Sample - Questionnaire on Refugees

Please tick the relevant boxes.

1. What sex are you?

   Male ☐ Female ☑

2. What age are you?

   11–15 ☑ 16–18 ☐ 19–24 ☐
   25–35 ☐ 36–50 ☐ Over 50 ☐

3. Most refugees are:

   Men ☐ Women ☑ Children ☐

4. Most people become refugees because:

   They are fleeing persecution ☑ They are looking for work ☐
   They come here to learn English ☐ Other ☐

5. Most refugees are in:

   Europe ☑ Africa ☐ Asia ☐ USA ☐

6. What percentage of asylum seekers get refugee status in Ireland?

   About 10% ☑ About 50% ☐ About 90% ☐

7. Do you think the government is doing enough for refugees?

   Yes ☐ No ☑ Don't know ☐

8. Would you be happy if a refugee family came to live in your area?

   Yes ☑ No ☐

9. Do you think Irish people have responsibilities towards refugees?

   Yes ☑ No ☐

10. Do you think that all asylum seekers should be allowed to work while waiting for their case to be heard?

    Yes ☑ No ☐ Don't know ☐

Fundraising

Raising funds for an organisation or cause you have found out about could be part of your action. Consider the following points on fundraising.

- Contact the organisation for which you wish to raise money and see if they are organising any events that you could take part in. They might also give you ideas about types of event you could hold to raise money.
- Your fundraising event could take the form of a cake sale, a sponsored walk/run, a raffle, a sports event, a sponsored silence, etc.
- See if you can get free advertising for your event from your local radio station or newspaper.
- Choose a date, time and venue for the event.
- Check out whether you need special permission from anyone before the event can happen, e.g. the school principal, local council or Garda Síochána.
- Check whether you need to be **insured**. This could be important for all events you take part in.
- Organise sponsorship cards if needed and collection of all the money when the event is over.
- Thank everyone who helped and let them know how much money was raised.
- Give the money raised to the organisation or cause involved.

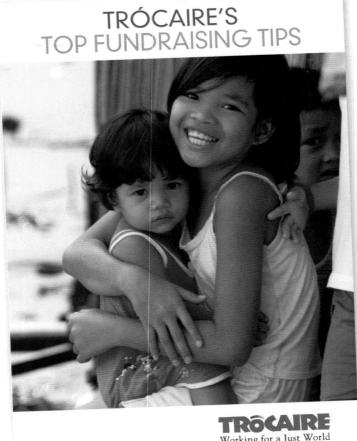

TRÓCAIRE'S
TOP FUNDRAISING TIPS

TRÓCAIRE
Working for a Just World

STUDY 61 A GUIDE TO WRITING A RAP

As part of your CSPE exam for your Junior Cert you must write about the action you took. This accounts for **60 per cent of the overall mark**. It is important that you write your report carefully and put the correct information in the right place. Read through the following pages to find out:

- the information needed for each section
- how each section is marked
- sample answers for each section.

Report on an Action Project (RAP)

Before you do the final RAP, follow these guidelines.

- Do a **draft** or **practice RAP** first. This will help you figure out what information you want to include in each section. You could get a photocopy of the Department of Education RAP booklet that is used for the report and use it to practise on.
- Make sure you **go back over your diary** or log to remind yourself of all the activities and information you discovered and were involved in.
- **Don't** include any extra pages or photocopies in the RAP booklet.
- You don't have to fill in every line of the RAP booklet.
- **Remember:** every student in the class must write their **own individual report**.

Sample Report on an Action Project (RAP)

This is a breakdown of how a RAP is marked and the kind of information the examiner is looking for in each section of your report.

Section	Maximum Marks Available
1 Title	3 marks
2 Introduction A) Identification and explanation of concept B) One reason	 4 marks 4 marks
3 Activities Undertaken A) Type of action and communication with people B) List and description of activities C) Detailed account of one activity D) Application of skills	 4 marks 15 marks 15 marks 15 marks
4 Summary of Information	30 marks
5 Reflections	30 marks
TOTAL	120 marks

Title (3 Marks)

- The title should give a **clear idea of the action** that has been taken. You could also mention here the **skill involved** in the action, e.g. 'a questionnaire investigating the issue of discrimination against people with disabilities' or 'learning about democracy by running a mock election'.
- Remember to **tick the box** beside the type(s) of action undertaken as part of the action project, e.g. visit, interview, etc.

Example: **The Title of My Action Project**

'Raising Awareness of the Importance of Fair Trade in My School'

Please tick ☐ the type(s) of action undertaken as part of the action project.

Survey/questionnaire	☐	Mock election/parliament	☐
Interview	☐	Fundraising	☐
Awareness raising	☐	Investigation	☐
Publication	☐	Student council activity	☐
Campaign	☐	Visit	☐
Designated day	☐	Other	☐
Guest speaker	☐		

Introduction (8 marks)

Part A (4 marks)

- Remember to tick the box beside the concept(s) your action project was based on, e.g. democracy, human dignity, etc.
- Explain how your action project was based on this/these concepts.

Example: **Introduction**

(a) *Please tick ☐ the concept(s) on which your action project was based.*

☐ Democracy	☐ Development
☐ Rights and responsibilities	☐ Stewardship
☐ Human dignity	☐ Law
☐ Interdependence	

Explain how your action project was based on this/these concepts.

My action project was based on these concepts because fair trade will help bring about development and dignity for the people of the Third World. Also, it is our responsibility to see that the rights of others are protected, as we should see ourselves as a global family all dependent on each other, or interdependent.

Part B (4 marks)

- Give **one reason** why you chose this action project.
- Give a clear reason why you did this particular action project. Avoid repeating what you said in part (a).
- **Avoid** phrases like, 'our teacher told us to . . .'

Give **ONE** reason why you chose to do this action project.

We chose to do this action project because in our CSPE class we were looking at reasons why the developing world was so poor. We realised that the world's trading arrangements made it easier for the First World to get richer at the expense of Third World nations and that a solution was to promote more fairly traded goods. We decided to do what we could to promote the sale of Fairtrade goods in our homes, in our school and in our community.

Activities Undertaken (49 marks)
Part A (4 marks)

- Remember to **tick the box** beside the people you communicated with in the course of your action project, e.g. students in my class, family, etc.
- Explain **why** these people were communicated with and how they were involved in the action project.
- Your answer should say **why the people or organisations** that became involved in your action project were **important or relevant** to the subject/topic of your action project.

Example: **Activities Undertaken**

Please tick the people communicated with in the course of your action project.

☐ Students in my class
☐ Other people in my school
☐ Person/people in the community
☐ Individuals/organisations involved in this issue
☐ Family

Explain why these people were communicated with and why they were involved in the action project.

We visited Oxfam to find information and to see their selection of Fairtrade goods. We went back another day and bought a lot of chocolate and other Fairtrade goods and sold them to the students in our school at lunchtime in the canteen.

Part B (15 marks)

- Write a **list and brief description** of the main tasks/activities undertaken as part of the action project.
- **What we did . . .** Each student should list the different activities they did during the course of the action project. This list will be the same for all students if the project was a group action, e.g. survey, interviewing, letter writing, collecting information, working in teams, etc.
- Include about **six activities**, writing **two to three sentences** to describe each one.
- In a group action, **all the activities of each group** in the class should be listed and described, even if you weren't involved in every one.

Example: ***(b) Write a list and brief description of the main tasks/activities undertaken as part of the action project.***

We did a brainstorm on the board of the possible jobs that we needed to do and then divided into six groups:

Group A (Research Committee): *Arranged visit to Oxfam to see what Fairtrade goods were on sale and buy some of their chocolate.*

Group B (Survey Committee): *Arranged survey to find out what other class groups knew about Fairtrade goods.*

Group C (Contact Committee): *Wrote to most well-known supermarket chains to ask that more Fairtrade goods be stocked.*

Group D (Petition Committee): *Arranged petition to be sent with the letters to the supermarket chains requesting that they stock more Fairtrade goods.*

Group E (Publicity Committee): *Made posters to go up around the school advertising Fairtrade goods sale on a certain day.*

Group F (Sales Committee): *Requested use of school intercom to advertise cards from Oxfam and Fairtrade gifts and sold a selection of what was available in the canteen at lunchtime on designated day.*

Part C (15 marks)

- Give a detailed account of **ONE particular task/activity** from the list in part B that **YOU undertook** as part of the action project.
- **What I did . . .** You should write out in detail an account of **one task** or activity you **did**.

- **Don't** write about a **number of different tasks** or activities that you were **involved in**.

Example: ***(c)* Give a detailed account of ONE particular task/activity from the list in part *(b)* that YOU undertook as part of the action project.**

My main task was to get as many students as possible to sign our petition requesting Irish supermarkets to stock more Fairtrade goods. To prepare for this task I was responsible for making out the petition sheets. I had to clearly type out what the petition was about at the top of the sheet. It said, 'We who have signed below ask that you stock more Fairtrade products in your supermarkets.' Underneath that there were spaces marked out for the person's name, address and signature. At the very bottom the petition said, 'We ask you to take into consideration the views of the students who have signed the enclosed petition.' I printed out the sheet and I photocopied one for each of my classmates and arranged clipboards that would make it easier for students to sign. I stood outside the canteen at lunchtime on a day we had agreed with our year head and I collected 150 signatures.

Part D (15 marks)

- Describe how **YOU** applied at least **TWO SKILLS** when undertaking the activity described in part C above.
- Write about **four sentences** on how **you applied/used each skill**.
- The skills you described cannot relate to the project in general. They **MUST relate to what you learned doing the task** or activity you described in part C of Section 3. For example, if you had described writing a letter in Part C, the skills described here might include how you improved your typing and computer skills and your knowledge of how to lay out a letter.

Example: ***(d)* Describe how YOU applied at least TWO SKILLS when undertaking the activity described in part *(c)* above.**

Persuasion skills: *I learned that the best way to persuade someone to sign a petition is to know the facts of your argument very well so that you can speak directly to someone without looking down at your page. I had written out a number of key points of information that explained what fair trade was all about and why it was so important.*

I practised it many times with other classmates before I had to face the rest of the school in the canteen. I also learned that you are more likely to get a good response to a request if you speak politely and try not to be too pushy.

Computer skills: *I learned how to format the petition in Word on the computer. I learned how to use a table and organise information on a page. I made three columns for the name, address and signature. I put 25 rows, so 25 people could sign on one page. I put the name and address of who we were sending it to on the bottom left-hand side. The title was in large bold letters at the top.*

Summary of Information (30 marks)

- Give **FIVE pieces of information** or facts that you found out about the subject of the action project.
- **Six marks** are given for **each** of the five relevant facts or pieces of information given.
- Do not include any personal opinion here.
- Sentences which begin with **I learned . . .**, **I discovered . . .**, **I found out . . .**, etc. are helpful.
- All facts **MUST relate to the concept/theme/topic/subject/unit** of the action project.

Example: ***Summary of Information***

Give FIVE pieces of information or facts that you discovered about the subject of the action project.

- *If the people in developing countries are paid a proper price for their work and their goods, they will be able to afford better health care and education for themselves and their children.*
- *Fairtrade is an international movement which ensures that producers in poor countries get a fair price for their goods so that they can live their lives in dignity.*
- *Oxfam's 'Make Trade Fair' campaign aims to change world trade rules so that trade can make a real difference to the fight against global poverty.*
- *If Africa, East Asia, South Asia and Latin America were each to increase their share of world exports by one per cent, this could lift 128 million people out of poverty.*
- *Many of the products that we depend on, like tea, coffee, bananas and cocoa beans (used in chocolate), are produced in poorer countries in the South or Third World.*

Reflections (30 marks)

- Think back on your action project and the different experiences you had while doing it. Give your **OWN thoughts** on these and explain why YOU think this way.
- This is where you make a number of statements. You must give **reasons for THREE of these statements**. In your reason or explanation say why you think or believe the way you do about the subject of the project, e.g. *'I think that the action project that I took part in has helped me understand how democracy works and why voting is an important part of a democracy'; or 'It is my opinion that voting in elections is a good thing, as it is one of the ways we take part in running our country. If you don't vote your voice isn't heard.'*
- Phrases like the following could be useful here:
  - ***I think . . . because . . .***
  - ***It's my opinion that . . . because . . .***
  - ***I feel that . . . because . . .***

- You could mention here how what you have learned could impact on you in the future and you could make recommendations or suggestions for future actions, e.g.
  - ***I recommend that . . . because . . .***
  - ***In the future it would be helpful if . . . because . . .***
- It is important that the views you express reflect the **human rights and social responsibility** dimension of the CSPE course.
- You can also make statements here about the **learning process and skills acquired** in doing the action project.
- Remember that it is not necessary that your action project had a successful outcome – sometimes things don't turn out the way we planned!

Example: **Reflections**

Think back on your action project and the different experiences you had while doing it. Give your OWN thoughts on these and explain why YOU think this way.

I think that fair trade really is one way to help the people in developing countries have a better quality of life and stop the inequality there is in the world. Doing this project made me aware of human rights abuses and also brought home to me what the idea of interdependence is all about – we live in a global village.

We need to think about all the things we use and where they come from and what kind of conditions the people who produce them live in. We discovered, for example, that a lot of the cocoa beans produced in the Ivory Coast in Africa involve slave labour. I think that we should be more careful about our choices when shopping. I was disappointed that some of the supermarkets that we wrote to didn't reply to our letters and I think that more pressure should be put on them. I really enjoyed doing the petition and I think it made me more confident about explaining important issues. I even persuaded my mum to buy Fairtrade tea and coffee at home.

Coursework Assessment Book (CWAB)

Instead of a RAP you could complete a Coursework Assessment Book (CWAB).

- A Coursework Assessment Book is a report on ONE module of work.
- A module is 12 to 15 weeks of work and includes an action project.
- The module of work can be done at any time over the three years of Junior Cycle.
- A module can be about a concept, unit or theme of work explored.
- The entire module must be based on ONE of the seven concepts in CSPE.
- The CWAB is divided into five sections.

The following is an example of a 12-week module on Human Rights and Racism in Ireland that could be undertaken and then written up in the Coursework Assessment Book (CWAB). This module focuses on the concept of Rights and Responsibilities.

Week 1 Examine the rights in the UNDHR and rank the Rights cards in order of importance.	**Week 2** Use Pastor Niemöller's poem (page 33) and debate whether the names of the groups mentioned in the poem could be changed to include groups that are denied their rights today.	**Week 3** Take part in a 'walking debate' to decide and reach a decision on what groups in Irish society get a raw deal or who have certain rights denied.
Week 4 Find out what organisations in Ireland are concerned with the rights of refugees.	**Week 5** Track stories in the newspapers that are about refugees and asylum seekers and see how these stories are reported.	**Week 6** Discover what international laws Ireland has signed in relation to refugees.
Week 7 Use a mix-and-match exercise of stories and definitions to find out what different terms mean, such as refugee, asylum seeker, etc.	**Week 8** Take part in a role-play or freeze frame about trying to enter another country with no official documents.	**Week 9** View the 'Know Racism' campaign video in preparation for the action project on racism in Ireland.
Week 10 Brainstorm and reach a decision on what action to take over the issue of racism in Ireland.	**Week 11** Organise into class groups to prepare for a guest speaker.	**Week 12** Visit of guest speaker from the Irish Refugee Council.

Remember, every student in the class has to complete their own Coursework Assessment Book (CWAB).

PHOTO CREDITS

For permission to reproduce photographs the author and publisher gratefully acknowledge the following:

© Alamy: 9, 68, 106, 157C, 157T, 157TCR, 162C, 163TL, 167BL, 167CL, 167TR, 17BL, 181BC, 181BL, 181BR, 34CR, 34T, 36BL, 38CR, 4BL, 50TR, 51CL, 51TC, 51TL, 52BC, 52CL, 52CR, 67BL, 78CL, 79TR, 97T; © Amnesty International: 29CR; © Amnesty International Ireland: 33, 29BL, 4BR; © Amnesty International UK: 29T; © Ashbourne Community School: 63T; © Barnardos: 134CLL, 45; © change.ie: 57, 56T; © Comhairle na nÓg: 90CR; © Comic Relief: 189BL; © Concern: 196, 226; © Control Arms: 206B; © Corbis: 114, 204, 119BR, 143TL, 157B, 164TL, 165TR, 167CR, 168BL, 16CL, 18CR, 36BR, 37T, 50BR, 50TL, 51CR, 66R, 18CL; © corpwatch.org: 203CL; © Cystic Fibrosis Association of Ireland: 153; © Dail na nÓg: 131; © DEA: 53; © digizen.org: 13B; © Donegal Youth Council: 90BR; © Dublin City Public Libraries: 85CR; © Earth Hour: 56C; © ECO-UNESCO: 65, 66L; © electionsireland.org: 108; © Europe Direct: 176; © European Communities: 60, 75, 166, 174, 175, 177, 118B, 161L, 161R, 162CR, 162TL, 163BC, 163BL, 163BR, 163CL, 164BR, 165TL, 171B, 171T, 172BL, 172BR; © European Community, DG ECHO: 169BL, 169BR, 169CL, 169CR; © Every Human Has Rights: 38BR; © Fairtrade Mark Ireland: 202, 200BL, 201C, 228TR; © Fianna Fáil: 115TR, 116BR; © Fine Gael: 115C, 116CR, 116CRR, 172C, 172CLL, 172CR, 172CRR; © Fine Gael/Benedicta Attoh: 103; © Focus Ireland: 134CRR; © Foróige: 81, 82, 82, 82, 82, 83B, 83T; © Free the Children: 195CL; © Getty: 30, 32, 211, 157TR, 162BR, 162CL, 165B, 168TL, 180TR, 185L, 18TR, 195TR, 197BL, 198BL, 20BC, 20CL, 34CL, 35B, 35T, 36CR, 37C, 50CR, 51BL, 51TR, 52BL, 52BR, 52T, 54T, 78TR, 87T, 97C; © GOAL: 134C; © GoodWeave: 193BR; © Gorey Echo: 94; © Green Party: 115BR, 116BRR; © greenbin.ie: 73; © greenschoolsireland.org: 63B; © Holocaust Educational Trust of Ireland: 22B; © Imagefile: 10, 119BL, 143C, 157BR, 15C, 162BL, 163TR, 168TR, 169TR, 17BR, 200CL, 54BR, 87B; © Irish Refugee Council: 134CR; © Irish Times: 23, 24, 74, 120, 123, 124, 186, 113T, 115CR, 116TC, 119TL, 119TR, 130CL, 133BR, 143B, 143T, 144C, 144T, 164BL, 164C, 164TR, 168CR, 22C, 28T, 43L, 4CL, 54CL, 55R, 79BC, 79BR, 79C, 79CL, 79TL, 84B, 84C, 84T, 85BR; © Irish Traveller Movement: 134CL; © ISPCC: 16BR; © James Connelly/PicSell8: 133BL; © JCDecaux: 86B; © John Quigley: 135; © Labour Party: 116CL,116CLL, 172CL; © Margaret Brown: 44; © Martyn Turner: 199C; © micandidate.eu: 117; © Muintir na Tíre: 147; © NCTE: 11; © NYCI © David Blake: 113B; © NYCI © Derek Speirs/Report: 132, 130CR, 18BL; © Panos: 208, 17BC, 187B, 187CL, 187CR, 188CL, 188TR, 189TL, 193BR, 193TR, 194CL, 194TR, 197TR, 201T, 203TR, 205BL, 207BL, 207BR, 207TL, 43R, 48BL, 50BL, 67BR; © Pavee Point: 25; © Pavee Point © John Byrne: 26, 27; © Photocall: 86T, 116BL, 116BLL, 128CL, 134B, 143BL, 146BL, 146CR, 146TL, 165CR, 4CR, 78CR, 79TC; © Photolibrary: 118T, 36T, 78BL, 80T, 85BL, 96CR; © PJ Browne Photography: 142; © Power of One: 55BL; © Press Association: 110TR, 198CR, 199B, 205TR, 228CR, 38TR; © Protect the Human: 31; © Report Digital: 6BL, 6BR; © Reuters: 110TL, 193CR; © Rex: 21CR; © Rising Tide: 48T; © Rock the Vote: 112CL; © Rock the Vote Ireland: 112CR; © Science Photo Library: 50CL; © SEI © Cassie Ann Wallace , Strabane High School, Co Tyrone: 64TL; © SEI © Daniel Eames, Portumna Community School, Portumna Co Galway: 64TR; © SEI © Dayle Kennedy Abbey Community College, Waterford: 64CL; © SEI © Murva Asad, Loreto College Cavan, Cavan: 64CR © Shepard Fairey and Earth Hour: 56B; © Show Racism the Red Card: 210TR; © Sinn Féin: 116TR; © Sportsfile: 15CR; © Student Council: 8BL, 8BR; © Tara/Skryne Valley Organisation: 136; © TEAM Educational Theatre Company: 13T; © The Equality Authority: 138, 210CR; © The Irish Independent: 139; © The Irish Traveller Movement: 28B; © The Ombudsman for Children's Office: 128B, 128CR; © TopFoto: 19, 21CL, 21TR; © Trócaire: 49, 218, 231, 192; © UN: 203BR; © UN Photo/Chris Sattlberger: 191TR; © UN Photo/Eric Kanalstein: 188BR; © UN Photo/Eskinder Debebe: 181TR; © UN Photo/Jenny Rockett: 181CL; © UN Photo/Mark Garten: 185R; © UN Photo/Paulo Filgueiras: 183, 38BL, 180B; © UNAIDS: 182TC; © UNEP: 182B; © UNHCR: 209, 182C; © UNICEF: 182T, 191B; © Urban Ballyfermot and Vincentian Partnership for Justice: 109CL, 109CR; © Wikimedia Commons: 162TR, 96CL, 15CL, 20TR; © World Aids Orphans: 190; © World Fair Trade Organization: 200CR; © Wrexham College: 210BR; A LONG WAY GONE by Ishmael Beah, Jacket design © 2007 by Jennifer Carrow, front cover photo by Michael Kamber/Polaris, used by permission of Farrar, Straus and Giroux, LLC.: 206T;

The author and publisher have made every effort to trace all copyright holders, but if any has been inadvertently overlooked we would be pleased to make the necessary arrangement at the first opportunity.